HEDGED

THE HISTORY OF COMMUNICATION

Robert W. McChesney and John C. Nerone, editors

A list of books in the series appears at the end of this book.

HEDGED

*How Private Investment Funds
Helped Destroy American Newspapers
and Undermine Democracy*

MARGOT SUSCA

**UNIVERSITY OF
ILLINOIS PRESS**
Urbana, Chicago, and Springfield

Library of Congress Cataloging-in-Publication Data
Names: Susca, Margot, 1976- author.
Title: Hedged : how private investment funds helped
    destroy American newspapers and undermine
    democracy / Margot Susca.
Description: Urbana : University of Illinois Press, 2023.
    | Series: The history of communication | Includes
    index.
Identifiers: LCCN 2023019469 (print) | LCCN 2023019470
    (ebook) | ISBN 9780252045462 (cloth) | ISBN
    9780252087561 (paperback) | ISBN 9780252055089
    (ebook)
Subjects: LCSH: Newspaper publishing—United
    States—History—21st century. | Press and politics—
    United States—History—21st century. | American
    newspapers—History—21st century. | Private
    equity—United States.
Classification: LCC PN4867.2 .S87 2023 (print) | LCC
    PN4867.2 (ebook) |DDC 071/.30905—dc23/eng/
    20230623
LC record available at https://lccn.loc.gov/2023019469
LC ebook record available at https://lccn.loc.gov/
    2023019470

For Zoe

"It's business" has come to be a legitimate excuse for hard dealing, sly tricks, special privileges. It is a common enough thing to hear men arguing that the ordinary laws of morality do not apply in business.

—Ida Tarbell, *The History of the Standard Oil Company*

Contents

Acknowledgments

At American University I am surrounded by colleagues shaping the future of higher education, journalism, and media studies. Patricia Aufderheide, Justin Bernstine, Kurt Braddock, Laura Denardis, Leena Jayaswal, Pallavi Kumar, Charles Lewis, Lynne Perri, Aram Sinnreich, John Sullivan, John Watson, and Sherri Williams have offered advice, encouragement, and friendship. Caty Borum provided important mentorship throughout this process, and I would not have finished this book—let alone have started it—without her help. I am especially indebted to Amy Eisman for her guidance, leadership, and support. She knew I would write this book a year before I did.

My book research over the years has had several distinct turning points; these were connections or conversations that moved both the interviews and the research direction forward in immeasurable ways. Honoring those pivotal moments, thanks are due to Tom Breen, John Carvalho, Nolan McCaskill, Christoph Mergerson, Marty Sanders, Sue-Ellen Sanders, Derek Simmonsen, and Rachel Simmonsen. Further thanks are owed to Jason Riccio for his patience early on explaining a 2-and-20. As the documents and interviews grew in number, I had help from several research assistants—Maggie Clifford, Nami Hijikata, Hanna Holthaus, and Aaron Schaffer—whose time finding, fact-checking, and organizing documents proved invaluable. Any faults are mine alone.

Thank you, Daniel Nasset, editor in chief at the University of Illinois Press, who saw promise in this work and graciously shepherded me through the process as a first-time book author. Peer reviewers provided other critiques and suggestions that strengthened the final manuscript. I am especially grateful to the dozens of citizens and journalists nationwide who provided insights that deepened my understanding of today's newspaper audiences and the threats private investment fund ownership and influence pose to democracy. As my concerns about ownership grow, they are balanced by the brilliance and tenacity of an army of former students working as reporters and researchers around the world. Among them are Alejandro Alvarez, Sophie Austin, Sommer Brugal, Brianna Crummy, Gabe Ferris, Rachel Hopmayer, Lindsey Leake, David Lim, Mason Peeples, and Trey Yingst.

No professor becomes successful without the time that other teachers have offered over the years. In Connecticut I had a stream of high school social studies teachers who inspired me to recognize the crucial role of journalism in democratic society. That list includes Jeffrey Gowdy and Thomas F. Howard, who died in 2016 before I could tell him thank you. At UMass that passion for journalism and cultural critique expanded thanks to professors Madeleine Blais, Peter Haas, Karen List, and Ekwueme Michael Thelwell. At the Columbia University Graduate School of Journalism Sandy Padwe taught me the importance of following the money and working a beat. At Florida State University Laura Arpan, Steve McDowell, Andy Opel, Jennifer Proffitt, and Art Raney fostered a deeper understanding of mass communication scholarship. I am a better teacher and researcher because of their expertise and patience.

I am endlessly grateful for my family and friends, who I would imagine by now are quite tired of hearing about the colossus known in our circles simply as "The Book." It has loomed large over every holiday and social interaction for years, so much so that it deserved its own seat at the bar. Kyle Quinn Pincince for nearly thirty years has been my best friend, and I am a better person because of it. Thank you, Ginevra Adamoli-Kalbli and Shawn Kalbli, Hillary Copsey Canan and Mike Canan, Azalea Candelaria, Carrie Pugh and Matt Felix, Scott Samples, Renu Schmoyer and Chuck Schmoyer, and Stephanie Susca for the support during these years and before them. To Warren Stern I offer a special thank you. To Eve Samples, a fearless environmentalist and loyal friend for two decades, "I love you!" Every cat video hit just right. I thank my brother, Mark Susca, and his wife, Sam Susca, for Fripp Island visits that provided much-needed breaks. My stepmother, Susie Susca, who makes a wicked good Derby pie, always offered a respite from the stress on visits south. My father, Peter Susca, is a retired Teamster who taught me to speak truth to power and showed me that collective action can force change. My mother, Patricia Susca, has made sacrifices throughout her life so that mine would improve. I am in awe of her compassion and strength. Finally, I offer a special acknowledgment to my daughter, Zoe. I finished my doctoral dissertation when Zoe was an infant, and I finish this book as she enters adolescence. Those eleven years provided many challenges and changes, but what remains is a boundless and unconditional love and the hope that she will know a more equitable and just world.

HEDGED

Introduction

What Crisis?

This book started to answer a question I couldn't.

In December 2017 the NBC News program *THINK* filmed me at American University, where I am an assistant professor of journalism, for a segment about broadcast policy, media consolidation, and newspaper profitability.[1] The month before, the Federal Communications Commission voted 3–2 along party lines, eliminating a decades-old prohibition against one company owning a television station and newspaper in the same market.[2] The FCC's order, which followed a petition from broadcasting giant Nexstar to bypass long-standing federal rules, also relaxed television and radio cross-ownership restrictions and created a path for companies to justify ownership of top-rated stations in the same market.[3] While the FCC's Republican majority claimed that the changes modernized rules and said minority ownership would be unaffected, Democrat Jessica Rosenworcel, now chair of the FCC, dissented, writing, "This agency set its most basic values on fire."[4] Prometheus Radio Project, an advocacy group against corporate media consolidation, sought to stop the loosened rules, concerned about core features of telecommunications policy, including competition, diversity, and localism.[5]

The case went to court. *Prometheus Radio Project v. FCC* became the latest in a long line of legal battles pitting the regulatory authority criticized for its alignment with powerful media companies against advocates concerned about the erosion of policies meant to protect the public. The US Court of Appeals for the Third Circuit ruled against the FCC, calling its analysis "so insubstantial" that it provided no justification to relax ownership rules.[6] In 2020 the FCC, with strong industry support, sought and received review from the most important court in America. The US Supreme Court heard oral arguments in January 2021.

The FCC doubled down that a weakened local newspaper marketplace, in part, warranted regulatory changes. Amicus briefs from groups with ties to the country's largest broadcasters, including the CBS Television Network Affiliates Association, supported the FCC's position. Gray Television, which operates or owns 162 stations covering 24 percent of US households, also filed an amicus brief in May 2020 in support of the FCC.[7] Its brief said that cross-ownership would allow synergies between broadcast outlets and newspapers in the same market because both "continue to shrink the amount of local news they provide."[8] That statement about the state of newspapers certainly is true. But a deeper document review reveals who is responsible for gutting local newspapers nationwide through its ownership, and it's the same hedge fund that also invested heavily in television companies supporting the relaxed rules. In early 2020 Alden Global Capital, by then in control of the Digital First Media newspaper chain, owned 986,300 shares of Gray Television.[9] Called a "destroyer of newspapers," Alden by June 2020 also owned 11.5 million shares of Tribune Publishing and 4 million shares of Lee Enterprises, a newspaper company founded in 1890.[10] Alden that year also owned shares of Nexstar, Sinclair Broadcast Group, and ViacomCBS.[11]

Despite concerns from advocates and the Third Circuit court's damning assessment of the FCC's methodology, the US Supreme Court in April 2021 unanimously sided with the FCC, heating up the media buying market and further consolidating ownership. Within months of the Supreme Court's ruling, Alden bought Tribune outright. By the end of 2021, two hedge funds controlled three of the most important newspaper chains in the United States. Two other publicly traded newspaper chains, including Gannett, the nation's largest, had millions of shares owned by powerful private investment firms, including BlackRock, which in September 2021 counted nearly $10 trillion in assets under management.[12] Through institutional stock ownership or outright control, private investment funds now hold sway over roughly half of all newspapers among the top twenty-five chains.[13] Apollo Global Management, which in 2019 financed a billion-dollar merger between Gannett and GateHouse / New Media and bought parts of Cox Media Group television stations, announced in February 2022 that, with another hedge fund, it intended to purchase TEGNA, one of the nation's largest broadcast chains, in a deal worth $8.6 billion.[14] Five years after the FCC's decision to deregulate, we have a newspaper and television news system owned and influenced by the ultrawealthy dismantling the very institution meant to give a voice to average citizens in a democracy.

In 2017 I did not know how much to blame on these funds. At that time, conventional wisdom noted that much of the local newspaper crisis could be attributed to "the internet," a catch-all boogeyman that suggested that the destruction of newspapers had been an unpredictable result of rapid technological innovation and shifting advertising revenue online. The internet became both an explanation for the destruction and a tool for newspapers' resurrection. We were just starting to learn more at that time about how hedge funds would operate as owners in a newspaper market in transition. Private equity firms, which are a different type of institutional investor, received even less attention as a democratic hazard. While advocates and scholars have studied the threats of media consolidation, the influence and power of these funds in the newspaper marketplace taken as a whole during this critical time period remained relatively uncovered when I sat down to chat with NBC producer Christine Nguyen. The dots—of ownership, of historical influence, of money, of impact, and of power—remained largely disconnected.

Back on my Washington, DC, campus one month after the FCC's vote, Nguyen used the term "crisis" when she asked me about newspapers.[15] I talked then about how a shrinking number of corporate media chains owned newspapers nationwide and explained that each chain was responsible for sharp cuts affecting city, county, and town government coverage. Since then, reporting staff has further contracted, meaning fewer people are paid to hold local politicians, government, and industry accountable for decisions that influence whether the wastewater treatment plant gets built near your house or if your property tax rate gets hiked to pay for it.[16] When Nguyen asked me, "What would make newspapers sustainable?" I answered that first we must reconsider what sustainability means for media companies, especially newspaper companies. I noted of chain television and newspaper owners that the question long has been about maximizing profit, or, as I said it then, "how much more money corporations bleed from these markets." I added, "It's not that they're not making a profit, it's that they aren't making enough profit." Nguyen asked how I knew that the loss of local reporting jobs and a never-ending stream of mergers were as bad for democracy as I suggested. Beyond personal newsroom experience and several dog-eared theoretical works, I will admit here that I could not cite how the consolidations, mergers, and layoffs so rampant in the newspaper industry over the last two decades had impacted local democracy. I theorized that it was bad, but how much did I really know? I started this book in order to answer that question. Along the way, it expanded into something more.

Private Investment Funds Are Everywhere

In early 2018 I started investigating American newspaper ownership, compiling over the next three years thousands of pages of bankruptcy court filings, congressional documents, corporate documents, trade reports, and regulatory forms filed with the US Securities and Exchange Commission. At the start of my research, I had been interested in examining layoffs and mergers at corporate newspaper chains, including Gannett, GateHouse, Digital First Media, Lee Enterprises, McClatchy, MediaNews Group, and Tribune Publishing, so that I could answer Nguyen's questions. I knew then that most top chains, by both circulation and the number of newspapers owned, were publicly traded, with shares bought and sold on the New York Stock Exchange or Nasdaq. Early on, I remained focused on the chains, not the investors influencing them, so I was surprised to see how much the newspaper companies shared something else.

The documents revealed that all of those newspaper companies listed above have private investment fund investment or ownership, some of which changed and strengthened during the writing of this book. Other newspaper companies I reviewed showed similar influence that dated back years before the internet upended the industry. While I started out studying the newspaper chains mentioned above, this book evolved into a study of the institutional investors and hedge fund owners who pushed for mergers and acquisitions that stacked debt at many of the top chains as the digital future beckoned. Private investment firms have exerted various levels of influence over corporate newspaper firms as institutional investors or managers or as part of other complex financing and debt restructuring after blockbuster mergers and acquisitions.[17] Looking at the state of newspapers today, Alden Global Capital has front-page magazine stories devoted to its predatory practices, but the calamity of its ownership is just an extension of what has existed for years: private equity greed and Wall Street influence in the name of profit.[18] As I traced that institutional investment, I also considered the impacts of private investment ownership and influence on reporters and audiences in a democracy. Across America, readers strive for newspaper substitutes, finding instead algorithmic-driven social media sites and ultrapartisan pollution online.

Perhaps to some, and, I'd wager, especially to readers from finance, this overarching finding of the seemingly boundless role that private equity firms and hedge funds play in today's chain newspaper market and over its last two decades is unsurprising. Bloomberg's New York bureau chief, Jason Kelly, opened his 2012 book, *The New Tycoons: Inside the Trillion Dollar Private Equity Industry That Owns Everything* by noting how much private equity influences daily life.

While on vacation at LEGOLAND California Resort with his son, Kelly remarked that the property is backed by private equity investment. His hotel and car rental company also were owned by different private equity firms, including the Blackstone Group, which is one of the nation's largest, with $619 billion in assets under management. At dinner with a friend who had run several major corporations, including Burger King, Continental Airlines, and Quiznos, Kelly noted that private equity firms had owned all of those, too. "The more I looked, the more I found it," Kelly wrote.[19] Such is also true of private investment fund influence in the American chain newspaper marketplace. The more you look, the more you find it.

Private investment funds include both private equity firms and hedge funds, and chapter 1 explains more about this class of business that has become so significant across so many sectors of the global economy. Penelope Muse Abernathy has deemed these hedge funds and private equity firms "the media barons of the 21st century."[20] Robert Picard first published on the role of institutional investors—a type of pooled fund that may include hedge funds, mutual funds, or private equity—in the 1990s.[21] His work since has expanded our understanding of media economics and ownership across fields and subspecialties both before and after the 2008 recession.[22] In 2011 he wrote, "The economics and financing of media companies are the foundations upon which all media activity takes place."[23] Despite this outsized influence—much of it buried between corporate chain monikers and tangles of financial and government documents—and outside of Abernathy's reports, there has not yet been a complete volume dedicated solely to the funds' history and control. With this book, I hope to add to an existing body of literature by tracing the last twenty years of private investment fund involvement and ownership at major chains. These firms' influence is so important that omitting them engages in a one-sided mythology that the internet and its hunger for newspaper advertising revenue are the only causes of the modern newspaper industry's strife.

Rich folks have owned newspapers dating back to colonial America, but chapter 3 explains what makes private investment fund ownership and investment so much worse than the family and chain ownership that dominated past eras of newspaper history. Pat Gauen, a retired *St. Louis Post-Dispatch* editor and columnist, has watched as the industry's watchdog function has eroded, telling me in an October 2020 interview: "There are governments that nobody watches. There are investigations that might have made major changes that are lost. Investigations that could have led to new approaches and policy, but there's nobody to call."[24] As such, the private investment fund trend is as pervasive as it is troubling, requiring a new classification, a new way to historically contextualize newspapers' role in democracy, seeing their diminished function under this for-profit regime. John Nerone and Kevin Barnhurst, who situated newsroom space and labor near the turn of the millennium, wrote about what they called "the corporate paper," noting that newsroom concerns then were a function of publicly held corporate owners. While not writing about private equity firms or hedge funds, the authors captured in 2003 the sense of the seismic shift I have sought to document: "The modern moment, and with it the reporter's or professional newspaper, has ended or is ending—it's hard to discern just where the caesura will rest."[25] I pinpointed what I see as the most pivotal moment in this recent history, looking back to when two private investment funds' entry into the newspaper market changed long-standing commercialism.

In 2003 the Blackstone Group and Providence Equity Partners reached a deal for a 40 percent stake of Freedom Communications, Inc., thus ushering in a new era of newspaper history that I call the private investment era. Over the two decades since, overharvesting for profits, mergers and acquisitions, debt, layoffs, and labor issues impacting reporters' role as a function of the Fourth Estate have defined and shaped this era, creating what I call the newspaper industry's neglected audiences: citizens unable to rely on local newspapers to stay informed about the inner workings of their local boards, commissions, and governments. In subsequent chapters, I explain and outline each of these features through an investigation of the industry itself and by talking to citizens and journalists most affected by the loss of local news this era has created.

Newspapers by design are meant to hold government leaders accountable to the people, so fundamental a mission and so fundamental to our democracy that journalism is the only profession with rights enshrined in the US Constitution. Picard recognized the vast scholarship on democracy and the press. In his words, the role of the press in democratic societies is to "set the citizen above the state."[26] Consider John Stuart Mill's viewpoint that democracy is achieved by those who can govern themselves; he counted on us being informed to make that process work.[27] Ida B. Wells, writing in 1892, decades before Black women secured the right to vote, said, "The people must know before they can act, and there is no educator to compare with the press."[28] The free press produces a product that is uniquely protected by the First Amendment because it is meant to help citizens make decisions about their political lives. C. Edwin Baker explained that normative role as the "institutional structure," a forum by which people gained knowledge and governed themselves.[29] Yet private equity first and now hedge funds alongside them have weakened that accountability role.[30]

Beyond reporting on local governance and providing civic knowledge, newspapers also printed a range of opinions, offered community calendars, and covered everything from the Little League schedule to road construction projects. Of local newspapers, Ayad Akhtar, a Pulitzer Prize–winning playwright and PEN America trustee, wrote: "Local news is local know-how defined. A healthy local news ecosystem provides communities with the information they need to live safe, healthy lives and participate in the democratic life of their communities."[31] My focus in this book on private investment funds' history and rise in the newspaper industry also considers something even bleaker than just their ownership and power. It considers the scorched earth they leave behind and what it means for the future of news and information in American democratic society.

On Theory and Methodology

The political economy of media provides the book's overarching theoretical and methodological lens in order to study the private investment era and its five defining features, but I also borrow techniques from investigative journalism to tell the story of the last twenty years and upend the myth that the internet alone destroyed newspapers. Robert W. McChesney has focused numerous critiques on the democratic impacts of our nation's for-profit media marketplace, writing in 2000: "A media system set up to serve the needs of Wall Street and Madison Avenue cannot and does not serve the needs of the preponderance of the population."[32] Baker called such practices of favoring business interests over citizen needs quite simply a "market failure."[33] Thomas Corrigan explained political economy's normative standpoint and its links to work on solutions benefiting democratic practices: "Where media systems fail to advance the public interest, PEC [political economy] scholars work to denaturalize those systems and transform both media and society along more just and equitable lines."[34]

Debates even between normative scholars exist, as do cyclical criticisms of the news media in general and its role in democracy specifically.[35] Scholars in past market analyses of media systems, often examining the reliance on advertising, see extreme profit at best as a financial benefit that may support better media but more often as a hindrance to its normative and editorial goals.[36] Ronald Bettig examined private equity's involvement in music, radio, and one newspaper deal: "I believe we need a greater awareness of how PE [private equity] affects media production and output and the ramifications of a further drift toward an entirely privately controlled media system based on the pursuit of profit rather than the promotion of democracy."[37] Modern critical political economy's focus on concentration of ownership, conglomeration, and the commercialism and commodification of audiences at the expense of media that is vital to the maintenance of a democracy is the lens by which I look at these issues. Political-economic critiques recognize the problems with for-profit production, and this book applies that lens to the funds in control of production. The power and, increasingly, the problems lie there.

My work also answers, in part, a call to expand both production and audience scholarship in this crucial area related to hedge fund ownership of and private equity investment in newspapers, recognizing that not all work in this important area is framed by political economy. In 2017 Rodney Benson offered this analysis of what he called an "ambivalent" critique of commercialism: "What we need now are better answers to that hedge funder's dead-end analysis: there's a huge problem, nobody's going to help, there's nothing we can do about it. We need a more thoroughgoing analysis of the causes and consequences of market failure, a better normative articulation of the tensions between democratic aspirations and market pressures, and a public policy analysis of what to do about it."[38] Through the construction of the private investment era and its five features, I sought to document those causes and consequences in the US newspaper market. In 2011 McChesney and John Nichols noted the fundamental problems unique to newspapers: "That newspapers are in crisis, and may soon become extinct after being central to the American experience through the country's entire history, is a fact now broadly accepted."[39] Victor Pickard, in *Democracy without Journalism? Confronting the Misinformation Society*, referred to the market inflicting "violence on the industry."[40] In setting an agenda for future research, Ignacio Siles and Pablo Boczkowski noted the need to historically situate the modern newspaper crisis and called for more empirical work producing original data.[41] I sought through primary financial, government, and judicial documents complemented by in-depth interviews to document these firms' control and to consider the impacts of that control on journalists and audiences in our democracy.

Other writers have also documented local newspapers in crisis using various terms to describe it. Margaret Sullivan, while a columnist at the *Washington Post*, wrote of the industry's trouble in *Ghosting the News: Local Journalism and the Crisis of American Democracy* using a house-on-fire metaphor: "The match was struck years ago, the kerosene poured, and the house is very much ablaze."[42]

A decade before that, Alex Jones considered "newspapers on the brink," while Christopher Anderson wrote about "local journalism on the brink."[43] Dean Starkman applied his Pulitzer Prize–winning research skills to the study of financial journalism and focused his critique on a business press that's a "watchdog that didn't bark."[44] While the terms and context may differ, academics and practitioners generally agree that newspapers are indeed in crisis. Who deserves the blame for putting them there is a matter of more debate.

The internet and now COVID-19 have been blamed for the newspaper industry's decline, for creating or exacerbating the crisis.[45] Not all newspapers are money losers, and some companies had digital revenue climbing as people sought more information about the global pandemic.[46] The journalism-in-crisis narratives often fail to address revenue and profit at several corporate chains. As an example, a January 2022 analysis showed that Gannett captured 28.2 percent of newspaper publishing marketing share and had 179 million unique monthly visitors online. The publicly traded company also saw a 40.9 percent increase in revenue in 2020, climbing to $5.9 billion in 2021.[47] Ken Doctor reported on a set of leaked Alden Global Capital financials showing that it had a 17 percent operating margin, earning $160 million in profit in 2017.[48] Elsewhere in the marketplace, others are profiting off a sophisticated system of financing and debt restructuring, with newspapers and their reporting personnel caught in the middle. The real story of what went wrong and continues to go wrong at the chains I studied is more nuanced, and central to its creation and maintenance are profit-minded owners and managers treating newspapers and their staff like any other disposable product in a capitalist society.

Beyond balance sheets and stock prices, the loss of an informed and engaged citizenry is the real consequence of these funds' ownership and investment, firms that also profit off the myth of newspaper insolvency. What we have is not a crisis of profit. What we have is a crisis of greed and growing inequality. Too much discussion on the well-documented crisis of local newspapers is framed as if the forces of its crisis were external, but my records analysis, complemented by 124 interviews, offers a different way of thinking about the crisis at several newspaper chains. In many ways an industry beholden to private investment funds both before and after the internet advertising crash and Great Recession created and maintained the crisis. And make no mistake: while a market crash implies devastation, by 2011 US newspapers still made $20 billion a year, an enviable target for many sectors of the economy.[49]

Not all American newspapers are owned or influenced by private equity firms and hedge funds, but the largest and most influential chains are, and this book hones in on the influence these firms exert, documenting their entry into the market, analyzing their current power, and looking ahead at how the future will look after they've sold off all the buildings, laid off more reporting staff, and cashed out on what's left of the free press.[50] It leaves out independent dailies and weeklies, as well as a number of family-owned chains. It also omits the *New York Times* and the *Washington Post*, both major brands themselves and each with different ownership structures, making them unique in the marketplace. Dan Kennedy examined private billionaire owners at the *Boston Globe*, the *Orange County Register*, and the *Washington Post*, noting that they could help the newspaper business.[51] While the *Post* appears better under billionaire Jeff Bezos's ownership, the *Orange County Register* under its billionaire owner received an unfortunate reality check. Alden bought the *Register* in 2016, and the hedge fund thwarted the efforts of another billionaire hotel tycoon to take over the *Baltimore Sun* and Tribune in 2021.[52] While billionaire owners in cities like Minneapolis and major philanthropic donations or shifts to nonprofit status are an interesting, albeit rare phenomenon, the more common influence of private fund ownership and investment focuses my critique.[53] I also recognize the existence, as Abernathy's astounding work has shown, of vast swaths of America that are "news deserts," places without any newspapers left. This book focuses on the history and current operation of investment fund owners and institutional investors where newspapers still circulate—Abernathy calls these "ghost newspapers"—and I predict that the role of these firms will widen until cities and towns with functioning newspapers inevitably turn into the news deserts that her work has drawn important attention to. It is, indeed, a crisis.

Looking over the last twenty years and using a variety of searches and databases generating thousands of pages of documents, I have been able to show not only the current influence of private investment funds but also how that influence has been rising steadily as it has changed. I used bankruptcy court records, federal court documents, trade reports and news articles, congressional and government communication, communication to shareholders, campaign finance records, and quarterly and annual forms filed with the US Securities and Exchange Commission to create a timeline and to chart this private fund power in the newspaper marketplace. Each chapter outlines key findings related to this investment and ownership crisis, but first I describe how I accessed these records. I hope that my explanation of how I accessed these records will help other researchers to replicate this hybrid critical and investigative work.

The SEC requires scant documentation from private investment funds, but publicly traded newspaper firms file more disclosures and documents.[54] These records are accessible from a number of locations, often directly from the SEC website. Examples of SEC files for private firms include a 13F, which is a disclosure of securities, and an ADV, which is a registration notification. Publicly traded companies file a 10-K, which is an annual report, and a 10-Q, which is quarterly. These forms generate a lot of information and data, some of them extraneous and some of them invaluable. Consider that Gannett's 2020 10-K is 166 pages.[55] The 2019 version reached 161 pages.[56] These forms include boilerplate language about a company and its management. They also list useful data for critical and journalism scholars such as information about assets, properties owned, executive compensation, and financial statements, including those related to equity and cash flow transactions. While some of the information in these forms may seem extraneous or pro forma, much information included in the pages of these reports is required by law and provides a window onto corporate media organizations' operations and leadership. Over time, patterns emerge.

While the twenty years of SEC files provide a huge trove of documents, as complements I conducted searches on the newspaper chains, as well as on their financial parent companies and major institutional investors where appropriate in other databases, all of which are available through my campus library. The Mergent Online database shows newspaper company data, including executive profiles, debt, cash flows, revenue, net income, cash from financing, number of employees, and dates of mergers and acquisitions. *Mergent Industrial Manuals* show in-depth company history, including corporation data, dates of acquisitions, and subsidiaries. The S&P Capital IQ database provides company information in the following categories: net income, capital expenditures, debt, and assets, as well as information on companies' executive leadership and board of directors. S&P Capital IQ also shows a company's institutional investors, and these can be charted over time. The Alliance for Audited Media's Media Intelligence Center provides ownership, print, and digital circulation figures at the owner/parent company level and at the newspaper level for dozens of newspapers, which acted as a complement to other reports. To access court records, I primarily used Bloomberg Law and LexisNexis. Tribune bankruptcy documents are voluminous, and access points exist from a number of locations online.

Outside of traditional database research, I also relied on public records requests, which can take months to be filled and require navigating a different type of bureaucracy. I acquired records related to Alden's use of pension funds, explained in chapter 6, through a Freedom of Information Act (FOIA) request I made to the US Department of Labor in October 2020. In November 2020 the department's Employee Benefits Security Administration responded by letter that no records were "responsive" to my request at the national office, noting that others may exist in its Kansas regional office. Several emails and phone calls were required to secure documents. Eventually, the US Department of

Labor produced documents in response to that FOIA request in April 2021. In June 2022 I filed a second FOIA request, which, three months later, generated more records about Alden Global Capital's financial practices, which, it appears, have been tracked by the federal government for years.

Searches must account for changes in ownership, subsidiaries, and rebrands. Tribune became Tronc and now is back to Tribune Publishing, which Alden owns. Alden operates its other newspaper chain as Digital First Media, and sometimes files fall under MNG, or MediaNews Group, a private chain that Alden first invested in more than a decade ago and now owns outright. Some SEC documents are under Alden Global Capital LLC, while others fall under Alden Global Capital Ltd. Its subsidiary, 21st CMH Acquisition Co., also appears. Gannett appears in some databases as Gannett (New) after its 2019 merger with GateHouse. Fortress Investment Group controlled both GateHouse and its New Media Investment Group rebrand. Fortress, a private equity firm, is part of a Japanese multinational conglomerate called SoftBank Group. Institutional investors own huge chunks of shares of Gannett and Lee Enterprises, two chains that, as of October 1, 2022, have held off hedge fund ownership. Chatham Asset Management, a New Jersey hedge fund, owns the McClatchy chain, which operates the *Miami Herald* and *El Nuevo Herald*, among others.

The records used for this book are like different puzzle pieces, and they have allowed me to assemble a picture of private investment funds' influence in the newspaper industry dating back to 2003, although it existed before that. Since shares fluctuate with capitalist markets, I have also noted that investment has differed year to year and even quarter to quarter. In reality, it can change day to day, although a financial website explained that this practice is "more like gambling than investing."[57] The records show that private equity first and hedge funds later have had different roles in the last two decades, but overwhelmingly, these firms' power and stake are growing as newspapers, and local democratic participation has been impacted.

This document work is complemented by 124 in-depth interviews generating 106 hours of material. These interviews form the foundation for the arguments and analysis in chapters 6 and 7. My years as a local newspaper reporter, first at a family-owned suburban Connecticut daily and later at a chain-owned Florida newspaper, have afforded other insights related to the importance of local newspapers' key functions in communities. These, alongside my scholarly credentials, are experiences I believe it's important for readers to consider.

Practicing Local News

I understand the role of local newspapers in civic life because I was a local newspaper reporter for several years after graduating from the Columbia University Graduate School of Journalism. As a twenty-five-year-old master's student, I took a fall 2001 seminar with Professor James W. Carey, who at first I underappreciated. I favored the reporting courses that sent me out to beats in the South Bronx and Sunset Park, Brooklyn. I can admit now, with twenty years of hindsight, that his doctorate gave him the appearance of existing in a nebular space far away from those of us who wanted to be practitioners. This felt especially true when I studied at Columbia during and after 9/11. I wanted to do journalism. I didn't want to analyze it. Yet on graduation day, weeks away from my first reporting job amid an economic downturn, there was only one person I sought out to discuss the future. I looked for Carey.

In an hour-long Illinois Public Media piece broadcast in 2006 after Carey's death at age seventy-one, the host said he had been an internationally recognized media critic, but he was revered as a teacher who loved journalists, which the host called "something uncommon among academics."[58] Just as there may be an assumed chasm between academics and journalists, I offer that another sometimes exists in journalists' understanding of the financing of the industry they work in or the reasons people like me now critique it. Carey understood this often myopic and Pollyannaish take journalists have on journalism: "The standard histories of journalism, which have come largely from journalism schools, are consistently whiggish in tone. They account for the development of the press against an assumed background for the expansion of freedom and knowledge."[59] I am cognizant of the ways this book offers a critique of the newspaper industry's corporate, private equity, and hedge fund realities, and that has upset some people I know who still work in the field and who fear it will be weaponized against newspapers and journalists. As news of this project filtered through my own social media network, a former Scripps Howard colleague emailed me to say, "I won't help you kill newspapers." Others reminded me of the long hours and investigative work that still gets done at newspapers nationwide despite the cuts and furloughs.[60] I hope this text offers a contribution to the field, bridging both the academic and the journalistic while drawing on methods from both. Journalism, when done well, is a public service and force for change. That does not mean that its history and contemporary practices are beyond reproach.

I worked as a local reporter from 2002 to 2007, spending the last four years at a Scripps Howard newspaper with offices in Fort Pierce, Stuart, and Vero

Beach, Florida. When people ask me when I worked there, I joke that it was "two owners ago." Gannett, influenced for years by private equity investment, owns it now. I covered education in St. Lucie County, Florida, a district plagued by achievement problems with a history of segregation. Nearly two decades after *Brown v. Board of Education* determined that separate wasn't equal, St. Lucie County schools finally desegregated.[61] The county was under federal monitoring of its schools' populations for another two decades. Rural cattle farms on one end, suburban in the middle, and urban in the northeast, not far from the beaches of Hutchinson Island, St. Lucie County was by the mid-2000s a minority-majority school district of more than forty thousand children. A data-driven investigation I did revealed that the system had resegregated its three dozen schools using a geographic busing model that leaders told parents was helping to maintain equality. My reporting forced changes, and it occasionally caused outrages, but it always was based on the premise that I was there to hold local government leaders accountable to the public.

I saw my role in local democracy as one that helped keep the community informed, and when it was time for school board elections, voters would decide if elected officials' decisions warranted keeping them in office. I am not unique in this role, and newspapers before corporate and private investment fund influence once employed more staff like me to do this important work. We were conduits between people and government, an important part of the local democratic ecosystem, though scholars such as Herbert J. Gans, looking mostly at national news, noted that this is flawed thinking about the journalist's role and actual citizen participation.[62] At the local level, I saw it work. And now I see it crumbling.

For more than four years, I had been one of three education reporters along Florida's Treasure Coast, each with their own county beat. When I left for a doctoral program in 2007, my schools beat was added to another staff writer's workload. A reporter I trained and mentored at American University took the revised K–12 education job in 2019. Alone, she covered education in all three counties, a region roughly the size of Rhode Island extending more than seventy miles along the Atlantic coast and inland to Lake Okeechobee. She is one of the most talented and committed young journalists I've supervised in fifteen years of teaching, but doing the work of three people takes its toll. It also means reporters make gut-wrenching decisions about which issues to cover and which meetings to attend, meaning that much of local government in these counties and cities goes unchecked and unwatched as people's stories go untold.

Using the Book

How did we get to a place where three top newspaper chains are controlled by hedge funds and two others are heavily influenced by institutional investors aligned in the same profit-motivated sector? This book aims to provide both historical perspective and contemporary context about the local newspaper crisis by focusing on newspaper chains' financing and ownership. It traces an arc from January 2003 to October 2022, examining the roots and rise of private equity and hedge fund power in the newspaper marketplace. It is designed to engage with American newspaper history, but the chapters that focus on the five core characteristics of the private investment era can be used individually.

Chapter 1 explains the key characteristics of the private investment era, as it explains how these firms operate as a sector of the US economy overall. Chapter 2 provides historical context, situating the era in this current period of financialization and in contrast to other time periods' commercial interests dating back to the eighteenth century. Chapters 3, 4, and 5, relying on trade reports, regulatory filings, and bankruptcy documents, investigate why and how we got here. Chapter 3 examines the era's first feature, which I describe as overharvesting, adapting a term from Philip Meyer's work on corporate news owners and profit motivation. Chapter 4 outlines twenty years of mergers and acquisitions, chosen by industry leaders influenced by private equity as an antidote to the rise of the internet as a tool to increase corporate newspaper power. Chapter 5 examines how, as advertising losses mounted, the debt that had resulted from mergers and acquisitions transformed the newspaper industry and created its own market for private investment funds interested in distressed companies. Chapters 6 and 7 examine the ownership effects for newspaper workers and local news audiences in a democracy, building a narrative and mapping concerns from a loss of trust to local government unchecked. Chapter 6 examines journalistic labor, contextualizing the loss of accountability journalism that results from newsroom layoffs. I interviewed thirty-eight current and former reporters and editors, including the president of the NewsGuild–Communications Workers of America, and their views are complemented by corporate, government, court, and trade documents dealing with labor issues such as layoffs, pensions, and unionization. Chapter 7 switches the book's focus from production and newsrooms to more deeply engage with newspapers' citizen—and, I argue, its neglected—audiences, synthesizing eighty-five in-depth interviews with current and past subscribers. The 124 interviews—the final one was conducted with a Tribune bond holder for chapter 5—totaled 106 hours of material, and transcripts stretched to hundreds of pages.

After conducting three years of research and spending another year writing, I can definitively say that if you want to fix local newspapers, you must eliminate the private investment funds. The bigger question lingers: How? The conclusion focuses on two solutions, updating work on the growing nonprofit news marketplace and arguing for greater antitrust enforcement of the small network of private investment funds hovering over the newspaper market that have helped dismantle it piece by piece. But before we can address solutions, I believe we have to understand the hidden power and map the overt crisis of private equity and hedge funds behind America's newspaper industry in crisis.

This book tells that story.

Chapter 1

The Private Investment Era

Warren Buffett's Berkshire Hathaway had a dalliance with the chain newspaper market, acquiring in 2012 dozens of newspapers from Media General, based in Richmond, Virginia, for $142 million and operating them as BH Media Group.[1] The deal registers as a blip in Berkshire Hathaway's 112-page annual report, which explained that the conglomerate that year "achieved a total gain for its shareholders of $24.1 billion."[2] With the $142 million media deal, BH Media Group took control of newspapers throughout Nebraska, North Carolina, and Virginia in addition to a number of other small and midsized titles, including the *Tulsa World* in Oklahoma and the *Morning News* in Florence, South Carolina.

News wasn't new to the Omaha-based company. Berkshire Hathaway had for decades owned the *Buffalo Evening News* and controlled shares of the *Washington Post*'s former parent company before buying the bulk of Media General's print properties.[3] In 2018 Lee Enterprises began managing BH Media Group's newspapers in addition to its own. Less than two years later, Berkshire Hathaway no longer appeared interested in the media sector despite Buffett being described as a longtime newspaper booster, and the investor known for long-term strategies called the industry "toast."[4] The *Wall Street Journal* headlined Buffett's exit: "Warren Buffett Is Giving Up on Newspapers."[5] Buffett's mega-company sold the newspapers to Lee for $140 million, and the Iowa-based chain grew larger, with print and digital products serving seventy-seven markets in twenty-six states.[6]

In January 2020 Buffett wanting out of the newspaper business felt like a severe blow, the final gasp in a long line of death rattles because the grandfatherly Nebraska billionaire couldn't or wouldn't help fix it. But like so many stories about newspapers, chains, and their problems, there's always more beneath the surface. Buffett may have given up on owning, but newspapers are still making Berkshire Hathaway money. The conglomerate provided financing for the Lee deal through its BH Finance subsidiary and refinanced its earlier debt.[7] Lee Enterprises is scheduled to repay Buffett's company $576 million at a 9 percent interest rate over twenty-five years.[8] The deal, built on Lee's newspapers and its debt, stands to make Berkshire Hathaway nearly $1.3 billion in interest over the term of the loan.[9]

This book isn't about Buffett, the world's sixth richest person, according to the Forbes 2021 World's Billionaires List; instead, it focuses on a different financial segment of wealthy private investment fund investors and owners who are profiting off newspapers as they simultaneously run them into the ground.[10]

The story of today's newspaper industry, as it has been throughout American history, in many ways is a story about money. American newspapers in the late twentieth century made stratospheric revenue, earning at the peak 20 to 30 percent profit margins, but that changed in the first decade of the new millennium as advertising revenues plummeted.[11] But newspaper companies even then pulled 8 to 15 percent profit margins, matching or beating the average earned by S&P 500 companies.[12] Still, today's narrative of newspapers in crisis belies this economic reality. Have a casual conversation with anyone about the newspaper marketplace, and it's likely to focus on the money lost. It'll veer toward advertising revenue lost to free internet sites, money lost when subscribers cut and run, and corporate newspaper stock prices plummeting. Someone will mention Buffett's exit from the business as a sign of its demise rather than a feature of distressed debt markets and the digital future.

In the last two decades, as private investment funds have taken a larger role in America's top newspaper chains, I would argue that it has become a story not just about money but about a lot of money. Billions of dollars have changed hands as newspaper chains have been swapped and sold. But I don't think the most important story of contemporary newspapers is a story of money lost, although ours is an industry in crisis. Its most important story is about money being made, often disguised behind the facade and tired trope of a failing industry. Consider that in May 2021, when hedge fund Alden Global Capital took full control of Tribune Publishing, the newspaper company was "profitable and [had] more than $250 million in cash."[13] While the operation of hedge funds has received notable attention in recent years—they've been called parasites, vampires, and vultures—private equity firms arrived to the newspaper marketplace first, pressuring newsroom managers for greater returns, stifling innovation, and pushing for mergers and acquisitions that inflamed the debt. For two decades, wealthy firms have chipped and chipped some more at newspaper companies by cutting coverage and staff to maximize their bottom line. And counter to those aims, good journalism costs money.[14]

The biggest winners since the private investment era began in 2003, capitalizing off what's left of the newspaper market and bleeding it dry, have been hedge funds like Alden and private equity firms like Fortress Investment Group, which took tens of millions of dollars in management fees from the GateHouse and Gannett chains.[15] These firms have profited off an industry in flux, an industry that for years failed to adjust and to pivot to the digital realities shaping today's media marketplace. This book examines the money circulating in and around the contemporary newspaper industry by looking at financial firms that own or influence chains, including Digital First Media, Gannett, Lee Enterprises, McClatchy, and Tribune Publishing, though it explains other chains affected by private investment funds, too, including those that no longer exist or were consolidated to form these chains. In reality, if you view these newspaper chains by their private investment fund owners and investors, a small group appears frequently over these last twenty years, sometimes in unison to finance blockbuster deals or sometimes against each other to fight out ownership in court. While in October 2022 three of the top newspaper chains are owned by two different hedge funds, both Gannett and Lee are influenced by institutional investors, too. Gannett has ties to private investment firms Apollo Global Management, BlackRock Inc., and Fortress. Alden in November 2021 put Lee on notice that it wanted to take over the company, and the fight went to court.[16] As of October 2022, Lee Enterprises won the latest round, but Nasdaq records based on 13-F filings show that institutional investors, among them BlackRock, still control nearly one-third of Lee shares.[17]

Not all American newspapers are owned or influenced by private investment funds, but the aforementioned chains are, and their influence in the name of profit forms the basis for this book's major arguments and my construction of the private investment era to tell this story. The private investment era has five defining features: overharvesting, mergers and acquisitions, debt, layoffs, and neglected audiences. These are unique yet interrelated characteristics that stem from private investment funds' influence and ownership, which have weakened newspapers' normative role in democracy. While there are many ways the information could be presented—chronologically or by the financial firms or the newspaper chains—I have chosen to write the chapters according to the issues

I see as the most prominent from the last twenty years as a way to chart the causes and consequences of this ownership and investment. Certainly, other issues—among them trust, analytics, and social media—exist. I would argue that those are by-products of the same power structures I have studied.

In situating the document and in-depth interview research that led me to conceptualize and chart the private investment era, I believe its five defining features act as a helpful heuristic and entry point to the overarching issues impacting newspapers over the last twenty years that have been influenced by private equity firms and hedge funds. It is my hope—in characterizing the influence of private investment funds in the marketplace as a newspaper era—that we have a more succinct model to understand the last two decades of newspaper history. These last twenty years have been similar to past newspaper eras, which have their own unique characteristics born of the economics, social conditions, and politics of their own times. This work examines and contextualizes the role of private funds in the newspaper marketplace before, during, and after the crucial period of advertising loss to free online sites and 2008's Great Recession.

Commercialism has been part of the US newspaper marketplace as long as we have had newspapers and, I would argue, has long been its defining feature. By the 1990s, public newspaper companies offered investors steady returns up to 20 percent, with larger takes in some markets.[18] Brian O'Connor, whose award-winning newspaper career spanned forty years and included a stint as a Knight-Bagehot Fellow in economics and business at Columbia University, worked at Tribune's South Florida *Sun-Sentinel*. "The only way you could have made more money was to have the printing presses crank out $10 bills," O'Connor remembered.[19] The commercialism of the private investment era should be understood as what it is: a natural extension and progression of the centuries of profitable American print journalism that came before it. Any story about extreme wealth must expand to examine inequality, including inequality between investors and newspaper staff writers who face near-constant pressure of layoffs and inequality between who gets a platform for their issues and who does not. And, crucial to the debate about newspapers in crisis, there is the inequality inherent between the information needs of citizens in a democracy compared to what is provided to them in the digital and print pages of newspapers beholden to private investment funds.

Into the twenty-first century, efforts to maximize revenue came amid a digital transition, with companies influenced or run by nonnewspaper managers who were seeking to save or to raise those stratospheric earnings that O'Connor remembered. When private equity billionaire Sam Zell used a complex system of leveraged financing to buy Tribune in 2007, internal company records from his leadership team showed their take on the business. In one memo dated August 9, 2007, an executive from his private equity company wrote to Zell about Tribune: "We want the company to move toward maximizing profitability."[20] That same document encouraged Zell to appoint someone to the board of directors: "His appointment signals that journalism is an important element of the business—not the only or even the most important element." Later, watching companies like Tribune destroyed by debt but still influential and profitable, hedge funds were the sharks that smelled blood in the water and struck, transforming the debt to equity and then dismantling the newspapers piece by piece. Hedge funds like Alden have earned reputations for redefining even the most cutthroat business practices, and now they're among the country's largest newspaper chain owners.

The Locusts of the Financial World

Before I discuss the role and growth of hedge funds and private equity in the newspaper marketplace, it is important to explain and to distinguish the two and to chart their growth as a sector of the US economy over the last two decades. These funds' growth is part of a broader period of financialization that Gerald Epstein in his 2005 book on the subject explained as "the increasing role of financial motives, financial markets, financial actors and financial institutions in the operation of the domestic and international economies."[21] Epstein coined the term "financialization" to describe the simultaneous loss of manufacturing and rise of the American financial sector in the 1980s. In her 2010 book on financialization's impact on the journalism industry, Núria Almiron explains the neoliberal roots of the explosions of these financial firms' money and power in the 2000s. The outcome is what she calls "periods of overcapacity" at the hands of a Wall Street overclass generating global instability in the name of profit.[22] Dwayne Winseck, writing about financialization and conglomerates in the Canadian media market, noted how influential these firms have been and how much the digital sphere gets blamed for the problems they have created.[23]

Although private equity firms and hedge funds are different from each other, both are types of pooled investment funds and alternative asset classes that share characteristics in this period of financialization. The US Government Accountability Office groups the two in its reporting on pension plans' investments.[24] Both fall under the broad umbrella of "institutional investors," which in addition to private equity and hedge funds may include pension funds, insurance companies, and mutual funds. There are differences, and that means differences exist in how private equity firms and hedge funds have operated and still do operate in the newspaper marketplace. What they share in the newspaper market is profit-motivated strategies that have negatively impacted the industry. Hedge funds typically focus on short-term transactions, often for a select group of wealthy investors. Private equity looks at longer-term investments, with firms frequently installing their own management in the private businesses they buy. Private equity uses a majority of borrowed or outside financing to make acquisitions.[25] Jeffrey C. Hooke, in his book *The Myth of Private Equity*, calls this type of deal a "no-money-down" commitment.[26] Firms can profit from those leveraged deals, while others have perfected profiting from the debt of distressed companies.[27] While private equity firms operate in three general areas—leveraged buyouts, growth capital, and venture capital—Hooke noted that their leveraged buyout deals now mark 65 percent of their business as a sector. Hooke also explained that hedge funds can and do leverage, but they tend to focus on publicly traded securities. Steven Drobny noted a decade ago that hedge funds' and private equity firms' use of borrowed funds separates them from the class of "real money" funds that oversee individual wealth, university endowments, and mutual funds.[28] In a 2019 report to the United Nations Economic Commission for Latin America and the Caribbean, Epstein explained that the largest asset management companies also control shares of US banks, and he showed that consolidation exists in those markets, too.[29]

Hedge funds and private equity firms have both their cheerleaders and their critics. Depending on your perspective, the anecdotes about the Miami mansions and black-tie parties dotting some nonfiction works are either motivating lore to emphasize endless possibilities in the market or cautionary tales signifying what's gone so terribly wrong. A book on hedge fund investing includes chapters titled "Learning to Scavenge" and "Looking for Prey."[30] Metaphors and anecdotes aside, the field is not without its darker side.[31] Reports and investigations have tied private investment funds to periods of great economic instability and losses for people who don't get invited to what professors Wulf Kaal and Dale Oesterle have called "the exclusive playground."[32] Aaron Glantz, investigating the 2008 housing crisis, put the blame squarely on these types of firms, which pioneered using mortgage-backed securities and bundles of debt to generate profit that left millions of Americans financially wrecked.[33] Ann-Kristin Achleitner and Christoph Kaserer wrote that hedge funds and private equity funds "have been compared to locusts, notorious for exhausting whole countries."[34] Peter Temple referred to hedge funds as "upmarket prostitutes" that have disabled the global financial system.[35]

Jennifer Oppold wrote that there is no accepted definition of a hedge fund; nevertheless, these types of pooled investment funds saw huge expansion in the 2000s.[36] The modern hedge fund concept started more than seventy years ago when Alfred Winslow Jones attempted to predict both undervalued and overvalued stocks, which he would "short."[37] Temple wrote that short selling is "a peculiar investment technique—selling securities one doesn't own, but has simply borrowed, in the hope of buying them back at a lower price to return to the lender, while pocketing the profit."[38] The strategy paid off for Jones. As Temple told it, a *Fortune* magazine headline in April 1966 described Jones's financial success as "The Jones Nobody Keeps Up With."[39] It's one of the financial magazine's favorite stories of all time, and it was written by retired financial journalist Carol Loomis, who explained Jones's ability to deliver returns above 600 percent.[40] By 2004 seventeen hedge fund managers were earning more than $100 million a year or more.[41]

As the returns skyrocketed, so, too, did the money invested in these funds. By 2006 more than a trillion dollars had been invested in hedge funds, accounting for nearly half the trading on two of the world's largest stock exchanges.[42] By the end of 2016, the global hedge fund industry, much of it headquartered in the United States with shelters in places like Bermuda and the Cayman Islands, had at least $5 trillion in assets under management.[43] The goal is to generate returns high above market averages.[44] Yet those returns aren't for everyone. Hedge funds limit the number of investors that can be a part of these pooled investments, often in order to shirk regulatory rules laid out in the Investment Company Act of 1940, which created rules, regulations, and disclosures to protect citizens after the Great Depression.[45] Hedge funds are also less flexible on when investors may cash out, and they take higher fees than those charged by mutual funds. According to the US Securities and Exchange Commission's Office of Investor Education and Advocacy, typical hedge fund fees are based on the 2-and-20 structure, meaning fund managers take a 1 or 2 percent fee based on the amount of assets under management, as well as 20 percent of the profits.[46] Regardless of performance, hedge fund managers keep the fees, according to Temple.

According to Steven N. Kaplan and Per Strömberg, private equity firms use leveraged buyouts, which in lay terms means that they effectively use borrowed money to make their acquisitions.[47] Kaplan and Strömberg also explained that there is a two-part expectation of the performance of the businesses that private equity invests in or takes over. There is a first period, during which private equity invests in the firm, and then an additional period, usually of five to eight years to turn a profit (basically, when firms need to show something to the investors). A newsletter dedicated to business coverage put that strategy into focus: "The private equity playbook is not overly-complex: raise capital from outside investors, acquire businesses and implement improvements, then divest (hopefully) at a premium."[48] Private equity looks to profit in other ways, Kaplan and Strömberg explained, including a fee generated from managing a company or from monitoring its assets. The cut from these management fees and from the profits can yield huge windfalls. Like the fee charged by hedge funds, it can reach 20 percent. The top five hundred private equity firms in 2018 managed $93.8 trillion in assets. Such rewards lead private equity managers to engage in high-risk behaviors, called "moral hazard problems" by Eileen Appelbaum and Rosemary Batt.[49] Yet in Appelbaum and Batt's view, when problems arise with private equity takeovers, it is the company that shoulders the blame rather than the investment firm engaged in the risky behavior.

As institutional investors' market power grows, so too have volatility and calls for regulation. In a 2021 article for *Management Science*, Itzhak Ben-David, Francesco Franzoni, Rabih Moussawi, and John Sedunov studied large institutional investors and determined that when these firms sell equity, they destabilize prices: "Excessive concentration in the asset management industry may pose a systemic risk."[50] William W. Bratton and Joseph A. McCahery explained that hedge funds' focus on short-term profits and their ability to exert influence over shareholder votes has raised allegations of unfair practices.[51] Henry Ordower explained in the *American Journal of Comparative Law* that hedge funds are "a managed pool of capital that would be an 'investment company' under section 3(a) of the Investment Company Act of 1940 but for the limited number and wealth characteristics of the owners of the interests in the pool."[52] Ordower noted that being registered as a hedge fund allows it to be exempt from the act's regulation, which oversees mutual funds. Tamar Frankel wrote in the *Rutgers Law Journal* that both hedge funds and the Wall Street banks that provide the funds' financing should be regulated, noting the confluence of these factors.[53] Yet calls for regulatory intervention have not made significant changes, in part because power in the financial industry hamstrings these efforts.[54] Luis Aguilar, a former SEC commissioner, said in a 2013 speech: "Too often, public company management and other issuers—represented by their lawyers, investment bankers, and industry groups—dominate the regulatory discussion."[55] Changes created by the Dodd-Frank Act ultimately led to new hedge fund disclosure rules, including a requirement to file the publicly available Form ADV to the US Securities and Exchange Commission. The ADV requires information about an investment advisor's operations, including ownership and clients, as well as statements about an advisor's business practices and fees. Yet despite increased scrutiny, Colleen Honigsberg, a Stanford Law School professor, called the regulation of hedge funds "light."[56]

The growth of the hedge fund and private equity marketplace is undeniable, and it remains the largely unregulated Wild West of Wall Street, with impacts on corporate social responsibility. Many firms operate with offices in the United States, but, like Alden and Chatham, they also have in the past or still do put money in off-shore accounts, "meaning they are less subject to national regulation and oversight."[57] Hedge fund managers also aren't restricted in how much compensation they can generate from the money they invest. Writing in 2008, Kevin Phillips in his book *Bad Money* called hedge fund managers "digital buccaneers" who are "hardly more restrained than their seventeenth-century predecessors."[58] Any company in any sector faces hedge funds' takeover tactics, so it's hardly a surprise that newspapers have fallen prey to them also. While profit appears to be the funds' sole target, it also leaves wide open the possibility for companies under private investment fund influence to operate in a way that is less community-minded. Researchers have shown that investments in sustainability, diversity, and community suffer when profit is the only goal; companies involved in those efforts to improve the world around them may actually inspire hedge funds to target them; hedge funds see line items in those businesses that, if eliminated, could lead to more profits.[59] Hedge funds can keep profits with little public disclosure required, and, different from many family-owned media companies, those profits aren't reinvested in communities or in their businesses, including newspapers, that were so desperate for change and innovation in the 2000s.[60] In the newspaper market, it has been a two-decade-long stretch to arrive here. I argue that the private investment era started in 2003, when two private equity firms and the privately held family media company Freedom Communications, Inc. struck a deal.

"Everyone Wins"

Tim Hoiles and his family reached a deal in 2003 that ushered in the private investment era and put this private investment fund strategy into sharp focus. The deal is also a case study in how private equity investment leaves a company vulnerable to hedge fund ownership farther down the road.

Twenty years ago, Tim Hoiles's immediate family owned 8.6 percent of Freedom Communications, Inc., the privately held media company founded by his grandfather R. C. Hoiles, who began his own newspaper career as an apprentice in 1905.[61] By the family's fourth generation, Freedom had grown to America's twelfth largest media company. At its peak, it operated eight television stations, thirty-seven weekly newspapers, and twenty-eight daily newspapers, including southern California's *Orange County Register*, considered then the

25

company's crown jewel and which a writer in 2002 described as "demographically blessed."[62] Daily circulation at its newspapers during Freedom's glory days reached more than 1.2 million subscribers. Four dozen adult family members—divided into three lines descended from R. C. Hoiles—owned shares in the company, and, like many extended families and family businesses, there were factions and alliances, squabbles and disputes most notably over whether the chain was operating in the libertarian tradition R. C. Hoiles favored.[63] Questions about how to handle shareholders' exit from the family business also loomed. These disputes peaked in the 1980s with a bitter, years-long court battle over how shareholders could cash out of the lucrative family business.[64] The issue remained unresolved for years.

Not everyone worked in the family business, but Tim Hoiles did, and he was named publisher of the Victorville, California, *Daily Press* in 1978. He previously had served as publisher of Freedom's Pampa, Texas, paper before taking the top job in Victorville. He had studied and practiced the ideals of the Fourth Estate, believing, as he told me his grandfather had also believed, that newspapers that did their job correctly interrogated both business and political interests in power in the name of democracy. Mark Hampton explained the concept of the Fourth Estate: "[It] signifies that, whatever the formal constitution, genuine political power resides in the informal role of the press, which in turn derives from the relationship between the press and its readers."[65] Tim Hoiles, in an hour-long telephone interview in January 2021, talked with me about this role and his family's place in the local democracies in the markets where they had operated TV stations and newspapers for generations: "My grandfather once said that a newspaper is very important, but it needs to take stands on issues that might affect its income, and it might affect the bottom line. He was willing to do that. I don't think a lot of people in the business are." Readers responded. Tim Hoiles grew Sunday readership in the western Mojave Desert city to fifty thousand before leaving the top post in 1990.[66] The editor of the *Daily Press*, Steve Williams, wrote in his own retirement column in 2015, "Tim made more wise decisions in the course of a month than most publishers I've known make in their entire careers."[67]

Market analysis appears to have been one of those strengths. After he left the *Daily Press*, Tim Hoiles continued as one of Freedom's board members, examining the family business and, by default, the newspaper industry from his home in Colorado. In the early 2000s, Tim Hoiles grew concerned after looking at the cost of durable goods in some of Freedom's key newspaper markets spread across eleven states.[68] He believed that advertising rates were not enough to sustain the newspaper business long term, and he felt that raising subscription prices to make up the difference would turn away customers. He also saw downward trends in three of the revenue streams most important to newspapers: apartment classifieds, automotive advertisements, and help wanted listings. Tim Hoiles saw trouble on the horizon. At that time and based on those price metrics, he considered the company "mature." It was time to sell. In 2002 Tim Hoiles sought to liquidate his Freedom shares, forcing a family shareholder forum, where he confirmed that he told the others, "I believe we are one of the most dysfunctional families that own a business in America." While it may have been dysfunctional, it was also—like other media companies and family chains founded in the twentieth century—riotously profitable.

Freedom, based in Irvine, California, the subject of a Northwestern Kellogg School of Management case study, in 2003 reportedly was worth between $1.5 billion and $2 billion, with $200 million in cash reserves. Tim Hoiles's desire to sell brought interest from other corporate and private chains, including Gannett, Journal Register Company, MediaNews Group, and Scripps Howard. "More than 50 outside bidders showed interest in buying all or part of Freedom, resulting in 26 preliminary indicators of interest and 10 formal offers," that Kellogg case study noted.[69] Freedom shareholders seeking to stay in the family business turned down one of those formal offers, a $1.8 billion bid from MediaNews Group and Gannett to buy the entire company. During this period, a London-based broker approached Tim Hoiles with a price. "My response was 'OK, I'm going to take that and run, but I don't believe there's any way they can sustain that,'" he remembered.

In 2003 two private equity firms, the Blackstone Group and Providence Equity Partners, ultimately won over family members with a $450 million offer to buy a 40 percent stake in Freedom.[70] The firms' share of the private media company eventually climbed to 48 percent before things fell apart. The Freedom/Blackstone/Providence deal closed in May 2004, and financial publications put its total value at $2.1 billion.[71] Alan J. Bell, then Freedom's president and chief executive officer, said in a joint press release announcing the deal: "It is that rare solution to a dispute in which everyone wins—including the 7,000 employees of the Company coast to coast who have followed every chapter of this widely discussed process."[72] While the deal may have seemed like a happy outcome to some, Tim Hoiles told me that he feared Freedom would never repay the debt. To make the deal, the company founded by Tim Hoiles's grandfather borrowed $771 million from megabank JPMorgan Chase, tripling Freedom's debt to $1 billion.[73] As the deal was being finalized, Tim Hoiles said he turned to his nephew, who was staying with the company, and told him to sell the *Orange County Register*, then responsible for about half of Freedom's revenue. If Hoiles's nephew decided to keep the *Register*, Tim Hoiles told him that he should offload the eight television stations to generate liquidity. It appears the family members remaining in Freedom held firm.[74] Five years later, Freedom filed Chapter 11 bankruptcy.[75]

Before that, the first two years went well, but bankruptcy court records show that private equity's influence and extreme profit motivation had had an impact. Blackstone took two Freedom board seats. Providence took two others.[76] As their power increased, so, too, did their profits. News reports from 2005 suggested that the partnership was prospering. One year after the deal, Freedom maintained cash flow margins of 25 percent, growing in spite of advertising losses throughout the industry. Richard Morgan wrote in *The Deal* that "Freedom has gotten ahead" and called its revenue flows, which bucked industry trends, "remarkable." He also noted that the company "has gone on to thrive."[77] A 2006 story in the *Los Angeles Times* written by Kimi Yoshino noted of the *Register*, "The paper remains profitable but not at the level that shareholders and investors expect, according to information provided to employees."[78] By September 2006, Freedom had started cutting staff at the *Orange County Register*, citing publicly a $20 million advertising loss at the newspaper in a region of southern California hit hard by the housing crisis as the reason for the layoffs.

The advertising losses posed a problem, especially for the private investment funds hovering over the balance sheets. Bratton and McCahery explained private equity and its aims broadly, finding the firms to be both active and vocal in the role they take in businesses they target, even those in which they have less than 100 percent ownership: "Private equity buyouts are governance interventions and anything but passive."[79] In documents filed in the US District Court for the Central District of California in 2011 related to the Freedom bankruptcy, private equity's role in what happened next is key. The firms and their profit extraction strategies played as important a role as those advertising revenue losses.[80] The documents explained that Freedom directors "continued to act in blind devotion to the equity holders' interest and engaged in self-dealing by both siphoning cash out of the Company, both in the form of dividend payments to shareholders and monitoring fees [to Blackstone and Providence], and improperly using the Company's assets as a bargaining chip with the [lenders] in an attempt to create value for insiders and out of the money equity positions at the expense of unsecured creditors."[81] Freedom sought to buy out Blackstone and Providence with money borrowed from General Electric, and news stories reporting on the terms of the deal—a deal that never materialized—put the two private equity firms' returns at 15 percent.[82] By August 2007 the southern California newspaper had cut three dozen newsroom jobs and forced out its publisher, N. Christian Anderson III, who was credited with driving the news-paper's Pulitzer Prize–winning coverage.

For the two private equity firms involved in the Freedom deal, the money and power only accelerated as the newspapers sank into chaos. In its May 2004 news release announcing the finalized Freedom deal, Blackstone noted that over the previous fifteen years it had invested more than $7 billion in equity, with one-third since its inception in "media and communications, including significant investments in the publishing and broadcasting sectors."[83] Providence, the other private equity firm, had at that time managed funds "with over $5 billion in equity commitments," including in Canada and in another holding company with other investments in Comcast Corporation.[84] Writing about Blackstone in the book *King of Capital*, David Carey and John Morris explained: "Private equity investing means burrowing into business and per-forming minutely tuned analyses. Could revenue be boosted a point or two? How much would pass through to the bottom line? What costs could be taken out to notch up the profit margin a fraction?"[85] Blackstone also was involved in the frenzied real estate market right before its crash in 2008. Glantz explained that Blackstone bought and then a few months later sold billions of dollars in real estate without improving the buildings or creating jobs. Of Blackstone's wheeling and dealing, Glantz wrote, "The public got nothing."[86] Considering Blackstone's operations in other sectors, it is not hard to imagine these firms' views on public-service journalism.

Yet both Blackstone and Providence expanded into other media sectors after Freedom. In 2007 Providence, with other private equity firms, secured a winning $12.7 billion bid for Univision, the Spanish-language news giant that turned down a $15 billion acquisition offer in 2017.[87] In 2007 Providence won a $1.2 billion deal for thirty-five of Clear Channel's television stations.[88] Blackstone at one time held stakes in textbook publisher Houghton Mifflin, radio conglomerate Cumulus Media, and the Weather Channel.[89] Blackstone, which went public in 2007, also was part of a private equity takeover of Dutch conglomerate VNU, which owned Nielsen Media Research. In 2006 Blackstone and the other firms signed a $10.3 billion deal for the company that included *Adweek*, *Billboard*, and *Computing*. In its press release announcing that deal, Blackstone wrote that the new ownership consortium "intends to keep VNU substantially together as an integrated company pursuing existing long-term strategy."[90] Months later, Nielsen laid off 10 percent of its staff.[91]

Despite Freedom's bankruptcy, both financial firms are thriving, but the newspapers in Freedom's portfolio fared much, much worse, spun off into dif-ferent private investment fund portfolios, including those run by Alden and Versa Capital Management.[92] Blackstone managed $619 billion in assets as of

December 31, 2020.[93] Its 2017 Form 10-K, which is a publicly traded company's annual filing made to the US Securities and Exchange Commission, noted, "In the U.S., economic growth and the passage of tax reform drove markets to new highs." Blackstone founder Steve Schwarzman has made *Time* magazine's list of most influential people, and in 2016 *Forbes* named him number 1 on its list of most influential people in finance. In 2017 Schwarzman earned a base salary of $350,000, yet his total compensation that year reached $125,519,429.[94] In Carey and Morris's book about Blackstone and Schwarzman, the failed Freedom deal is seemingly so insignificant that it gets just one mention. For newspapers, Freedom and its deal shifted the focus from profit to profit and control, regardless of the fact that the product being produced is linked to democracy. The *Wall Street Journal* reported in July 2004: "The newspaper business has been a hot sector for private-equity companies, which value the industry's high gross margins and consistent cash flow."[95] There was no turning back.

Freedom was the canary in the coal mine that showed how private investment funds' trajectory would play out in the newspaper industry. Eventually, parts of Freedom ended up in other private investment fund portfolios. An online financial publication that summarizes mergers and acquisitions noted that Freedom was sold to a "consortium" of financial buyers in 2010, and six years after that it was sold to a "strategic buyer" for just over $52 million.[96] In 2010 Alden, with Angelo, Gordon & Co. and Luxor Capital Group, took ownership of Freedom's twenty-six dailies, seventy weeklies, and eight TV stations.[97] It sold off the TV stations to Sinclair Broadcasting for $350 million.[98] The private investment firms also converted debt to equity, transforming the bankruptcy into ownership.[99] The Digital First Media newspaper chain, an arm of hedge fund Alden Global Capital, was the strategic buyer in 2016; it ultimately bought outright big pieces of the fractured Freedom, which included its California properties, the *Orange County Register* and the *Riverside Press-Enterprise.*[100] Despite concerns about its hedge fund ownership, Alden in 2021 grew larger, buying Tribune.

It's a similar story across the corporate chain newspaper landscape: early private investment and influence that either grew, impacting the state of operations, or, in deference to it, ultimately led to the elimination or consolidation of those chains entirely. Hedge funds then got once-venerable chains or parts of them on the cheap, putting these funds in control of one of America's oldest and most important industries, the only profession with rights enshrined in the US Constitution.

Chapter 2

Democracy for Sum

America's newspaper history can be divided and studied according to its major eras, the first before we were even a nation. The eras broadly defined in chronological order are the colonial era, the partisan press era, the penny press era, yellow journalism in the late nineteenth century, and the commercial mass market era, which existed for much of the twentieth century. Indeed, lingering public perceptions, axioms, and viewpoints about the press and its role in society are often held over from or rooted in these past eras. They are marked by different characteristics involving ownership and stability, distribution and technology, content and cost, relationship to audiences, economics, politics and partisanship, and the social conditions the newspapers both reflected and created at the time. Looking at profitability specifically, newspapers have generally been a good business, often concerned with commercialism but still motivated by a desire to inform and, in some cases, to persuade.[1] Critics and scholars, among them, C. Edwin Baker, have long studied ownership as a crucial factor in the performance of a free press and its connections to, as he called it, "the health of democracy."[2] I believe it is important to explain profit motivation historically in the newspaper industry. In this chapter I focus on commercialism of the different historical time periods, aiming to provide a contrast to the commercialism we have and have had during the private investment era.

The Colonial Era

In the colonial era, both informing the public and creating "the profit of the publisher" were motivations for newspapers' growth, rooted in the creation and distribution of pamphlets and one-page sheets popular at the time.[3] The economics of the newspapers largely relied on political involvement through subscriptions and advertisements plus ancillary printing contracts. Profitable advertising in the colonial era launched the demand of dailies, when advertising-supported weeklies could not fill the needs of those who wanted the information supplied by the press. Writing in 1936, Edwin H. Ford remarked on newspapers' growth in the colonial period: "The man who had opinions on public affairs in Colonial America needed plenty of space in which to air his views."[4] There also was a darker side to this advertising and the profit generated during the period, according to Jordan E. Taylor's work.[5] Taylor showed that the profitability of early American newspapers was, in part, due to reliance on advertisements promoting and profiting from the sale of enslaved people.

In terms of ownership, the names atop the mastheads of the colonies' most important newspapers will look familiar even to those who know nothing about newspaper history.[6] Benjamin Franklin apprenticed for his older brother, James Franklin, who started the *New England Courant* in 1721. The *Courant* entered the marketplace in stark contrast to other newspapers published in Boston, which required British authorities' approval.[7] Benjamin Franklin eventually moved to Philadelphia, taking over the *Pennsylvania Gazette* in October 1729 and possessing, according to Albert Henry Smyth's 1906 work, "a large circulation and advertising patronage."[8] Edwin Emery wrote: "That is how he began his rise to fame. That is the base upon which he built his fortune. He had concluded at the very beginning of his career that the quickest way to acquire influence was to gain wealth. There was nothing new in that idea, except that Franklin chose to make the press his medium for reaching that estate. That *was* a new idea."[9] Sidney Kobre wrote that by 1750 Franklin's *Pennsylvania Gazette* "was a respectable, established and prosperous paper ... and the sheet was filled with news, news, news, and advertisements."[10] Upon Benjamin Franklin's exit from the newspaper to handle other affairs, he was to be paid 1,000 pounds a year from the newspaper's profits, an amount equal to just over $238,000 in today's US dollars.[11]

While advertising was important, newspapers also relied on postal subsidies, which led to the diffusion of newspapers throughout the country.[12] Robert W. McChesney wrote: "The Founders themselves had implemented enormous printing and postal subsidies to spawn a vibrant press; they were under no illusions that a free press could be generated by letting rich people try to make as much money as possible in publishing and hoping you lucked out."[13] Victor Pickard has argued that this shows that government support of media is not just possible but rooted in America's history.[14]

Through the expansion of newspapers, public knowledge spread, too. Mark Feldstein explained that the *National Gazette*, which was "the paper of Thomas Jefferson's Republican Party," actively sought and exposed the corruption of the rival Federalist Party, including the activities of the staff at Alexander Hamilton's Treasury Department. The newspaper's actions led to Hamilton's aides being convicted of insider trading.[15] In 1775 thirty-seven newspapers existed in the colonies with a total weekly circulation of 1.2 million. But by 1810 just eight of these remained, many having stopped or suspended publication during the Revolutionary War.[16]

The Partisan Press Era

In the late eighteenth century, the idea of the informed voter took hold as political parties, including the Democratic-Republicans and the Federalists, took their messages to the public through events that newspapers covered during the partisan press era. Publications fell into two camps. First, political parties ran them. Second, businessmen paid for "trade journals."[17] After Jefferson became president, he believed so strongly in citizen participation that he brought Samuel Harrison Smith to Washington to report and disseminate the news. Smith launched a four-page triweekly called the *National Intelligencer*, which covered Congress and other news from the district.[18] In terms of generating public knowledge and support, Jeffrey L. Pasley explained, "From the 1790s on, no politician dreamed of mounting a campaign, launching a new movement, or winning over a new geographic area without a newspaper." Such was a crucial link in the formation of the American newspaper system and democracy, though Pasley rightly acknowledges that it was most often a link between newspapers and elite white politicians and citizens.[19]

From the end of the eighteenth century, the fluid lines between newspapers and political parties dominated by the partisan press era signaled how important the American press was to party politics for more than a century.[20] Most important in the partisan press era was the underlying thread of political involvement, which by default captured an eager audience. Pasley has written that newspapers were so crucial at the time because many were founded before a political movement started in order to boost its causes and ideas: "A newspaper subscription might be the only corporeal link that a citizen had to his chosen party."[21] Criticisms of partisan political leanings, Pasley argued, are wrongly viewed through the objective lens of the twentieth century. If anything, one of his strongest arguments in *The Tyranny of Printers* shows that the involvement of printers in both politics and news made for more robust debate and active and engaged participants in the process. Newspaper editors at the time were, therefore, beholden to the political parties they relied on for income—parties they also were openly members of. Those connections were so important that wealthy men who supported newspaper endeavors were called upon to furnish loans to keep the newspapers running.

Andrew Jackson's 1828 election brought new roles for the press and new power for newspapers in democracy, as it also deepened the partisanship of the newspapers at the time. In the wake of the Revolutionary War, western expansion spawned new communities, and newspapers were started outside traditional colonial hubs in Illinois, Indiana, Kentucky, and Ohio.[22] Jackson elevated Kentucky editor Francis P. Blair to a prominent position as one of his most trusted advisors. Pasley wrote that Jackson owed his presidency to newspaper editors, eventually naming more than fifty to key administrative posts.[23] George H. Douglas has shown that having a newspaper in western communities was actually the first part of development there, not a result of the development.[24] Not all newspapers of the time survived, let alone thrived, but those that did generated huge wealth for publishers in cities such as Chicago, Cincinnati, St. Louis, and St. Paul.

The Penny Press Era

The leap from the partisan press era to its successor, the penny press era, was marked by changes in both economics and production, as well as changes to the audience itself. Douglas has written on the century between 1830 and 1930, explaining that "newspaper fever had swept the land and no self-respecting town could afford to be without its own newspaper."[25] As technology improved and literacy spread, in 1833 the penny press era was born, so named for its price drop from six cents per issue down to one cent.[26] Benjamin Day's *New York Sun* was committed to the idea of a press that could reach more than the elite, an idea that spawned the lower cost.[27]

To generate and sustain interest and to thwart competitors, Day turned to sensational content, saying at one time, "We newspaper people thrive on the calamities of others."[28] He also covered corruption, providing valuable coverage on the scourge of the underclasses. As this era kicked off, a more accessible and commercial press faced threats to the constitutional foundations that guaranteed its freedoms.[29] John Nerone has argued that the formula of the period centered on "sensational news with mass market appeal, large-scale industrial production, and economies of scale" and that each of those hallmarks appears in news long after the era's end.[30] Andie Tucher has argued that the development of the penny press, which mirrored the internet as a supposedly democratizing force, was notable specifically because it broke free from political parties and was seen as a media tool for those other than the political elites.[31] Tucher wrote that the founder of the penny press *New York Herald* was physically attacked six times, accused of debasing American journalism, but he also was credited with early investigative prowess and compared to William Shakespeare.

Profits—eventually—rolled in and with them the modern urban daily. Frank W. Scott, in *A History of American Literature*, explained the growth of newspapers at the time: "The growth of these papers meant the development of great staffs of workers that exceeded in numbers anything dreamed of in the preceding period. Although later journalism has far exceeded in this respect the time we are now considering, still the scope, complexity, and excellence of our modern metropolitan journalism in all its aspects were clearly begun between 1840 and 1860."[32] Adam Tuchinsky, writing about Horace Greeley and his *New-York Tribune*, said: "Newspaper production became hierarchical and specialized, its ownership corporate, and its consumption democratic."[33] At the start of 1830, nationwide there were 65 daily newspapers and 650 weekly ones; a decade later, the numbers had doubled.[34] Day sold the *New York Sun* to Moses Yale Beach in 1838, and the newspaper "exposed influence-peddling and bribery in the judicial system, and . . . crusaded against slavery."[35] Greeley, an abolitionist editor and founder of the *New Yorker* and the *New-York Tribune*, thought it immoral for newspapers to profit off crooked or devious advertisers, and he questioned, as noted in Gamaliel Bradford's 1924 history, "[If you] allow yourself to be subsidized by rich and unscrupulous advertisers, what becomes of the independence of journalism?"[36] There is a special irony in considering his views on independence; Greeley held an ambition to hold elected office, eventually running unsuccessfully for president against Ulysses S. Grant. But his newspaper, the most widely read in 1860, provided a robust and necessary forum for antislavery views. Before the Civil War his *Tribune* had 250,000 subscribers and reached many more nationwide.[37] About Greeley, James M. Lundberg wrote, "In making the *Tribune* into a clearinghouse of information as well as ideas, he made reform-minded, opinion-driven journalism commercially viable, and invented the persona of the crusading journalist."[38] Greeley, using his newspaper and magazine, crusaded against worker mistreatment and unemployment.[39]

Newspapers that garnered more income from advertising saw more independence from political parties, ultimately leading to ideas of press independence that would subsist long after that era's end.[40] Stevens reminded us that the break represented one from party subsidies, not party politics.[41] Newspapers also made money. Studying data from newspapers published between 1880 and 1885, Maria Petrova used a database contemporary to the period that was meant to connect advertisers with newspapers. She found that newspapers, once they became independent of political parties, generated more revenue from advertising.[42] Stevens explained that two New York penny papers were influenced by the advertising revenue brought in by New York's "best-known abortionist," Madame Restell.[43] The period also offered the viewpoint of Edwin Lawrence Godkin, a late nineteenth-century editor and founder of *The Nation* who criticized the cheaper newspapers of the period: their focus on lowbrow sensationalism in order to generate more subscriptions failed readers in a democratic society.[44] The Civil War found new missions for the newspapers of the penny press era, boosted by readers seeking out information about a nation divided.[45]

If anything, the competition between newspapers and the need to expose social conditions forced better reporting. Greeley fought for progressive changes; there was no so-called wall between business and editorial functions, an idea that was popular at least in theory throughout twentieth-century newsrooms. Liberal reforms aside, Gregory A. Borchard wrote that Greeley, through his media properties and capitalization on changes to technology, including the telegraph, saw his newspapers as both social democratic forces and a means to achieve wealth.[46] Michael Schudson explained that penny press newspapers were rife with shipping news and advertisements—money makers and "bulletin boards for the business community"—but he also noted that the pages were places for "partisan, provocative, and ill-tempered" editors to spread their ideas.[47] Schudson explained that the key difference between politically subsidized newspapers of the past and those of the penny press era pivoted in how advertisers paid for spots the masses would read. And newspaper publishers—even those who thought themselves more moral than others—infrequently turned away the dollars generated from advertising. News, as Schudson explained, became about politics, about foreign affairs, about domestic issues, about police blotters, and even about private citizens.[48]

Yellow Journalism

It wasn't until after the Civil War that newspapers became big businesses and the real shift from revenue generated from political parties to advertising was completed. Newspapers also shifted the importance from circulation to advertising revenue.[49] Full-page advertisements became standard parts of the newspapers of the 1890s, and post–Civil War papers also began generating revenue from classified advertisements.[50] My American University colleague W. Joseph Campbell has written incisively on the period and its mythologies and realities. In his book *The Year That Defined American Journalism: 1897 and the Clash of Paradigms*, Campbell wrote: "American newspapers probably were never more popular or integral than they were in the late 1890s."[51] The publishers of the time—William Randolph Hearst, Adolph Ochs, and Joseph Pulitzer among them—earned both money and political power through their ownership. Gerald Baldasty argued that newspapers became a commodity in this period, which shaped the advertising-supported model long into the future.[52]

The Pulitzer and Hearst media empires were planted during this era, documented in Kenneth Whyte's 2009 book *The Uncrowned King: The Sensational Rise of William Randolph Hearst*.[53] The men not only earned their money through circulation battles but also showed it off, buying yachts and building skyscrapers as they competed for shares of the growing and crowded New York City newspaper marketplace. Excess reigned. Aurora Wallace has written of the link between architecture and the journalism of the time: "Pulitzer's *New York World* may have started readers daily with the precarious conditions of modern life and the city's infrastructure, but it offered its own 309-foot tower as a safe harbor. The media industry as embodied in tall towers is an argument for relevance, an inescapable structure that stands as a testament to the vitality and utility of the endeavor."[54] The *New York Times*, too, saw the seeds of its profitable future planted during the era of yellow journalism, although Ochs's *Times* was seen as "dull" compared to its yellow competitors, according to David Halberstam's *The Powers That Be*.[55] Schudson has explained this shift in content—I imagine it as a historical turn away from what we think of as today's clickbait to more serious coverage—from a "story" model to an "information" one.[56] Joyce Milton called it "the time of the great reporter."[57]

More readers at the turn of the nineteenth century meant more money for the powerful newspaper owners. Emery explained the period's growth: "From 850 English-language, general circulation dailies in 1880 to 1,967 in 1900; from 10 per cent of adults as subscribers to 26 per cent—these were the statistical evidences of its arrival as a major business."[58] Ochs bought the *New York Times* for $75,000 in 1896 when its circulation neared nine thousand.[59] By 1900 circulation at the *Times* had hit eighty-two thousand after the Spanish-American War made yellow newspapers wildly popular. But the *Times* stood in contrast to Hearst and Pulitzer papers by seeking out a more influential, intelligent, and high-brow audience. Halberstam explained that Ochs published key news on retailers in New York City's booming fashion industry, making the *Times* the de facto advertising home for retailers at the start of the new century. Finally in the black and by World War I, the *Times* under Ochs syphoned those profits into serious war coverage. Between the start and end of the war, the *Times'* daily circulation increased more than 100,000, to 352,000. Sunday circulation in the same period rose by 328,000.

After he inherited the *San Francisco Examiner* in 1886, Hearst doubled its circulation, then sought to create a newspaper chain, moving east to battle Joseph Pulitzer, who founded the *St. Louis Post-Dispatch*.[60] Hearst eventually acquired dozens of newspapers, becoming the largest chain newspaper publisher in America.[61] Albert Pulitzer, Joseph's younger brother, earned $100,000 a year from his ownership of the *New York Morning Herald*, which sold for one penny. A long-standing rival to Joseph, Albert sold his newspaper to Joseph McLean for $400,000. McLean was a wealthy businessman with family ties to both the *Cincinnati Enquirer* and the country's major industrial centers. Joseph Pulitzer, meanwhile, ran the *New York World*, which sold for two cents, ultimately becoming so wealthy that he was able to found the Columbia Graduate School of Journalism and the Pulitzer Prizes, a way to restore a legacy clouded by his circulation battle with Hearst and what many believed was a period that "darkened" his reputation and that of his largest newspaper too.[62] Still, his wealth at the time of his death stood at nearly $20 million and represented "one of the largest ever accumulated in the newspaper field."[63] After reckoning with the failures of sensationalism, he demanded that his staff produce hard-hitting reporting that would operate in the public interest. Joseph Pulitzer's top industry rival, Hearst, died in August 1951. Hearst's will, which reached 125 typed pages, put his worth at $59.5 million.[64]

The Mass Market Era

As newspapers grew and industrialized, they did so along with other businesses. Douglas explained: "Huge corporations, more powerful than any known in history, were being forged into still larger corporations."[65] Competition between newspapers and a focus on their local communities meant newspapers resisted the corporatization and conglomeration of the other businesses of the time. More to that point, Emery explained that newspaper publishers and reporters actually resisted the monopolies in "steel, oil, copper, sugar, tobacco, and shipping" and the conditions they witnessed that were born from them.[66] Newspaper owners were quite content with the wealth and influence owning newspapers afforded them. David Croteau and William D. Hoynes have argued that by the end of the mass market era, commercial interests had become a unique form of censorship, and they explained that markets do "not necessarily meet democratic needs."[67]

Newspapers at the time were profitable and controversial, but even with those constraints, newspapers and magazines became agents for democracy, putting pressure on elected officials to act and address the ills of the time period. Still, and despite their criticisms of profit seeking, newspaper historians believe that newspapers also cemented their role in democracy in the early twentieth century. Douglas explained: "It was the muckraker and the editorial writer who gave birth to civic reform and the progressive era, not the politician or the government regulator. . . . The newspaper was the way that people encountered the world around them. It was also the only regular source of interpretation and analysis that could make sense of the cascade of events that constitute life in a democratic republic. The newspaper made public response possible."[68] Hearst, seeing the power of muckraking in long-form magazine articles, bought *Cosmopolitan* in 1905, adding to his print empire.

By the first years of the twentieth century, the muckraker mantle had been taken primarily by magazine writers attacking the robber barons, stock market plungers, and their excesses as newspapers continued providing a voice to social abuses. *Cosmopolitan* produced stories on US Senate corruption contemporary to Ida Tarbell's Standard Oil exposé, which was published as an 815-page book in 1904 after it was a magazine series called *The History of the Standard Oil Company*. Writing about Tarbell's work, which targeted John D. Rockefeller, one of America's great industry robber barons, Steve Weinberg said it "created a social maelstrom that built and destroyed reputations, altered public policy, and changed the face of the nation."[69] *The World* employed Elizabeth Cochran under the pen name Nellie Bly, who covered systemic abuses in mental health facilities and sweatshops.[70] Ida B. Wells's coverage of lynching in her Memphis newspaper earned her a crucial platform in the United States and the UK.[71] John Hersey's "Hiroshima," which outlined the horrors of the atomic bomb and foiled American censors, filled the entire August 23, 1946, issue of the *New Yorker*.[72] Yet muckraking—used synonymously here with the terms "investigative reporting" and "watchdog journalism"—was not consistent or even visible across the field.[73]

The mass market period ushered in new standards of objectivity as it offered readers journalism that held government accountable *sometimes*, just as scholars have argued that the influence of advertising and profit motivation clouded watchdog reporting. Lucia Moses has explained that this relationship between public service and business has long been an uneasy one for journalists working in the public interest.[74] Edward Herman reminded us in 1981 that Left-oriented criticism of large corporations "underestimated ownership and family control."[75] Family owners of the twentieth century built wealth on their newspaper ownership, but they also funded staff who were empowered to hold government accountable even if they skirted responsibilities covering industry and business, as Baker has studied. Robert G. Picard explained the ascent of both money and good journalism in the second half of the twentieth century: "Money was plentiful, journalists were relatively well compensated with wages and benefits, and resources existed for many of the kinds of reporting that journalists cherish."[76] Families and chains at least seemed concerned about their products' role in democracy even if they also were concerned with profit and were beholden to both government and advertisers that acted in some ways as censors, as Baker explained in his 1994 book *Advertising and a Democratic Press*.[77] As I lionize a very specialized type of national reporting, I also note that Herman, with Noam Chomsky, called much of the same period of war reporting a key feature of newspapers' propaganda model, one that forwards ideas of good victims and bad, and one that sees even the laziest journalists rise to fame for republishing or rebroadcasting the official spin.[78]

There were bright spots, and it is these stories that show not only the power of journalism done right but also the power of what is lost when profit becomes paramount. Pickard explained a period in the 1940s when political and judicial rulings emphasized that "the press's commercial concerns were not as important as its democratic obligations to the public."[79] Reporting during and after the Vietnam War stands out as one of journalism's finest hours. The highlights include Halberstam reporting on the political missteps in Vietnam that led President John F. Kennedy to seek Halberstam's removal from his post there and Seymour Hersh uncovering US forces' massacre of hundreds of civilians in My Lai.[80] Reports on both the Pentagon Papers and Watergate were published under the leadership of wealthy family owners. Katharine Graham, *Washington Post* publisher during Watergate, published the investigative work that brought down President Richard Nixon.[81] Idolized in journalism history, Graham was not without her own critics. She was burned in effigy outside the *Post*'s downtown offices by union pressmen picketing the newspaper after its shares went public. The pressmen thought the family's 15 percent profit targets had made them "greedy."[82]

As families sold to chains during this time period, Ben Bagdikian, who had been a *Washington Post* assistant editor during its publication of the Pentagon Papers, explained that newspaper chains made "cosmetic" changes.[83] Those tweaks were meant to revamp the overall look of newspapers to justify subscription and advertising rate hikes as the cuts to actual coverage began. Bagdikian reported that study after study from academics and think tanks beginning in the 1970s and onward, including from the Brookings Institution, showed that chains charged more for work that delivered less. McChesney, writing in the foundational volume *The Political Economy of Media: Enduring Issues, Emerging Dilemmas,* noted that newspapers had become among neoliberalism's staunchest defenders as they, like other business-centered operations in the 1980s and 1990s, developed profit-first stances: "Corporate media apologists say not to worry, now that everyone is blogging we have the journalism we can handle and then some. Digital technology will eventually solve the problem the pundits tell us; in the meantime just let the media conglomerates buy up all the media they can, lay off reporters to become 'efficient,' and rake in monopolistic profits so they can expand the economy and create jobs. You know the drill."[84] Pickard more recently reminded us that throughout the twentieth century newspapers and other media were supported by advertising; advertisers sought the attention of people paying for newspapers. News was, in his words, a "by-product" of this commercial exchange.[85]

In many ways, this was different from Greeley's success in the mid-1800s and Ochs's and other families' successes that followed; for them, the news came first, and the wealth followed. The appearance of credible, objective news was a function of profit motivation.[86] Newspaper revenue between 1994 and 1998 grew at a nearly 8 percent compounded annual rate.[87] Yet readers throughout the twentieth century still relied on this commercially successful news and found trusted sources in it. Knight Ridder, which owned three dozen newspapers until its merger with McClatchy in 2006, employed national reporters who were among a minority of journalism voices discrediting the Bush administration's trumped-up claims about Iraq's weapons of mass destruction after 9/11.[88] Moses Ofome Asak and Tshepang Bright Molale, writing about the history of authentic news sources and fake news, explained of readers during the twentieth century: "They trusted mainstream media structures because they knew journalists were trained professionals in the production and dissemination of news."[89] Many cities had competing newspapers, even under corporate chain control, but the newspaper industry was far from being as fragmented or distressed as it is today.

By the 1980s institutional investors had gained traction as major stockholders in financial markets. Philip Meyer and Stanley Wearden wrote about this shift in the newspaper market in 1984. They explained at the time that managers sought long-term profitability but short-term recognition of the company's value in the form of high-performing shares. They found that "product quality, editorial quality, and managerial quality seem to be the chief concerns of newspaper people, whether their papers are privately owned or publicly owned. Analysts, on the other hand, were most concerned with financial considerations."[90] John Soloski and Picard wrote in 1996 that newspaper companies should understand the role institutional investors play in "calling the shots."[91] Steven Drobny wrote that as a sector these funds are "important and worth analyzing because: (1) they are some of the largest pools of capital in the world" and "(2) they have a direct impact on the functioning of society."[92] Institutional investors industry-wide often operate "behind the scenes" and are often concerned with a company's liquidity and profit-making performance.[93] Picard showed in a 1994 study that institutional investors in newspapers provided "the bulk of capital invested through stock markets" and "pursue specific strategies for capital preservation and growth."[94] In his review, institutional investors' money in the newspaper companies at that time "exceeded $20.6 billion."[95] Of course, at the time of his study, newspapers still were steady and profitable investments, doubling the performance of manufacturing sectors. It is perhaps interesting to note that in the nearly three decades since that study was published, several of the seventeen publicly traded companies Picard reviewed no longer exist, merged into others or taken over by private equity firms and hedge funds.

Another period of consolidation marked the end of the twentieth century in newspapers and across other media industries. In 1983 Bagdikian sounded the alarm when fifty firms controlled a majority of broadcast and print media in the United States. Two decades later, Bagdikian pointed to what he called "The Big 5," documenting the tremendous shifts and contractions in ownership power and a new media oligopoly that had emerged since he published his first edition.[96] Looking more broadly at consolidation and its impacts, Herman and Chomsky explained that news was a function of the wider mass media system, and they looked at profit motivation and ownership to arrive at the first filter of their propaganda model. The two traced "the routes by which money and power are able to filter out the news fit to print, marginalize dissent, and allow the government and private interests to get their messages across to the public."[97] Included in their critique is a recognition that the size of the most powerful media firms effectively limits the opportunity of other firms to enter the market. They also noted that media systems operate in tiers, with the most successful, often marked by size, setting an agenda for the tiers below them.

In the new millennium, new challenges emerged, among them, of course, the internet and the loss of classified revenue. But more important, as I argue in chapters 3, 4, and 5, are the challenges that arise from overharvesting profits, the debt born of mergers and acquisitions, and the greed of private investment funds. By 2003 research studying seventy-seven dailies with circulation between twenty-five thousand and one hundred thousand found that publicly traded newspapers generated more profit than those in private portfolios. Among the study's findings, authors Stephen Lacy and Alan Blanchard noted that a push for profit to satisfy shareholders was taking a toll, including at the company known until 2008 as Thomson: "The Thomson study and this research should be considered a warning about the long-run negative impact of very high profits on the quality and circulation of daily newspapers."[98] Dean Starkman explained that the public was uninformed about the major economic collapse of 2008 and the corruption of the financial system. According to Starkman, the failure rests with financial journalists: "Missing are investigative stories that directly confront powerful institutions about basic business practices while those institutions were still powerful. The watchdog didn't bark."[99] I would add that it's not so much a failure of the business press as the fact that, by that point, the business press was being influenced by the same Wall Street firms and lenders that accelerated the fall of newspapers. Aeron Davis has written about this structural reality, focusing on communication power and financial elites and linking the simultaneous rise of both.[100]

The interest in newspaper companies as money-making tools did not, of course, begin in the twenty-first century with these pooled investment vehicles or major shareholders voicing concern and hammering management for increased profit margins. Venture capital and mutual funds had been involved in publicly traded newspaper companies dating back to the 1970s, but investing in a company and betting on its success looks different from carving it up with little regard for its future.[101] The sale of Freedom Communications, Inc., described in chapter 1, wasn't the first big-money merger that illustrated newspapers' tremendous profitability. But the Freedom deal showed something else: private investment funds were now deep in the game, with short-term strategies and nonnewspaper managers installed on boards and in executive positions that would mark disaster as the industry faced innovation and managerial challenges in the mid-2000s as the inevitable internet transition loomed.

Into the new millennium and not long after the ink dried on the Freedom/Blackstone/Providence deal, investors started making other deals, and they also started exerting pressure. How private investment funds work in the newspaper marketplace varies, but it is worth noting that there still is money in this market despite the fact, quite paradoxically, that it is an industry in crisis. In 2020 Marc

Edge wrote: "Why are newspapers still here? It's very simple. Newspapers are still here because they still make money."[102] It's the money and the crisis that make newspaper companies a target.

This book also traces the years of ownership and financial influence as it considers how the industry under private investment fund ownership and investment is reaching its terminus as newspapers hit their bottom line. The book also shows how today's private investment fund interests are influencing the public sphere by eliminating access to crucial news essential to the creation and maintenance of local public opinion. Douglas wrote of the largess, lessons, and sensationalism of the penny press era, and I believe his analysis can be attributed to the period we live in now, a period I have recast as the private investment era: "It may have served as a kind of wake-up cry to a somnolent and indolent America. It might also have served to remind Americans that the road to good newspapers is always a difficult one, fraught in each generation with fresh dangers that, once they infect the air, are not easily overcome."[103] A decade ago, Núria Almiron's *Journalism in Crisis: Corporate Media and Financialization* showed that private equity's influence in cable, broadcast, and print media treated the news and news organizations like any other product in a capitalist society.[104] In 2009 Matthew Crain focused on private equity and leveraged buyouts in a critique focused widely on the American media sector, looking at cinemas and radio in addition to newspapers.[105] It was written before hedge funds burrowed into the newspaper market, gaining traction over the last decade, but Crain saw the warning signs. Leveraged buyouts have received their due in other industries. Bryan Burrough and John Helyar wrote arguably one of the greatest works of twentieth-century business nonfiction in their telling of private equity firm KKR's $25 billion takeover of RJR Nabisco in *Barbarians at the Gate: The Fall of RJR Nabisco*.[106] KKR-backed Axel Springer, a German publisher, bought Politico in August 2021.[107]

A positive development stems from these last twenty years. These firms' power and control have also forced innovation in the formation of unions and in the growth of the nonprofit sector as reporters seek to throw off the yoke of these funds' influence. The question for me is how much that has been lost in these last two decades can be resurrected or restructured using alternative business models. That loss also raises questions about what deserves to be preserved.

Chapter 3

Overharvesting

I recognize, as Robert W. McChesney has for decades, that in order to understand and to transform the news media system we first must identify its contours of wealth and power. This raises an important set of questions about the newspaper industry's commercial realities as a part of the financialization of the overall economy. Yet if commercialism has been part of the US newspaper landscape since the days of Benjamin Franklin, then what makes the private investment era any different? Or, in reality, what makes it any worse? This chapter offers information on investment firms' strategies within and outside the newspaper sector, amplifying the impacts of their ownership and influence and identifying other financial dealings that show that these firms have incentives to minimize newspapers' investigative role in democratic society.

Philip Meyer wrote about harvesting in 2004, borrowing a term from Harvard University's Michael E. Porter. As Meyer described it, harvesting meant that managers were "raising prices and reducing quality so they can shell out the money and run." Meyer said that cutting the amount of news and the staff who produced it was a hallmark of harvesting in the newspaper industry. In practice, Meyer warned that harvesting meant less community engagement and public service.[1] To me, the term "harvesting" also implies growth or, at least, the ability to reap something from a healthy crop. But like any field that has been overworked and undernourished, overharvesting eventually leads to a barren wasteland. Over the last twenty years, overharvesting has decimated local newspapers. Profit in the name of democracy looks much different from profit made in spite of it.

Behind newspaper chain names like Gannett, Digital First Media, and McClatchy are wealthy fund managers calling the financial shots as newspapers nationwide wither on the vine. Alden Global Capital, the hedge fund owner of the Digital First Media and Tribune chains, is arguably the most maligned of America's private newspaper owners, and it made its own headlines in 2018 after its *Denver Post* staff publicly blasted it. Joe Pompeo explained its ownership strategy in a *Vanity Fair* article: "The ensuing publicity threw Alden's draconian playbook into sharp relief: buy distressed newspapers on the cheap, cut the shit out of them, and reap the profits that can still be made from print advertising."[2] While Alden gets a barrage of negative attention, other investment firms, including Fortress Investment Group, which owned the GateHouse chain and acted as its manager, also play or have played a key role in overharvesting profits, impacting coverage in cities and small towns nationwide.

Advertiser influence and commercialism in the late twentieth century negatively impacted newspapers, but today's private investment funds' overharvesting has kicked an industry that is already down. But down does not mean out. US newspaper publishing industry revenue in 2021 reached $20.9 billion, with profit margins just below 4 percent.[3] Publicly traded newspapers in 2020 generated $8.8 billion from advertising revenue and another $11.1 billion from circulation.[4] As I consider the multi-billion-dollar revenue remaining in the print and digital newspaper market, I want to point out that in 2021 the revenues of private equity firms, hedge funds, and other investment firms as their own sector of the US economy reached $230.6 billion, with profit margins above 36 percent.[5] Newspapers as an industry are adjacent to one of the country's wealthiest sectors, yet they still remain in crisis. What's worse, newspapers helped buoy some of those funds' portfolios through what was left of advertising revenue, but newspapers also allowed these funds to profit through aggressive cuts, asset sales, debt financing, and management fees. As the funds as their own sector grow larger and more profitable, newspapers have descended further into crisis. Studying today's corporate newspaper chains means studying the private equity firms and hedge funds that influence or own them, and it means considering further that the product being traded, like any other in capitalist markets, is the most important in American democracy.

Studying the hedge funds and private equity firms in conjunction with newspaper chains has allowed me to track the last twenty years of history and consider newspapers' diminished role in democratic processes as a quotient of overharvesting. As a way to study private investment funds' profit motivation, government documents and trade reports point to control of shares, control of boards, and cutthroat strategies used to maximize profit at any cost. Hedge funds and private equity firms are notoriously impervious, but records we can access, including bankruptcy documents and US Securities and Exchange Commission records, show that they often exploit long-standing subscriber relationships in communities like the Tribune-owned *Hartford Courant,* a newspaper so old that it predates the nation.[6]

Overharvesting at private and publicly traded chains is, of course, tied to the other core features of the private investment era. How debt accumulated in the wake of disastrous mergers and acquisitions, why reporters were laid off, and how audiences stopped seeing value in their daily newspapers are tied to profit and the sometimes absurd decision-making of newspaper company executives to maximize it. At the chains beholden to private investment funds, the pressure to outperform prior years marked disaster in a crucial time period that should have been dedicated to a digital pivot. Between December 2008 and December 2009, ten newspaper companies, including those influenced by private equity (among them Freedom Communications, Inc., Journal Register Company, and Tribune Publishing), filed for Chapter 11 bankruptcy protection.[7] By 2010 MediaNews Group, constrained by nearly $1 billion in debt, joined them. Hedge funds own all of them today.

Lean Dean

William Dean Singleton founded MediaNews Group four decades ago. Rising to become the country's second-largest newspaper company, Singleton's MediaNews Group by the time of his retirement included respected titles, among them the *Denver Post,* the *Salt Lake Tribune,* and the *San Jose Mercury News.*[8] Stories about Singleton over the years show a newspaper executive similar to others forged from the late twentieth-century fires of competition and advertising largesse. Like R. C. Hoiles and other family founders, Singleton started with a small newsroom job and became wealthy from decades running newsrooms. How wealthy? A 2003 *Columbia Journalism Review* profile described his primary home having eleven bathrooms, a fact eclipsed by the mention of his Westwind II private jet.[9] In September 2021 the University of Denver awarded him its 2021 Journalism in the Public Interest Award, noting his "contributions to journalism and public life, along with his dedication to the industry from a young age."[10] The Denver Center for the Performing Arts' theater is named for him.

Alongside the anecdotes of philanthropy and news savviness are tales of his merciless accounting procedures and an acquisition strategy that built MediaNews Group into a private powerhouse with fifty-four dailies, not all of them supported like the *Denver Post*. In 1995 MediaNews Group bought the *Brattleboro Reformer* in Vermont, where Randy Holhut had worked as a sports reporter since 1989. Holhut recounted in an email that he was "not retained when I did not accept the new terms of employment under MNG."[11] But he returned in 2004, working as a night editor and editorial page editor for six years. Holhut refers in both emails and conversation to his two stints at the *Reformer* as "tours," which elicits the feeling of battle even before private investment funds took over. During his second tour, when he was working under MediaNews Group management, Holhut watched as the newsroom staff was cut. Singleton's MNG stopped paying for a water cooler in the break room, and then the 401(k) match disappeared. In his second stretch, Holhut as an editor was privy to more knowledge of the newspaper's financials. "We were profitable," Holhut said. "We were still being squeezed to make more money. That was the cycle the paper was trapped in. We were just bled dry."[12] He left in 2010, when he said that little hope existed that conditions would improve. Today, Holhut is editor at a Brattleboro nonprofit news outlet called *The Commons*, part of Vermont Independent Media, Inc.[13]

During our November 2021 interview Holhut recalled that period just before hedge fund Alden Global Capital took seats on MediaNews Group's board. Before private investment funds took over, many corporate newsrooms faced cuts and resource issues like the ones Holhut remembered. A September 1999 profile described Singleton as a "ruthless" leader who "slashes salaries, cuts staff, and publishes papers that will never be known for their editorial quality."[14] Many journalists I interviewed thought the first decade of the new millennium represented the bottom because of chain owners' greed. They watched as leaders like Singleton acquired newspapers nationwide as a business strategy, one that in Denver pitted MediaNews Group against Scripps Howard's *Rocky Mountain News* in a "battle for dominance."[15] But those acquisitions, alongside advertising losses, also burdened MediaNews Group with $930 million in debt.[16] By 2008 MediaNews Group bonds traded as junk.[17] Two years later, Chapter 11 bankruptcy followed, and lenders traded debt for equity.[18] Alden filled executive slots after the bankruptcy restructuring.[19] By 2013 Alden Global Capital owned the newspaper company outright.[20] Conditions were about to get much worse.

Alden took complete control of MediaNews Group, eventually merging it and Journal Register Company under the Digital First Media moniker. Since then, Alden's hedge fund leadership at Digital First and Tribune newspapers has made Singleton's cuts and tactics look downright trivial. In 2018, the year he dissolved his association with the *Denver Post*'s editorial board, Singleton said of Alden's ownership, "I don't know that they understand how damaging they've been to the newspaper and how damaged the newspaper is in the local community."[21] Consider that this statement came from the guy whose newsroom cuts earned him the nickname "Lean Dean."[22]

Despite aggressive cuts at MediaNews Group before Alden's influence and ownership, people paid attention to Singleton's opinions about the field. By 2007 he was chairman of the Associated Press.[23] In 2012 *Salon* called him a "mogul."[24] A *Denver Post* article announcing his retirement at age sixty-two cited the paper's five Pulitzer Prizes during his tenure as a signal of his successes, not to mention the quality of the chain's arguably most important newsroom.[25] In the early 1990s Singleton predicted that just three major newspaper companies would be "left standing."[26] He wanted MediaNews Group to be among them. It is, kind of. But the big three landscape Singleton envisioned looks much different today.

The Private Investment Plutocracy

Three private investment funds—Alden Global Capital, Chatham Asset Management, and Fortress Investment Group—in recent years have sat atop this private fund newspaper plutocracy as owners, though they are not alone nor have they appeared since the start of the era. This section focuses on these three private investment funds of the last twenty years as it maps how newspapers became part of their portfolios. Other private investment firms, including Angelo, Gordon & Company, Apollo Global Management, Ariel Investments, Aurelius Capital Management, BlackRock, Blackstone, Cerberus Capital Management, Oaktree Capital Management, and Providence Equity Partners, have exerted various levels of influence in the newspaper market over the years, and their influence also is detailed in this chapter.

Fortress Investment Group: The Phantom

For nearly two decades, Fortress Investment Group has been a steady private equity presence in the newspaper industry and beyond it. If Alden is a vulture, then Fortress is a phantom, lurking behind the newspaper scenes but hiding in plain sight. Fortress maintains headquarters on the forty-sixth floor of a building on Avenue of the Americas in New York City. From there, Fortress has played a role in both Gannett and GateHouse / New Media Investment

Group. In 2017 Japanese conglomerate SoftBank paid $3.3 billion in cash for the fund company, and for more than a decade before that Fortress owned—and slashed—newspapers nationwide.[27]

Fortress formed in 1998, and its initial public offering nearly a decade later hit $29.7 billion. A business-to-business publisher described its IPO this way: "Yale University endowment chief David Swensen criticized the firm's principals for the conflicts of interest inherent in their deal, and joked that a section on 'greed' was absent from Fortress's SEC offering document."[28] The first day of trading saw its shares jump 89 percent, effectively making cofounder Wesley Edens and other Fortress partners billionaires.[29] *Forbes* wrote of Edens, "He spun out four new listed firms between 2013 and 2015 that manage assets in media, mortgages, senior housing facilities and golf courses—and which pay Fortress hefty fees."[30] Fortress's amended annual report filed in April 2017 with the SEC revealed some of its principals' wealth. It showed that Peter Briger Jr., like other top executives, earned a base salary of $200,000, but he pulled $27 million in total compensation, including bonuses, stock awards, and insurance premiums.[31] Edens, who is the former chairman of New Media Investment Group, a principal at Fortress, and Fortress fund FIG LLC's principal and director, had compensation in 2016 of $7.7 million.[32] Edens, who is also co-owner of the NBA's Milwaukee Bucks, in 2020 dropped $20 million on a penthouse in New York City's Chelsea neighborhood.[33] Despite Fortress's premium payments to its top brass, the business-to-business publication *Institutional Investor* described the State Teachers Retirement System of Ohio as being among the biggest losers of Fortress's operations.[34]

Fortress—through its FIF III Liberty Holdings LLC—entered the newspaper business in 2005 with its $530 million purchase of Liberty Group Publishing.[35] A press release announcing the deal explained: "The majority of the Company's paid daily newspapers have been published for more than 100 years and are typically the only paid daily newspapers of general circulation in their respective non-metropolitan markets."[36] At the time of the purchase the *Wall Street Journal* noted that Fortress offered no expertise in media or running newspaper companies: "Nonetheless, buyout shops are keen to scoop up newspaper assets because they generate consistent cash flow and can be loaded up with debt to pay for the initial purchase."[37] Liberty Group consisted of small, local newspapers and shoppers, sometimes called "pennysavers" or "free sheets," filled with advertisements.[38]

The free and penny monikers belied the importance of these newspapers. The company's newspapers circulated mostly in rural and suburban areas, but reporter Leon Lazaroff explained that as the Liberty chain was going up for sale in 2004 those shoppers and small newspapers were "attractive because they face little competition for local advertising dollars and generate consistently high cash flows. Though few of Liberty's community newspapers has a circulation of more than 20,000, the group posted in 2003 sales of close to $189 million on a readership of about 2.3 million per week."[39] Liberty was first incorporated in Delaware in 1997 "for the purposes of acquiring a portion of the daily and weekly newspapers owned by American Publishing Company."[40] American Publishing was the brainchild of Conrad Black, jailed for three years for fraud related to the operation of Hollinger International Inc.[41] In 1998 Hollinger sold Liberty to Leonard Green & Partners, described as a "leveraged-buyout firm," for $310 million.[42]

Once in Fortress's hands, the Liberty chain was rebranded under the Gate-House moniker, and GateHouse went public in 2006.[43] GateHouse's initial public offering of 13.8 million shares was expected to raise $200 million, which a business publication noted was "either the most counter-intuitive IPO imaginable, or a case of dreadfully bad timing."[44] That story noted, however, that GateHouse was leaning on the record of its owner, Fortress, in the market.

Fortress's investments have transcended industry boundaries from newspapers to railroads to real estate. Real estate news site the *Real Deal* wrote, "Fortress provided pop singer Michael Jackson with a mortgage on his Neverland Ranch."[45] When it deepened its role in the newspaper marketplace, Fortress also was heavily invested in assisted-living centers and cell phone towers.[46] Fortress has a diverse portfolio, including investments in nonmedia and the operation of other funds, such as the FIG LLC (run by Edens), Fortress Japan Income Fund, the Fortress Japan Opportunity Domestic Fund, and the Global Opportunities Fund. Its company profile in the financial database S&P Capital IQ explained in September 2021 what Fortress looks for: "In distressed situations, the firm will seek to secure corporate ownership or control by working with a company's board of directors or creditor's committee. It prefers to have majority stake in companies. The firm invests in distressed and undervalued assets and tangible and intangible assets such as real estate, capital assets, natural resources, and intellectual property. The firm primarily provides its services to individuals. It also provides its services to high net worth individuals."[47]

In 2006, when GateHouse went public, it reached 330 markets across twenty-one states. By 2007, then in 383 markets across twenty-three states and with 73 percent of its daily newspapers having a history of one hundred years or more in some communities, GateHouse appeared ready to exploit that long-standing relationship, thinking it had to do little to keep readers paying based on that history. After acquiring Massachusetts properties, GateHouse executives almost instantly enacted layoffs.[48] Its 2007 annual report explained: "We believe that the longevity of our publications demonstrates the value and relevance of the local information that we provide and has created a strong foundation of reader loyalty and a highly recognized media brand name in each community we serve."[49] GateHouse's total circulation—combining its dailies, weeklies, and free shoppers—reached above 4.7 million. Yet its cuts and poor management at the newspapers it took over earned GateHouse the nickname "OutHouse" among some staffers I talked with. As it cut reporting and editing staff and consolidated operations, GateHouse also kept paying dividends worth up to forty cents per share to shareholders.[50] That meant that it kept paying itself, because at that time Fortress owned 42 percent of GateHouse stock through its FIF III Liberty Holdings LLC.

The advertising revenue drop hamstrung those profit-motivated efforts, but Fortress remained as a key shareholder and manager in the newspaper market, extracting lucrative fees from GateHouse and, later, New Media and Gannett. Specific to newspapers, GateHouse's strategy has long been about maximizing revenue, putting power and control into Fortress executives' hands, sometimes at the expense of other shareholders. Its Form 10-K filed for the calendar year 2012 explained: "Fortress will continue to have effective control over fundamental and significant corporate matters and transactions, including but not limited to: the election of directors; mergers, consolidations or acquisitions; the sale of all or substantially all of our assets (or any portion thereof) and other decisions affecting our capital structure; the amendment of our amended and restated certificate of incorporation and our amended and restated by-laws; and our dissolution. The interests of Fortress may not always coincide with our interests or the interest of our other stockholders."[51] As its portfolio and debt grew, it offered little in the way of innovation.

In 2013 New Media Investment Group managed by Fortress was founded as a holding company after GateHouse filed Chapter 11 bankruptcy. New Media's annual report for 2013 said: "Our Manager does not have any prior experience directly managing our Company or media-related assets." The report continued: "We have agreed to pay our Manager a management fee that is not tied to our performance."[52] New Media's filings show that it took 1.5 percent of GateHouse's total equity; its cut in 2013 was worth about $6 million.[53] A May 2014 New Media Investment Group investor relations statement noted that the chain's portfolio had risen to 429 community publications spanning 356 markets in two dozen states.[54] New Media counted $670 million in assets that year. By April 2016 the *Boston Business Journal* wrote that New Media reported $1.2 billion in revenue and $67.6 million in profits, when Fortress again took a 1.5 percent fee based on

New Media's equity plus a cut of the profits.[55] New Media's 2016 annual report shows that Fortress was paid at least $32 million in fees.[56]

For these funds, newspapers have been a very good business. And in 2019 Gannett and GateHouse merged into America's largest newspaper company in a deal worth $1.3 billion.[57] Although still under the Gannett name, the company is effectively GateHouse, the newspaper group long run by Fortress and "known for hollowing out American newsrooms."[58] While Gannett laid off reporters and cut coverage, it still paid Fortress both dividends and management fees. In 2018 and 2019 "Fortress and its affiliates were paid $1.0 million in dividends," according to Gannett's 2020 annual report.[59] In 2020 the private equity firm was still extracting millions of dollars in management fees. In 2020 alone Gannett paid $16.3 million in management fees, with another $16.9 million in "management fee expense" listed in documents filed with the SEC. In an April 2021 Gannett document filed with the SEC, executives explained that Fortress and its affiliates, which are listed as the "Former Manager," had been paid an annual management fee of 1.5 percent of total equity plus 17.5 percent of the adjusted profits.[60] As of June 30, 2021, across its holdings Fortress counted $53.9 billion in assets under management, more than double what it had at the time it started in the newspaper marketplace.[61] Gannett's staff has been cut in half since the merger.[62]

Alden Global Capital: The Vulture

In 2007 Alden, an offshoot of power broker Randall D. Smith's financial universe, got its start. R. D. Smith & Company was described as a hedge fund "profiting from other people's misery by trading the stock and debt of troubled companies, both for itself and its customers."[63] Smith installed Heath Freeman to lead Alden, and before long, it was buying shares of newspaper companies and other sectors, too. The Securities and Exchange Commission requires institutional investors like Alden to file a form called a 13F. That form provides information about the companies firms invest in and how many shares firms own.[64] As an example, in its Form 13F filed after the close of the 2010 calendar year, Alden Global Capital Ltd. reported its institutional investments in Bank of America, Build A Bear Workshop, Ford Motor Company, Motorola, Playboy Enterprises Inc., and Wells Fargo, among others.[65] The form noted that Alden owned 1.3 million shares of McClatchy, 314,158 shares of Journal Communications Inc., and 9.3 million shares of Gannett, an increase of more than a million from the year prior, when it also owned 356,100 shares of Lee Enterprises and 165,500 shares of Citigroup.[66] Alden isn't the only hedge fund in the newspaper business, but its power in the industry is growing with its purchase of Tribune.

Industry watchers have long been concerned about Alden's involvement in the newspaper industry, and workers at its properties and others in which Alden owns shares have publicly protested and unionized against Alden's ownership and influence.[67] (These issues are covered in more detail in chapter 6.) Its 2020 filings show that its LLC arm had $764.7 million in assets under management.[68] In September 2019 Alden owned just over 9 percent of Gannett, although by December 2020 it had dropped its shares below 2 percent, according to records available on the S&P Capital IQ database. Since late 2019 Alden had owned about one-third—or 11.5 million shares—of Tribune, and in a December 2020 SEC filing called a 13D, Alden first put shareholders on notice that it wanted full control.[69] The *Financial Times* wrote at the time: "Alden, the hedge fund trying to buy Tribune, was on track to make a profit from newspapers last year despite the pandemic. Alden's holding company made 20–25% operating margins in 2019: more than double that of peers such as Gannett or even The New York Times."[70] Alden also owned shares of Gray Television, Nexstar Media Group, Outfront Media, Sinclair Broadcast, and ViacomCBS, where it also made money. A Sinclair executive, looking ahead to the 2020 elections, said on an earnings call in 2019: "In 2020 we are not going to be able to get out of the way of the money. It's literally going to be hand over fist."[71] In another twist of fund fate, Sinclair bought Freedom's television properties after its bankruptcy.[72] By 2016 Alden's MediaNews Group had $1 billion in annual revenue.[73] In 2015 it had turned an estimated 10 to 12 percent profit largely by making deep cuts.[74]

Tribune, too, made money in the last few years before Alden bought it when it was a major investor. Tribune's 2018 annual report noted that operating revenues had increased 1.5 percent—worth $15.2 million—over the prior year for a total revenue of $175.3 million, up from $40.2 million in 2017.[75] At the end of 2020 Tribune took in $96 million from its portion of the sale of BestReviews LLC.[76] Little reinvestment exists when revenues are up, certainly none that would improve journalism. Often, profit-motivated strategies rely on disconnecting from the community, as newsrooms are commercial real estate, seen as capital line items that can be sold to increase the bottom line. In December 2020 Tribune closed the *Hartford Courant*'s newsroom, and it will not open another.[77] Also in 2020 Tribune sold its Norfolk, Virginia, real estate, earning the company $9.5 million.[78]

One of the oldest newspaper companies under review also is not without its own private equity and hedge fund influence. Institutional investors hold more than twenty-five million shares of Lee Enterprises, the newspaper company that was founded in 1890 and that publishes the *St. Louis Post-Dispatch*.[79]

Lee, traded on the Nasdaq stock exchange, counted 49 million unique visitors to its web properties in June 2021, with 337,000 digital-only subscribers, up 50 percent over the prior year.[80] In that quarterly report, Lee listed $820.7 million in total assets, including buildings, land, and cash. Private investment funds have paid attention. In September 2021 one of Lee's ninety-four institutional investors was MNG Enterprises, which is also a part of Alden Global Capital's hedge fund empire. In business databases as of September 2021, Alden is listed as a separate Lee investor, and in December 2021 Lee's board rejected a twenty-four-dollar-per-share takeover bid from Alden.

Chatham Asset Management: The Least Worst

The Tribune sale to Alden came less than a year after New Jersey hedge fund Chatham Asset Management bought the McClatchy newspaper chain, which by the time of its sale counted fifty-four Pulitzer Prizes among its newsrooms.[81] Chatham beat Alden, which also wanted McClatchy, and Alden tried unsuccessfully to stop Chatham's purchase through the courts.[82] Chatham bought chunks of McClatchy shares in 2017, the year McClatchy sold CareerBuilder for $73.9 million.[83] A Chatham Form 13F from August 2017 explained that the hedge fund, run by Anthony Melchiorre, and Chatham Asset High Yield Master Fund, Ltd., owned 387,516 McClatchy shares, which were traded on the New York Stock Exchange. A report filed to the SEC two months later revealed that Melchiorre and Chatham had sole voting power over 540,531 shares, roughly 10 percent of McClatchy. By the end of November 2017, a different SEC document called a Form 4 showed that Chatham owned more than one million McClatchy shares.[84] In July 2018 Chatham lent McClatchy more than $350 million at a time when the newspaper company showed $64.5 million in assets.[85] Its quarterly report documenting that period explained: "We began to actively market for sale the land and buildings at two of our media companies."[86] In September 2020 Chatham closed on the McClatchy chain, bringing the company out of bankruptcy in a $312 million deal and putting it in control of newspapers in fourteen states, including award-winning publications such as the *Charlotte Observer*, the *Miami Herald*, and the *Sacramento Bee*.[87] As of September 2021, Chatham also owned sixty-two million shares—equal to two-thirds—of Postmedia in Canada. Chatham, its financial profile explains, also paid $514 million in July 2014 for the publishing company now called A360 Media LLC, which publishes the *National Enquirer*, *The Star*, and *OK!* Omega Advisors is listed as Chatham's coinvestor in A360, which lists $421 million in assets and $221.3 million in total revenue.[88]

Chatham as the newest hedge fund to the newspaper game has revealed less about its strategies in the marketplace than other firms such as Fortress and Alden, both of which have a longer history, although what happened to Christina Lords helps frame part of the picture of what likely lies ahead.

Lords remembered a McClatchy executive visiting Boise when the *Idaho Statesman* still had a newsroom to announce the newspaper chain's bankruptcy.[89] Seeing that Chatham Asset Management was a likely contender to buy the chain, that McClatchy executive told the *Idaho Statesman* newsroom that the New Jersey–based hedge fund effectively would be the least worst option available. By then, Alden Global Capital's ownership at other chains in cities such as Denver and Oakland had generated such fear that reporters everywhere were concerned. In Boise the tone of the corporate executive's message that Chatham was not Alden left Lords feeling far from reassured.

When she became the *Statesman*'s editor in February 2018, Lords said that half the staff was over forty years old and half was younger than forty. It was a good balance that was tipped as layoffs accelerated. Younger journalists were pressured to learn more quickly and to work longer hours, and editors were forced to constantly work in training mode. When in September 2020 Chatham bought McClatchy, Lords noted that she was officially down four positions.[90] In 2021 she had found a seating chart of the newsroom from 2000 that indicated where one hundred journalists would sit. When she pulled this chart from a box while preparing for a move, the newspaper staffed just twenty people, and Idaho growth had exploded. US Census figures noted that Idaho was the second-fastest-growing state in the decade between 2010 and 2020, experiencing a 17.3 percent population jump.[91] The state's Hispanic population spiked in that time period, growing to 13 percent. Lords hired a Hispanic affairs reporter to cover issues impacting the growing communities. She built partnerships with former competitors.[92] She also worried almost constantly about staffing. "The mission was: keep journalists," Lords told me. Lords increasingly grew concerned that neither McClatchy executives nor Chatham hedge fund managers would understand the needs and concerns of the community she fought to cover, not to mention the needs of a staff living without cost-of-living increases as housing costs skyrocketed.

The thirty-five-year-old had worked for a short stint at a Seattle weekly publication but returned to Idaho, the state her family has called home for five generations. Lords grew up in eastern Idaho, went to school in northern Idaho, and worked in southwestern Idaho before landing at the Boise-based *Idaho Statesman* as a breaking news reporter in 2017. She described the differences in the state's regions, among them distinctions in agriculture and in economies, but she explained that Idahoans statewide often share a mistrust of the federal government despite two-thirds of the state's landmass being designated as federal public lands.[93] These are the intricacies of local communities, and covering these unique characteristics is built through homegrown knowledge and experience. Lords understands the important role of accountability journalism, but she knows about day-to-day community reporting, too, and how it binds. From 2009 to 2011 she worked for the *Moscow-Pullman Daily News,* and a short story she wrote about the loss of federal funding for Meals on Wheels generated so much attention and so many donations that the service restarted. "It sure taught me a lot how developing good sources in a small community will lead to good tips and how one story can make a huge difference to everyday folks if we take time to pursue them," she told me. To pursue them, Lords knows you need reporters.

On daily morning calls with other McClatchy editors after the Chatham takeover, Lords became what she called the "squeaky wheel," asking more and more about when positions would be filled. When a talented young reporter who covered the city of Meridian asked for a raise, her request was denied. She quit. "I guess we're not covering Meridian anymore," Lords thought at the time. By then, the *Statesman* employed one full-time photographer. Lords made choices about whether to ask the photographer to cover a 9:00 a.m. meeting or a high school sports game that night, because to do both meant a twelve-hour day without overtime compensation. "We started to rack up all these open positions. I was walking around with six open positions in my newsroom," Lords said. "How are we going to cover the beats that are expected of us? Who the hell was going to cover that?" At this time, the pandemic also peaked, as did calls for social justice after the murder of George Floyd.

After six months without a statehouse reporter, McClatchy allowed Lords to hire one, a talented journalist who, two weeks into her job, asked for Microsoft Excel. McClatchy had eliminated the Microsoft Office suite from newsroom computers the previous year. Excel is so fundamental to investigative reporting that not having it in a newsroom would be like sending a carpenter to a construction site without a hammer. As the state and federal government began releasing US Census and COVID data, Lords understood the need and advocated for the reporter's access, which would have been provided through licensing. She emailed the IT department, which responded by asking if Excel was necessary. Lords said "yes." IT talked to the reporter. "They tell her no, and I'm like OK, but when we talk to people about the journalism that doesn't get done, when we tell them they don't have robust coverage, this is what we mean," Lords recalled. She noted that McClatchy had tried to push a community-funded focus similar to what the *Seattle Times* has had success with through its impact journalism initiatives.[94] Think of it as crowd-funded work paying for a team to investigate an issue of community concern, and Boise was ready to try it. Lords wasn't interested in bashing McClatchy or Chatham, but she was thinking of a changing and growing community that would benefit from stories found through a reporter's probe of data using Excel. Her fear turned to missing stories, and as editor she knew the ones that drove traffic and subscriptions. "We know through analytics these stories get read," Lords said. "I'm putting out these editor letters that say, 'support local journalism,' and here is a tangible example." She opened Twitter.

She fired off a tweet expressing frustration and hoping for the community's support. Her tweet, since deleted, read: "We're now fighting with @mcclatchy IT to get excel added to an investigative reporter's laptop. To review census data. At some point, this death by 1,000 cuts has to stop. Support your local newspapers, people. Get a digital subscription. This is genuinely what we are up against."[95] Her Friday tweet, which would go viral, also led to her Monday firing. McClatchy executives told Lords she was fired over misuse of the company's social media policy. She had spent the weekend refreshing her knowledge of the handbook, nervous about corporate retaliation, but she failed to find her misstep articulated in the document. She ultimately deleted the tweet after a McClatchy executive said she had to.

After McClatchy fired Lords, the unionized newsroom at the *Statesman* wrote a letter to Tony Hunter, McClatchy CEO, and to Kristin Roberts, then chief content officer, in Lords's defense. The Idaho News Guild wrote, "To fire an editor for advocating for resources and encouraging people to subscribe is a remarkably disappointing decision by McClatchy management. This is a devastating blow to the morale of a newsroom that is already chronically understaffed."[96] Eventually, McClatchy offered Lords, who has more than a dozen journalism awards, her job back. She refused and founded the *Idaho Capital Sun*, a nonprofit newsroom she runs with several other news veterans.[97]

Microsoft Excel would have cost McClatchy less than $160, with other options costing around $6.99 a month. Consider that McClatchy's hedge fund owner, Chatham Asset Management, in 2020 managed $6.9 billion in assets. Its compensation arrangement, disclosed in a May 2021 ADV filing, noted that Chatham staff get paid through a combination of a percentage of its assets under management and performance-based fees.[98] A 2 percent annual fee on the management of those assets—if it followed standard hedge fund procedures described in chapter 1—would reach $138 million.

Like other private investment funds, Chatham is involved in other sectors of the economy beyond media, and by exerting pressure on those firms, it can wring out profits there, too. Chatham invests in the Mohegan Tribal Gaming Authority and in the health care sector.[99] With Blackstone and another private equity firm, in February 2020 Chatham took a principal position in One Call, based in Jacksonville, Florida, and described in trade publications as "the nation's leading provider of specialized healthcare solutions for the workers' compensation industry."[100] Chatham, as an institutional investor, also has sought governance initiatives. In September 2021, as owner of 14.9 percent of the marketing and brand company R. R. Donnelley, Chatham called for a restructuring there. RRD's website pushes for diversity and inclusion, environmental health, and sustainability, and it includes a section on its open-door ethics hotline.[101] RRD has also shown massive revenue gains. In August 2021 the company reported a 442 percent jump in its stock price between July 31, 2020, and July 30, 2021.[102] Yet in a letter to shareholders, Chatham wrote of RRD that "fresh perspectives are sorely needed in the boardroom," continuing, "As RRD's largest equity and debt holder, our interests are aligned and our primary goal is the maximization of stockholder value."[103] In February 2022 Chatham completed its acquisition.[104]

An Evolving Marketplace

Two hedge funds today own three of the top newspaper chains in the United States: Digital First Media, McClatchy, and Tribune Publishing. Still other institutional investors or private equity firms appear at different times in the private investment era at the largest remaining publicly traded newspaper companies, which are Gannett and Lee Enterprises, and at others that are gone. It is also helpful to view today's hedge fund ownership and financial constraints as a path from private equity investment. At McClatchy and Tribune the road to hedge fund ownership goes straight through private equity. At MediaNews Group, hedge fund ownership goes through the greed of millionaire founders—Icarus-like owners who chose mergers and acquisitions as a strategy to maintain high revenues from the end of the twentieth century.

Private investment funds or the private equity divisions at corporate banks— even if they aren't the owners—have been involved in publicly traded chains like Gannett and GateHouse for decades levying varying degrees of influence. The private equity divisions of some of the world's largest banks brokered a deal at Tribune that led it straight to bankruptcy. Other private investment firms entered the market in this period offering little experience in running the news companies that are so crucial to communities nationwide. Penelope Muse Abernathy has explained that the newspaper chains Civitas, BH Media, and 10/13 Communications were all founded between 2009 and 2012.[105] Versa Capital Management, which Abernathy showed had $1.4 billion in assets under management, led the Civitas chain and its ninety-eight newspapers until it sold off most of them in 2018.

As early as 2005 business scholars spotted a convergence between how the two types of pooled investment firms operated in the newspaper industry, an important contrast to family owners and less aggressive shareholders without ties to private equity and hedge funds.[106] A 2006 *Editor & Publisher* piece explained: "Institutional investors have been in the ownership mix for decades, but now some newspaper executives are looking uneasily at these stockholders, concerned that their demands for ever-increasing returns threaten the very existence of some storied companies."[107] Julie Reynolds, a freelance investigative reporter, has studied the funds in the newspaper industry: "Hedge funds often act like private equity owners to the extent they buy up companies using borrowed money and then pay themselves fees and dividends while stripping the actual newspaper."[108] Pressure from shareholders, including institutional investors, means pressure at newspapers nationwide to produce more with less. In 2006 the *New York Times* wrote about the rise of private equity in the industry: "Many people also talk about another alternative: private equity. Steven Rattner, a principal of the Quadrangle Group, a private-equity firm specializing in media companies, contends that firms like his are no less demanding of results than public shareholders are."[109] Other notable deals involving private investment funds moved forward in the name of profit.

Years before Alden, Chatham, and Fortress would transform the newspaper landscape, two major deals showed the early threats of private investment fund investment and ownership. They also revealed how distressed debt markets would be another factor that would transform the industry, which chapter 5 addresses. In 2006 Avista Capital Partners paid $530 million for the *Star Tribune* of Minneapolis, buying the paper from McClatchy. John Hoff called Avista Capital Partners, a private equity firm with offices in Houston and New York City, "the devil" for its brief ownership and operation of the *Star Tribune* in Minneapolis.[110] Alex S. Jones wrote that Avista appeared poised to harvest the Minneapolis daily.[111] At the time, the Minnesota newspaper had been very profitable, "generating more than $1 billion in cash flow since McClatchy bought it."[112] Graydon Royce, sixty-six, worked at the *Star Tribune* from 1980 to 2016 and at one time headed its employee union. He remembered how McClatchy sent one executive, who arrived wearing a black suit, to tell the newsroom about the Avista deal. Royce described the mood as "somber":

> We felt a great sense of betrayal from McClatchy. We knew that private equity was not a good option. It just was not; there were so many things wrong with that. To me, a New York hedge fund just smelled wrong from day 1. You're a private industry. This is one of the complexities of newspapers. You are a private industry, but you are performing a civic responsibility. You are part of a civic life of a community. You are a community resource. And we were told, "Avista will come in and do a fine job." You know, the usual malarkey. I never got a sense of comfort.[113]

Royce remembered that the newspaper lost more than a quarter of its staff in the years after the sale.

Cuts started soon after Avista's takeover. In May 2007 the *Star Tribune* announced the elimination of 7 percent of its workforce.[114] In 2008 the newspaper hired the Blackstone Group's advisory arm to help it restructure its debt, paying a $150,000 monthly fee for Blackstone's services.[115] In 2009 Avista Capital Partners II reported in a Form D to the US Securities and Exchange Commission the sale of nearly $3 billion in "limited partnership interests" with a minimum buy-in of $10 million.[116] Yet despite that money, by 2009 the *Star Tribune,* called one of America's "great regional newspapers," had filed for bankruptcy.[117] Wayzata Investment Partners, another private equity firm, for a years-long period became with GE Capital the *Star Tribune*'s majority owner after a swap allowed for the exchange of its debt into equity.[118] Billionaire Glen Taylor bought the paper in 2014, and he has owned it outright since, telling readers in an opinion piece published in May 2020 at the height of the coronavirus pandemic that the paper's community role was "critical" as he thanked advertisers, staff, and subscribers.[119] While Taylor picks up the pieces, Avista, as of March 2021, managed $3.6 billion in assets for twenty clients.[120]

As the Avista sale formed, farther south in Chicago, Ariel Capital Management, which was at the time one of Tribune's largest shareholders, increased its stake in the company by 5 percent. Tribune owned nearly a dozen newspapers, including the *Baltimore Sun,* the *Los Angeles Times,* and the *Orlando Sentinel.* The website Black Entrepreneurs & Executives explained that Ariel's increased stake was due to the profit anticipated from its eventual sale: "Ariel along with one other major shareholder raised their stakes in the Los Angeles Times ower [*sic*], in anticipation of a sale or breakup of the company."[121] Private equity billionaire Sam Zell bought the chain in 2007.

The year before, Charles Bobrinskoy, the vice president of Ariel Capital Partners, discussed with reporter Lowell Bergman in *Frontline*'s "News War" documentary the role private equity firms like his played in the newspaper marketplace, highlighting the profits: "Again, private equity firms are going to pay good prices for these companies. The business is not nearly as bad as many people think." He stopped short of saying that his investment firm, which was Tribune's fifth largest shareholder at the time of the interview, held any sway over decision-making. When Bergman reminded Bobrinskoy that the Los Angeles daily was profitable, the financier answered: "There's a difference. Making a return for your shareholders."[122] Profits alone don't register for institutional investors seeking maximum revenue, and Bergman's reporting in that series showed how newspaper companies steadily cut further and further into news staff and coverage to boost profits. In 2006 the *Wall Street Journal* noted that Ariel, which had $530 million invested in Tribune, had reacted positively to the news of a leveraged buyout, which ultimately put the venerable chain into a protracted bankruptcy.[123]

Throughout this era, board seats at various newspaper chains went to private equity or hedge fund managers, who gained powerful say over whether to reinvest in a newspaper company and its products or instead try to dismantle newspapers and sell them off for parts during those shaky years of the new millennium and after the 2008 Great Recession. Edward Herman has explained that real corporate control rests with its board of directors.[124] Vincent Mosco has explained that boards that lack labor voices and diversity facilitate "elite corporate interaction."[125] Alden's Heath Freeman had a seat on the boards of Journal Register and the Philadelphia Media Network and in 2011 took a seat on the MediaNews Group board. Bruce Schnelwar, another executive with ties to Freeman's hedge fund mentor, also took a seat on MediaNews Group's board.[126]

When one private equity firm exits, it provides opportunities for others, some as managers but often as major shareholders or bond holders exerting market pressure in other ways. Sometimes the funds deal with each other, too. In the 2019 merger with Gannett, Fortress hovered in the background of that deal along with private equity firm Apollo Global Management, which provided financing.[127] Apollo, an alternative investment firm based in New York City, manages $455 billion in assets, a figure that ballooned by a factor of seven in a decade.[128] In December 2021 Apollo also was reportedly about to loan $4 billion to Fortress parent SoftBank after already having loaned Fortress's New Media $1.8 billion at an interest rate of 11.5 percent to finance the Gannett merger.[129] In 2020 Gannett's annual report explained that financing meant new roles for the private equity firm: "As of December 31, 2020, the total gross leverage ratio exceeded certain thresholds, whereby Apollo had the right to nominate one voting director."[130] By its April 2021 proxy statement, which is a document required to be filed with the SEC as a method of communicating with shareholders, Gannett's filings show that BlackRock Inc., a global asset management firm, owned 14 percent, the equivalent of 19.9 million shares.[131] By September 2021 that figure had jumped above 21 million shares.

BlackRock, according to Harvard University's Future of Media Project ownership database, as of May 2021 controlled shares in brands or parent companies including ABC News, CNN, Fox, Nate Silver's 538, NBC News, the *New York Times*, and Sinclair.[132] Its assets under management, as of December 31, 2020, reached nearly $9 trillion.[133] News reports expected that figure to grow by another $1 trillion in 2021.[134] BlackRock's assets under management led researchers in the journal *Business and Politics* to call it among finance's "Big Three." Jan Fichtner, Eelke M. Heemskerk, and Javier Garcia-Bernardo wrote, "These findings support the thesis that the Big Three may exert structural power over hundreds, if not thousands, of publicly listed corporations in a way that is 'hidden' from direct view."[135] BlackRock's 2020 Investment Stewardship annual report explained: "We look to boards and executive management to serve the interests of long-term shareholders and other stakeholders."[136] Fichtner, Heemskerk, and Garcia-Bernardo found that BlackRock held at least 5 percent in more than half of all publicly listed US companies, and it has been successful swaying corporate leaders to take positions it considers favorable. Now we wait to see how it will sway Gannett leaders, who have long-standing ties to Fortress.

Private investment funds that appear frequently in this decades-long period sometimes appear together, like Alden Global Capital and Cerberus Capital Management, named for the three-headed dog in Greek mythology that guards the gates of the underworld. While it appears that the firms act as competitors, in reality a tight and exclusive group of financial firms has been involved in the newspaper market for two decades.

In the 2010s Cerberus was involved in Irish debt markets, prompting one business reporter there to write: "You don't name yourself after the three-headed dog that guards hell if you want a reputation as nice guys."[137] In 2011 a group of Massachusetts nurses rallied to criticize Cerberus for financing a hospital chain that was "squeezing patients and workers for ultra-profits."[138] In 2010 Cerberus was part of a small group of lenders with Alden and Angelo, Gordon & Co. that took equity positions in the Philadelphia Media Network Inc., the name given to the restructured *Daily News* and *Inquirer* that put Alden's Heath Freeman on the board.[139] Cerberus, which owned an 80 percent stake of Chrysler when it was rescued by a multi-billion-dollar taxpayer bailout, has been called a "secretive private equity fund."[140] In 1995 Cerberus provided a $13 million loan to Penthouse that generated 19 percent in interest and fees.[141]

It also owned a number of television stations, selling in 2011 for $200 million to Sinclair.[142] Cerberus has also provided financing for an Ohio-based paper company that supplied both magazines and newspapers.[143] Alden owns Digital First Media, which both Cerberus and Apollo Global Management sought for a period in 2015.[144] In Alden's May 26, 2021, form filed with the SEC after it bought Tribune, Alden borrowed $218 million to finance its Tribune acquisition from several lenders, Cerberus 2112 Credit Holdings LLC, Cerberus ASRS Holdings LLC, and Cerberus FSBA Holdings LLC among them. Cerberus Business Finance Agency, LLC, is the agent for the first-tier debt.[145]

Local newspapers don't have a profit problem. They have an ownership and investment problem. The crisis has, in part, been created by these firms' money-making strategies and their entry and expansion into the newspaper market, sucking profit away and creating conditions that have confined newspaper companies that should have been focused on the impacts of the internet. In his 2011 book, *The Deal from Hell: How Moguls and Wall Street Plundered Great American Newspapers*, James O'Shea explained: "Capitalism built the American newspaper industry, but it was the sort of capitalism embraced by men and women who wanted to build something that would endure, employ people, and make the founders rich by providing a vital service. I don't know that the kind of capitalism evolving in America holds the same promise."[146] Hedge fund ownership and private equity dealings threaten newspapers, their workers, and the audiences who rely on these local newspapers to stay informed in a democracy. They have been threatening operations for decades, although hedge fund ownership shifted our understanding of just how bad it can get. Increasingly, due to mergers and consolidations and debt, local newspapers nationwide are owned or influenced by an oligarchy of hedge funds and private equity interests with a profit-first mentality that offers citizens in those communities little to no local news, often because of staff cuts conducted to maximize profits. This era, which started with the Freedom deal described in chapter 1, illustrates that newspapers and newspaper chains now are nothing more than assets under management, widgets to be bought and sold by a small clique of financial firms with little interest in a healthy functioning press or its relationship to democracy.

Chapter 4 explains more about the mergers and acquisitions of the 2000s that left companies in debt as private equity tried to get its cut contemporary to the rise of the internet and the loss of classified advertising revenue. Even after failed mergers, companies kept consolidating as digital loomed large.

Chapter 4

Mergers and Acquisitions

In 2007 $20 billion was spent to acquire newspapers.[1] Between 2008 and 2019 US firms spent $10 trillion in mergers and acquisitions, with newspapers among the products swapped and traded as firms looked to consolidate and synergize.[2] Bullied by private equity firms operating as institutional investors or owners at major chains like GateHouse, corporate newspapers sought mergers and acquisitions as the overarching strategy to handle the loss of advertising revenue and the inevitable digital transition. In 2009 Jonathan A. Knee, Bruce C. Greenwald, and Ava Seave wrote in *The Curse of the Mogul: What's Wrong with the World's Leading Media Companies* that bad acquisitions were a prime reason for media companies' underperformance: "In a world where economists can be found on as many sides of an issue as politicians, it is a relief to find a topic on which there is effective unanimity. Mergers and acquisitions (M&A) do not create value."[3] Efforts to maximize profits and decisions made in deference to private investment firms and institutional investors eager to strip newspaper company profits take us to the second feature of the private investment era: mergers and acquisitions.

In reality, these mergers and acquisitions mark a period of great instability born of this investment influence. Yet, facing innovation demands and shifting consumer behavior, newspaper companies cut investment in digital and forged ahead with M&A as a key strategy throughout the private investment era. Power in the newspaper market changed and shrank into a handful of companies, but the debt that resulted proved disastrous, setting a vector for deeper investment fund influence and control. Despite concerns about mergers and acquisitions, newspapers and newspaper companies in this era have been sold and consolidated, cut and cast off from their communities as corporate chains beholden to investors sought more profit through synergies and, eventually, layoffs. As some private equity firms sought to extract newspaper profits from the chain marketplace, others, like Fortress Investment Group, became owners, acquiring hundreds of local newspapers and gutting them. Not every private equity firm and hedge fund played the same role in this period, but the roles they played—and continue to play—had and continue to have impacts.

This chapter considers the last twenty years of M&A at major newspaper chains as it demonstrates the digital transition that never materialized as a result of private equity pressure. It should be noted that the newspaper chains themselves have faced dramatic changes through mergers and acquisitions or consolidations in this era, so the analysis of documents and trade reports related to other chains pushed into the history books, including Journal Register Co. and Knight Ridder, also are included to study the broader impacts of the era's M&A. As an example, studying GateHouse's acquisitions and mergers of the era allows for a deeper understanding of the role that Fortress Investment Group and its debt accumulation played in that chain leading up to its 2013 bankruptcy and, six years later, its $1.3 billion merger with Gannett. Similarly, studying the Knight Ridder and McClatchy merger from 2006 also shows the private equity interest leading up to that pairing, which ultimately set an ownership vector for hedge fund Chatham Asset Management.

Some of the most spectacular mergers and acquisitions to ever hit the newspaper industry came in the last two decades, and they rolled out the red carpet for billions of dollars in debt, distressing companies and putting chains at risk of hedge fund control. The next chapter reviews the debt that resulted from these decisions, but in this chapter I begin with a definition of M&A and then move on to a broad overview of consolidations and chains historically before engaging in a discussion of M&A in the corporate chain newspaper market that happened as digital development withered.

Chains, Consolidations, and Corporate Media Power

In the preface to their 2003 book *Winning the Merger Endgame*, Graeme K. Deans, Fritz Kroeger, and Stefan Zeisel wrote that a merger is not so much a blending of two companies as it is when "one entity consumes another."[4] I believe a key quotient of M&A in the private investment era is instability born of these corporate actions, a flip from past eras that saw consolidations grow family power with money reinvested in journalism in small and large communities nationwide. Alex S. Jones explained that at the *Los Angeles Times* under Chandler family ownership, its profits were reinvested in journalists and their assignments, increasing quality. In his book *Losing the News*, Jones, a former director of Harvard University's Shorenstein Center on Media, Politics, and Public Policy, wrote: "If newspapers lose that sense of obligation and stewardship to the communities they serve, then the survival of newspapers is of little importance, because they will be just another business."[5] As more families exited the newspaper marketplace, Jones became increasingly concerned about the loss of public service mission.

M&A are inevitable in any industry and have appeared for much of the last century in the newspaper market, and funds are cutting into that mission. In his foreword to *Winning the Merger Endgame*, James K. Glassman explained: "Viewed up close, business—like war, football, or childhood—is chaos. But step back a bit and patterns emerge across space and time."[6] His is a notable observation that also can be applied to the newspaper industry, seeing that it is, above all else, a business. The patterns that emerge related to private investment fund influence and ownership as they relate to M&A can also be traced, and they reveal little in the way of public service mission.

In the earliest years of the new millennium, private equity firms expecting huge windfalls bought in and started making decisions about newspaper operations, including taking seats on newspaper boards. Private investment funds started influencing decision-making in that way or through the ownership of large percentages of shares traded on public indexes. Advertising losses caused panic, and mergers and acquisitions were seen as one remedy to steady sinking profits. Bigger, it would seem, would be better, with cost effectiveness maximized through consolidation and contraction. Yet Paul Boselie and Bas Koene wrote: "Fewer than 25 percent of mergers and acquisitions achieve their financial objectives."[7] Mergers and acquisitions in the media world have become more noticeable because of their sheer scale and perhaps because of the collapse that followed, one that seemed impossible, given the money generated by generations of family owners.

Throughout the twentieth century, families entered or expanded their place in the chain newspaper landscape, among them Bancroft, Bingham, Chandler, Cox, Gannett, Hoiles, and Scripps.[8] In a March 1910 letter that is part of a collection of his writings held by Ohio University, E. W. Scripps wrote: "A newspaper fairly and honestly conducted in the interest of the great masses of the public must at all times antagonize the selfish interests of that very class which furnishes the larger part of a newspaper's income."[9] Edwin Emery explained that Scripps sought to create newspapers for the working classes that he described as the "people's papers" which after his death turned away from covering labor issues and adopted a more conservative tone.[10] That newspaper chain, one piece of what would become the E. W. Scripps Company, eventually expanded to include properties like HGTV that existed, it seemed, solely to connect cable audiences to advertisers.[11] Scripps's consolidated revenue in 2013 reached $432 million, and by 2015 its television properties reached 20 percent of American households.[12] Gannett bought what was once the Scripps print division in 2016, one of a series of acquisitions that transformed newspapers and their public service mission as profit, once again, became paramount.

Notable families exiting the newspaper marketplace generations after their founding and looking for billion-dollar sell-offs brought new interest from corporations and, eventually, private investment funds in both newspapers and broadcast markets. Cox in 2019 sold a huge chunk of its broadcast properties to a group of private equity funds managed by Apollo Global Management.[13] The Cowles family sold the *Des Moines Register* in 1985 to Gannett. Another significant Gannett acquisition was its 1986 purchase of the seventy-year-old Bingham family chain, which marked the end of that family's newspaper ownership, meticulously described in Susan E. Tifft and Jones's book *The Patriarch: The Rise and Fall of the Bingham Dynasty*.[14] That deal followed Gannett buying other major and influential US dailies, including the *Cincinnati Enquirer* and the *Des Moines Register*. Included in the $1 billion Bingham transaction was the sale of the chain's flagship, the *Louisville Courier Journal*, in Kentucky. At the time, Gannett CEO Allen H. Neuharth used a horse-racing metaphor to describe the confluence of deals, saying it was "like winning the Triple Crown."[15] The sales in that period put Gannett's paid circulation at six million, according to *Associated Press* reporting from 1986, and marked the end of a $1 billion rush to consolidate or gobble up smaller, profitable chains and dailies. Philip Meyer called Gannett's accumulation of newspapers, swinging from good to bad economic times, laying off staff, and slashing the amount of news, as "Al's money game."[16] Gannett triggered other newspaper companies to view layoffs and surface coverage as ways to boost profits. By the 2000s, Gannett had institutional investors and private equity firms demanding more as its power in the industry accelerated.

By 2002 Gannett had flexed that power successfully, fighting alongside other companies in federal court for relaxed ownership rules as media democracy advocates like Robert W. McChesney cried foul.[17] It also demonstrated most notably that consolidation in the newspaper marketplace would not benefit citizens who relied on those newspapers for stories about their communities' civic, political, and social lives. Above all else, it showed that consolidated companies were willing to fight battles to forge new profit strategies, and it showed that they would win. If anything, those earlier consolidation strategies appeared to provide a roadmap for private equity and hedge fund investors to see what was possible in the newspaper market while they looked at ways to grow larger.

In 2019 Gannett merged with GateHouse to form the country's largest newspaper company, in control of more than 200 dailies. While under the Gannett name, the company is run by New Media Investment Group / GateHouse executives with strong and long-standing ties to Fortress Investment Group. Before and since that merger, Gannett has also seen some of the largest influence of powerful private equity shareholders, some of whose behavior in the market could at best be described as questionable. As an example, Omega Advisors, Chatham Asset Management's coinvestor in Canada, owned 13 percent of Gannett in March 2014. In 2016 Omega was accused of illegally using insider information, and its founder paid $4.95 million in penalties before retiring and scaling back the fund in 2018.[18] As of November 2021, Gannett's largest institutional investor is BlackRock, which has an even larger position than Omega did in the 2010s.

Concerns about consolidations and merciless profit-motivated strategies existed, of course, before deep private investment fund engagement in the market, in part due to advertiser motivations and also because of Gannett. Penelope Muse Abernathy's studies of the newspaper industry led her to conceptualize three types of owners. She referred to the "founders" of the nineteenth century; she charted the "corporate newspaper managers" of the second half of the twentieth century; and then she put a moniker on the private investment funds that are so powerful today, calling them "the new media barons."[19] Even during the corporate newspaper period before the turn of the millennium, links between newspaper boards and other financial sectors posed problems, including over advertising influence at thirteen publicly traded chains.[20] Suzanne M. Kirchhoff wrote in a September 2010 Congressional Research Service report: "Between 1960 and 1980, 57 newspaper owners sold their properties to Gannett Co. By 1977, 170 newspaper groups owned two-thirds of the country's 1,700 daily papers."[21]

Consider that by the start of the private investment era consolidation had empowered nearly two dozen newspaper companies to control 70 percent of the country's circulation. It's a pattern that began with businesses, shifted to families, and then moved on to institutional investors, slowly sliding toward fewer and more powerful firms in control.[22] Abernathy explained that by the end of 2004, the three largest newspaper companies owned 187 daily newspapers. Twelve years later, her work showed that the three largest companies' ownership stake had jumped to 296 dailies and brought with it a combined daily and weekday circulation of 12.6 million.[23] By early 2018 America's two largest newspaper chains were owned by a private equity firm and a hedge fund, respectively.[24] In the four years since, consolidation has deepened, as Gannett, the largest chain, now owns nearly as many dailies as the top three did in 2016. Today four top chains—Gannett, Digital First Media, Lee Enterprises, and Tribune—control as much circulation as two dozen companies did twenty years ago. That means control by the hedge fund owners and private equity investors also has been consolidated.

The M&A of the last twenty years helped create this new newspaper oligarchy. Many of the largest newspaper mergers and acquisitions of the twenty-first century have been motivated by profit rather than any kind of strategy that would benefit citizens in a democracy.[25] And these consolidations and mergers arrived at the cusp of the shift to digital. In 2011, as Alden Global Capital took a substantial piece of MediaNews Group, MNG's outgoing CEO, Dean Singleton, noted the influence of institutional investors in the marketplace: "There are institutional owners of Gannett, institutional owners of McClatchy, institutional owners of other newspaper companies. Our job is to make stock ownership grow in value, that's what we have been doing, and that's what we'll continue to do."[26] Yet as a strategy, M&A shifted control away from the local communities the newspapers were trying to serve.

The effects of a shift in local control were magnified as the M&A strategy continued. Consider that in March 2000 Tribune paid $8 billion for Times Mirror Co., then parent company of the *Los Angeles Times*, long owned and run by the powerful Chandler family, worth $4.2 billion in 2015.[27] The 2006 *Los Angeles Times* obituary for former publisher and scion Otis Chandler said: "The Chandlers had no rival as the most powerful family in Southern California. They owned vast landholdings and used their influence with elected officials and the business elite to shape the region's development."[28] David Halberstam wrote this of the Chandler family: "They did not so much foster the growth of Southern California as, more simply, invent it."[29] That 2000 merger created the third largest newspaper company in the country, which would eventually force some workers into lawsuits against Tribune for what was promised to them as employees of Times Mirror.[30] It also earned Los Angeles at that time the ignoble title of being America's largest city without a major daily newspaper published by local owners, a fact that two decades ago was newsworthy.[31] It hardly would be today.

Baltimore, Boise, Chicago, Denver, Hartford, Miami, and Sacramento are defined by daily newspapers that are owned by hedge funds with no presence in those communities. Gannett, headquartered in McLean, Virginia, but under GateHouse leadership, owns the *Arizona Republic* in Phoenix, the *Cincinnati Enquirer*, the *Detroit Free Press*, and the *Tennessean* in Nashville. It also owns smaller newspapers nationwide, among them the *Abilene Reporter-News*, with a Sunday circulation of 7,195 in central Texas, the *Beaver County Times* in western Pennsylvania, with its 8,634 weekday subscribers, and the *Burlington County Times*, with a daily circulation of 13,098, in New Jersey.[32] At hundreds of other local newspapers nationwide, including in Allentown, Pennsylvania, and Peoria, Illinois, it's the same story: private investment fund control with little regard for local coverage. In January 2006 Mark Fitzgerald and Jennifer Saba wrote: "Americans used to know who owned their hometown papers."[33] Few do today. Universally, these chains run or influenced by private investment funds lay off reporters and cut coverage as they seek out more opportunities to expand across the country.

M&A Frenzy

A decade before Journal Register's first bankruptcy case, on August 25, 1999, the *Wall Street Journal* ran a 210-word story under the headline "Journal Register Co. Hopes Shares Attract Institutional Investors."[34] At that time, the story noted that Journal Register owned twenty-five daily newspapers, servicing 645,000 paying subscribers mostly in the Northeast and New England, with other properties and readers in Ohio and St. Louis. The Journal Register Company, formed in 1990, owned the *Times Herald* of Norristown, Pennsylvania, which was founded in 1799 under a different name six months before it published George Washington's obituary.[35] Its history mattered little to its profit-generating potential for owners and investors: in 1999 the chain also had nearly eight of its ten shares—equal to 36,335,123 shares—owned by Warburg Pincus Capital Corporation, affiliated with the private equity investment firm E. M. Warburg Pincus & Co., which managed $7 billion in investments.[36] In 1990 Journal Register was formed from the fallout after high-risk junk bonds felled a different chain owner.[37]

With Warburg Pincus, a key newspaper shareholder in 1990, bankers with Goldman Sachs sought to repackage and resell the newspaper company's debt. A Goldman banker "hung onto the new bonds, confident that if bankruptcy befell the company the senior position he'd negotiated would ensure a 100-cents-on-the-dollar recovery."[38] In 1999 the newspaper company was seeking more liquidity, and in doing so, it intended to float 10 percent of its stock, the profits of which would flow back to "Warburg partners and affiliates." In 1999 Journal Register posted solid earnings, part of an industrywide ad revenue boom worth more than $43 billion.[39] In 2002 Warburg Pincus had doled out 2.5 million Journal Register shares to its partners.[40] That same year a small percentage of its shares were owned by Ariel Capital Management, which had stakes in other newspaper companies, including Lee Enterprises and Tribune.[41]

In 2003 Journal Register was winning awards for its newspapers' work in Woonsocket, Rhode Island, and Ardmore, Pennsylvania. Executives eyed more acquisitions. By July 2004 Warburg had $14 billion in assets under management and had considered making a bid for Freedom Communications.[42] Journal Register was also generating money. On an earnings call in 2004 with Journal Register shareholders, then CEO Robert Jelenic told investors that net income was up $14.8 million, an increase of 6 percent. Advertising revenues, he said, were up 14.5 percent. Pretax net income: up. Retail performance: up. Connecticut cluster: up. Philadelphia cluster: up.[43] In July 2004 Journal Register bought the 21st Century newspaper chain, owned by a group of private equity investors, including Goldman Sachs.[44] Industry publications described the deal this way: "Pontiac, Mich.–based 21st Century has rolled up several of these titles since its founding in the mid-1990s. Capital for those buyouts came from private-equity firm Kelso & Co., and Goldman Sachs's Capital Partners II investment fund, which founded the company along with Chairman and Chief Executive Frank Shepherd."[45] By 2005 reporters covering the industry called Journal Register's acquisition appetite "voracious."[46] That year, an industry-wide M&A hot streak started.

A dizzying frenzy of M&A gripped the newspaper industry. Lee Enterprises bought the Pulitzer chain for $64 a share in a deal worth $1.5 billion.[47] MediaNews Group bought Diversified Suburban Newspapers. Gannett bought HomeTown Communications Network, Inc., in March 2005.[48] HomeTown was described in a news release as a "community publishing company" with revenues in 2004 expected to hit $86 million.[49] Fortress bought the Liberty chain, which would become GateHouse.[50] Knight Ridder offloaded the *Detroit Free Press* to Gannett. In 2006 Journal Register bought Suburban Lifestyles Community Newspaper Group, which had revenues the year prior of $2.2 million.[51] GateHouse spent $400 million on 124 newspapers near Boston.[52] Less than a year after acquiring GateHouse, Fortress sought $762 million in "debt financing."[53] GateHouse, owner of hundreds of local newspapers, including the *Patriot Ledger* in Quincy, Massachusetts, focused on markets that larger chains passed over.[54] And GateHouse's strategy, the *Wall Street Journal* reported in 2006, was "making acquisitions."[55] Yet the biggest deal of 2006 was McClatchy's

June merger with Knight Ridder, which also was influenced by private equity investors. The staggering $4.5 billion merger saddled McClatchy with billions in debt. Industry analyst Ken Doctor called the deal "disastrous" and noted that it "burdened [McClatchy] with a price-tag held over from the good old days, just as they were ending."[56] Corporate debt climbed.

At Knight Ridder, private equity investors caused a shakeup in 2004 that tipped the first domino leading to its failed merger with McClatchy. Knight Ridder was once a venerable and profitable newspaper chain with reporters committed to accountability journalism in the name of democracy. Its Washington, DC, reporting team was "virtually alone in their questioning of the Bush Administration's allegations of links between Saddam Hussein, weapons of mass destruction, and international terrorism."[57] In 2004 Knight Ridder was the nation's second largest chain, and its board of directors meeting in July of that year was held at the Ritz-Carlton in San Francisco's Nob Hill neighborhood. These were not lean years. Knight Ridder's 2004 Form 10-K showed a company with $4 billion in total assets and $1.4 billion in debt. Shareholders averaged a 22.2 percent return on equity investments.[58]

Charles Layton, writing for the *American Journalism Review*, reported in 2006 on what was headlined "Sherman's March."[59] Layton outlined what happened in the hallway of that San Francisco hotel during the 2004 board meeting. Knight Ridder's three largest shareholders "camped outside the door," angry about stock performance and a price per share of about sixty-five dollars.[60] It had peaked at eighty dollars per share a few months before. One of those shareholders was Bruce S. Sherman, a Naples, Florida, wealth management executive who owned through his Private Capital Management firm 19 percent of Knight Ridder and lived in a $9.5 million, 12,050-square-foot penthouse with Gulf of Mexico views.[61] At the time, Private Capital Management managed $32 billion in assets, and Sherman had been called in business publications a Wall Street luminary.[62] Layton wrote:

> He had built a reputation for producing returns of 20 percent and even 25 percent a year for his investors, but now he wasn't even outperforming the market indexes, which themselves were sluggish. He needed a way to rescue his investment. Simply selling the Knight Ridder stock would likely depress its price, sinking him even deeper in the hole. However, he and his fellow mutineers believed that Knight Ridder in its entirety could be sold outright, just auctioned off, for more money—and maybe a lot more—than they could get by selling their shares on the stock market. So Sherman had decided to bully the company into putting itself up for sale.[63]

Sherman's Private Capital Management firm also owned shares in Gannett, Mc-Clatchy, and the New York Times Co.[64] In February 2006 Sherman and Private Capital Management with another of the firm's executives held 12 percent of Gannett shares. The document filed describing the transaction—called a Schedule 13G—noted: "In these capacities, Messrs. Sherman and Powers exercise shared dispositive power with respect to shares held by PCM's clients and managed by PCM."[65] A November 2005 profile of Sherman explained: "Sherman has said his investment style is built around preserving the wealth that his clients have amassed. The goal is for clients to double their assets every five years."[66]

Inside that San Francisco meeting room, facing pressure from Sherman, the Knight Ridder board voted to increase shareholder dividends and buyback ten million shares as a way to steady the sinking stock price. The hikes to shareholders like Sherman came after a decade of layoffs. The most notable influence over Knight Ridder came from Private Capital Management Inc., then its largest shareholder, which also pushed for aggressive profit-maximizing strategies.[67] *National Public Radio*'s David Folkenflik reported that Knight Ridder had "endured wave after wave of budget cuts as it attempted to placate investors seeking greater profits."[68] *The Economist* reported in November 2005 that Knight Ridder's former boss Tony Ridder was maligned for his newsroom cuts, but it noted that those cuts were never deep enough to keep shareholders happy.[69] Less than two years after that Nob Hill board meeting, Knight Ridder faced its unsuccessful merger with McClatchy as yet another way to mollify investors.

Knight Ridder wasn't the only newspaper company trying to survive the internet transition and disruption from M&A as investors fumed. John Soloski explained in 2005: "Most institutional investors live quarter to quarter and are unable to take a long-term view of an investment."[70] By April 2006 MediaNews Group had entered into a deal with Hearst and the now larger McClatchy worth $1 billion and involving four newspapers, including the *San Jose Mercury News*.[71] By 2007—the year before the Great Recession and as the digital transformation gripped the industry—researchers alongside journalists working in large and small newsrooms nationwide grew concerned about the price of profit, including how it manifested in several high-profile mergers and acquisitions and, later, newsroom cuts. Rem Rieder, writing in the *American Journalism Review*, stated: "No sooner had McClatchy sealed the deal than it cast off the Knight Ridder papers deemed to be in slow-growth markets and/or incapable of making enough money. The message was clear: Quality journalism is fine, but only when it's lucrative."[72] More acquisitions followed. Gannett bought Central Ohio Advertiser Network from Journal Register.[73] MediaNews Group spent $290 million on three newspapers from Hearst.[74] By 2007 Journal Register, too, was consolidating operations after a fourteen-year period that saw it complete thirty-one acquisitions. That year, despite revenues of $463.2 million, Journal Register was paying roughly 10 percent—or $43.6 million—in interest on its debt.[75] Executives that year were forced to sell the corporate jet.[76]

GateHouse, under Fortress's control, also continued M&A. Its plan for the future, articulated in its annual reports, centered on growing, with no plans to navigate the internet. GateHouse's 2007 annual report noted: "Since our inception, we have acquired 395 daily and weekly newspapers, shoppers and directories. This strategy has been a critical component of our growth, and we expect to continue to pursue it in the future."[77] GateHouse spent $115 million for more than a dozen Morris Publishing Group newspapers and inked other deals.[78] *Editor & Publisher* reported on GateHouse's acquisition of Morris, noting that its business strategy was to "grow free cash flow, often with acquisitions, to fund dividends considerably higher than peer companies."[79] It spent $380 million on nine publications from the Copley Press.[80] The acquisitions grew GateHouse's reach from nineteen US states to twenty-three.[81] It grabbed newspapers in Heber Springs, Arkansas, and Sleepy Eye, Minnesota, including some that boasted profit margins of 40 percent.[82] It also bought yellow page and white page directory company SureWest Communications. Outside of these, GateHouse's 2007 annual report mentions forty additional publications acquired for $27.5 million it called "tuck-in acquisitions."[83] *Bloomberg Businessweek* reported in February 2007: "Quietly and methodically, the New York private equity firm has assembled the largest collection of small-town newspapers in the U.S."[84] It was expected to generate more than $23 million in profits off of $400 million in revenues that year.

Near the turn of the millennium, news companies began experimenting with the internet. In November 1999 Knight Ridder "joined the 'dot-com' craze."[85] At the time its newspapers generated more than $3 billion in revenues, and its internet activities were expected, at first, to lose money. Investors flinched, uncertain how that investment would play out even as some media analysts pushed for innovation. In August 2006 Scarborough Research issued a white paper showing huge bumps in audience use of newspaper websites: "The paper identified several key factors that contribute to audience growth online, including unique website content, high local-market internet penetration, heavy cross-promotion, and integration of the website into the core newspaper business."[86] But institutional investors always demanded more, and their demands put high-quality investment in digital on a shelf. In July 2000 the *Wall Street Journal* reported: "Investors have become more cost-conscious as their love affair with the internet has waned. Traditional accounting methods contribute to their dilemma. Because newspapers are valued on the basis of the ratio of their stock price to earnings or cash flow multiples, investments in lossmaking internet units hurt valuations."[87]

Mergers and acquisitions were seen as the antidote, and newspaper executives were unable to focus on the digital transition that loomed nor did they try to recreate or improve online classified listings. At a company like Knight Ridder, then in control of the *Miami Herald* and the *Philadelphia Inquirer,* the shortsightedness by 2005 had left it without a digital strategy, or, as *The Economist* put it, Knight Ridder was without a "national paper which can hold its own on the internet."[88] By April 2007 the financial magazine *Barron's* reported that "takeovers are changing the face of the newspaper-publishing business."[89] Over and over, executives beholden to private equity investors stalled innovation, and over and over there were people warning against it or trying to guide them down a smarter path. Plenty of people I interviewed for this book knew that their newspaper company was doing a terrible job preparing for the inevitable transition online, and many knew that it was due to the basic day-to-day bean counting that began to corrupt newspapers as private investment funds gained more power. Mergers and acquisitions were seen as a strategy to fight the impending internet battle, evidenced most notably by the merger of Tribune and Times Mirror in 2000.

"Build a Culture Using Allegories"

Tribune bankruptcy exhibits include a plan for its first one hundred days under private equity billionaire Sam Zell's ownership in 2007. These exhibits show a company both ill prepared to take on a media company of its scale and status, not to mention a group of private equity executives unsure how to navigate the digital transition upon them. In an August 9, 2007, memo, William Pate, an executive with Zell's Equity Group Investments, focused on corporate strategies related to its Tribune takeover. One, listed under the subhead "Print will prosper," reads: "We cannot be in a business where more than a third of the value is embedded in newspapers and also walk around saying that print is dying. It won't die if we find solutions to help it prosper. If employees or managers think print is dying, they should resign and seek work elsewhere."[90] That month, Randy Michaels, a former radio shock jock who rose to Tribune chief executive, wrote to Pate and copied Zell with a plan for the first one hundred days of Zell's ownership.[91] The email attachment, called "TRIB FIRST 100.doc," noted that Amazon, AOL, eBay, Google, Travelocity, and Yahoo had successful online businesses, and under that a bullet point reads, "Steal from them." Michaels also wrote, "Learn the language of print," to which someone responded using what looks like Microsoft Word's track changes feature: "More important than google and yahoo . . . is the emergence of blogosphere." Michaels's draft included other ideas and goals, among them "share stories and anecdotes"; "build a culture using allegories"; "eliminate most of the HR department"; and "famous people writing columns." Another point in the document asked: "What's wrong with a section that holds the news up to a fun house mirror?" That garnered this response: "We should buy The Onion," referring to the satire website, which one might think could be described as a business strategy if parts of the entire document didn't read like satire. Under Michaels's plan for "DAYS 90–100" there are two bullet points. The second one says: "Develop a plan for the next 100 days."[92] There's little evidence of how any of these strategies—if you can call them strategies for a media company that reached 80 percent of Americans—played out in the first one hundred days or at any other time. A year later, Tribune filed Chapter 11 bankruptcy, besieged by $13 billion in debt. The debt, some of it brokered by private equity sectors at major banks and that newspaper companies like Tribune took on during this flurry of mergers and acquisitions, eventually made companies both attractive and vulnerable to later private equity investment and hedge fund ownership.

At Gannett, GateHouse, Lee Enterprises, and MediaNews Group former journalists I interviewed remembered unsuccessfully pushing for a transition strategy. Kurt Greenbaum arrived at the *St. Louis Post-Dispatch*, owned by Lee Enterprises, in mid-2002, which he described as a time when many print reporters and editors still scorned digital in the years after the dot-com bubble burst.[93] Greenbaum, age fifty-seven at the time of our interview, took a position in 2002 as online news editor in St. Louis. He remembered feeling at first like an outsider pushing for digital to be taken seriously. "To some people in the newspaper industry I was an insurgent," Greenbaum told me. "And I represented a problem. I feel like I was a voice crying out in the wilderness saying, 'We better be prepared for it. And we better invest in it and make our peace with it. It's coming.'" We talked in September 2020 about that time period at newspapers before the worst of the recession, and Greenbaum remembered the newspaper earning 25 percent profit margins. He explained that newspaper management should have devoted resources to the digital transition, but those profit targets hindered long-range planning. He thought Lee executives should have devoted resources to aid the transition online, similar to having a dedicated staff to handle photojournalism. "I shouldn't have been put in the position where I represented more work," Greenbaum said. "We should have taken 15 percent profit margins instead of 25 percent profit margins, so we could do the work getting the resources we needed."[94] Greenbaum left in 2010.

I was eager to see how Lee's corporate documents matched Greenbaum's memory of those years. While Lee's 2005 annual report discussed the move online and the internet, it made no mention of any investment in those activities. If anything, it explained that its majority stake in investments, including TownNews.com, provided opportunities for revenue, not exactly a strategy representing a shift toward the digital future. Its sections titled "Operation Expenses and Results of Operations" and "Liquidity and Capital Resources" failed to mention online as a place for expenditure or development. Lee's 2005 Form 10-K showed the financial impacts of its buying spree, its way forward, like that of so many others, intent on using M&A. That document noted that on Sundays in its markets spread over twenty-three states, including Arizona, California, Hawaii, Nebraska, and Wisconsin, three-quarters of adults read its newspapers. Its purchase of the Pulitzer chain pushed it into fourth place based on the number of newspapers owned and seventh by circulation. Its "cash required for investing activities" hit $1.2 billion in 2005 due to that major acquisition and $27 million the year before. Its six strategic priorities included "accelerate online growth," but neither the annual report nor its glossy message to shareholders listed any investments in how it expected to achieve that acceleration. But its investments in acquisitions past and future were clearly articulated: "One measure of the success of the Company's strategy to grow through acquisition is its enterprise value, which is defined as the market value of its equity securities, plus the principal amount of debt outstanding, less cash assets."[95] At that time, Lee, like other publicly traded newspaper companies, had private investment funds as major investors, among them Ariel Capital Management and Private Capital Management, which had wreaked havoc at Knight Ridder.[96] PCM had nearly a 20 percent stake in Lee, though it never publicly churned dissent.[97]

Private equity, by then intent on maintaining profit, hampered other efforts to innovate and pushed for further acquisitions. Gannett's 2005 annual report explained: "Within the publishing segment, the company continues to diversify and expand its acquisitions."[98] Brian O'Connor remembered a similar situation at the *Detroit News,* which in 2005 was sold by Gannett to MediaNews Group. In that period, O'Connor sat on an informal digital advisory board, and in the 2000s he proposed ideas that included an email newsletter. "We were told, 'Our software isn't set up. We don't have the money for that.' Everything was 'We can't do that.' The great digital future was upon us, and we were told we can't even do a newsletter if it made money," O'Connor said.[99] Once Alden took over board seats and started managing MediaNews, the situation deteriorated at that chain. Gabi Boerkircher went to MediaNews' *Boulder Daily Camera* in late 2010 not long after graduating with a journalism degree from the University of Colorado Boulder. By 2011, with Alden executives on the board, Boerkircher said that cost-cutting and money became all anybody could talk about. A designer at that time and twenty-three years old, Boerkircher suggested apps that would capitalize on the region's booming brewery scene. "We were told, 'What's the click rate? What's the return on investment?' It just took the joy out of it. We had to twist it to say that we could sell advertising," she remembered.[100] Even then, talks to engage local audiences stalled.

By November 2013, Fortress's New Media had focused on small to medium-sized businesses, called SMBs in its filings.[101] New Media's Form 10-K for that year explained, "Many of the owners and managers of these SMBs do not have the bandwidth, expertise or resources to navigate the fast evolving digital marketing sector, but are increasingly aware of the need to establish and maintain a digital presence in order to stay connected with current and future customers." New Media's strategy was basically to suck out whatever advertising revenue remained through a platform called Propel, and its annual report appears unapologetic about its strategy: "We have acquired over $1.7 billion of assets since 2006. We have acquired both traditional newspaper and directory businesses. We have a very scalable infrastructure and platform to leverage for future acquisitions." New Media operated in 352 markets, a new debt-free newspaper powerhouse overseeing 421 community print publications reaching more than 12 million people each week. Its stock was traded on the New York Stock Exchange under the NEWM symbol.[102] And for the years between 2014 and 2019, the company appeared to want to repeat the cycle all over again, spending more than $1 billion to acquire newspapers in Florida, Ohio, and Texas.[103]

When Fortress's GateHouse bought the *Beaver County Times* Kristen Doerschner by then had risen to assistant managing editor, and staff there worked to deepen the western Pennsylvania newspaper's use of video and expand its award-winning designs.[104] The Press Club of Western Pennsylvania recognized those efforts in May 2017, one month before GateHouse bought the newspaper.[105] In 2016 the newspaper started a video series meant to drive conversations in the region's Black communities. "We were on an upswing, and we were proud of the work we were doing," Doerschner said. When GateHouse bought the newspaper in June 2017, Doerschner remembered two men from the company visiting the newsroom, which at that time still had a central location in the community where offline community engagement was the norm. Neighbors played fetch with their dogs out front. They brought in story ideas. For some octogenarians, their morning walk to pick up the paper represented both social interaction and connection.[106]

Then, GateHouse. "They said, 'Don't worry, this is going to be such a good thing. We'll bring in so many resources,'" Doerschner remembered. The first shift was to change the website and the content management system that powered it. Doerschner asked how the new platform would handle stand-alone video, noting the resources the staff had devoted to the site and its community engagement impacts. The platform didn't support video. "When you are about to lay off all the photographers and videographers, you don't need to support stand-alone video, it turns out," she said. Within three months Doerschner called the newspaper "unrecognizable." It turned out that GateHouse didn't see a need to stay in the Bridgewater borough either, moving the newspaper to an office park on the outskirts of the community. The *Beaver County Times* had a Sunday circulation of 45,000 when Doerschner started there in 2005. When we talked in October 2021, I read her figures from the Alliance for Audited Media's database that showed at that time that Sunday circulation had dropped to 12,458. Doerschner gasped. After a moment, she said, "You just can't blame craigslist and advertising. It's certainly a lot more. And a lot of people got really rich off of what happened here."

We got here through bad newspaper management and a predisposition to tilt decision-making toward consolidations and profit motivation rather than innovation and audience-centered needs. By the 2010s, corporate chains' digital strategies still floundered as news organizations indebted to private funds wrestled with whether public interest reporting mattered at all. Dean Starkman criticized a group of journalism thinkers who for years pushed solutions he said failed to address journalism's core mission: "Public-interest reporting isn't just another tab on the home page. It is a core value, the thing that builds trust, sets agendas, clarifies public understanding, challenges powerful institutions, and generates reform. It is, in the end, the point."[107] Starkman has covered the financial press, weakened by and complicit in covering the warning signs of the Great Recession of 2008, and he has lamented the loss of investigative reporting in the years since. As accountability reporting dried up, news organizations acted as de facto supporters for these funds. Jeffrey C. Hooke in *The Myth of Private Equity* wrote that both mainstream news and trade publications' reporting are part of the problem of private fund power, with reporters elevating the status of fund managers and putting a "positive spin" on coverage: "Even experienced journalists fall victim to the buyout funds' public relations efforts."[108]

I don't wish to minimize the impact of the internet transition or the loss of revenue as factors upending the industry. But newspaper companies beholden to private investment funds and the financial industry itself should get more of the blame over what has transpired in these years. By December 2004 industry analysts had pushed consolidation as a strategy as retail ad revenue dropped. Nearly five years later, David Simon, the Baltimore newspaperman turned television writer, testified before a US Senate Commerce Committee hearing on the future of journalism: "In short, my industry butchered itself and we did so at the behest of Wall Street and the same unfettered, free-market logic that has proved so disastrous for so many American industries. And the original sin of American newspapering lies, indeed, in going to Wall Street in the first place."[109]

Wall Street–focused M&A was a failed strategy for growth and the digital transition, yet the internet gets blamed for the industry's greed, and that means that many of our solutions to address the local news crisis are likely off course, too. James Fallows in a September 2019 *Atlantic* article recognized this: "But what 'everyone knows' about the main source of the problem may be wrong—or misleading enough to divert attention away from a possible solution."[110] What gets mythologized as a solution fails to recognize the financial conditions created by private investment funds, whose power grows every year. Newspaper companies still turn to M&A as media researchers have called for skepticism of the deals that put newspaper companies in debt as the advertising industry crashed.[111] Lauren Fine is a former Merrill Lynch newspaper and media analyst who, *Editor & Publisher* noted, "has the ability to move markets."[112] Merrill provided the financing for the 2007 budget-busting leveraged sale of Tribune to Zell.[113] By 2008, amid the recession, Fine was researching the industry for *CBS News*, writing in one piece: "Newspapers are still profitable!"[114] In a separate column, Fine wrote: "Watch the media companies that financed recent acquisitions with debt, in particular newspaper companies."[115] That debt, as chapter 5 explains, drives its own private investment fund frenzy.

Chapter 5

The Debt

Frank R. Kauders wrote to Kevin J. Carey, then chief judge of the US Bankruptcy Court in Delaware, on December 12, 2008. While institutional investors control the vast majority of market trading volume, Kauders is part of the minority known as retail investors, nonprofessionals who buy and sell on equity or bond markets.[1] Four days after Tribune filed Chapter 11 bankruptcy, Kauders wrote that he and his wife were "distraught and devastated, being the unfortunate owners of 50,000 matured Tribune Company bonds, the ones they reneged on redeeming on December 8."[2] Kauders's letter became two pages in a trove of Tribune bankruptcy case exhibits, which ultimately stretched out into a battle over its assets and its debt. In October 2021 Kauders told me by telephone that despite signs that Tribune was in trouble and might have problems meeting future debts as they came due, there was no outward indication to him of trouble with the bonds. Additionally, he explained, Sam Zell offered reassuring public statements. Kauders remembered that the company was not illiquid at the time of the bankruptcy, that the bonds he and his wife owned had held their market value, and that they were listed at 97.5 cents on the dollar on the day they were due, which was also the day Tribune declared bankruptcy.[3] Kauders wrote to Carey, "All we know is that in our minds there is no doubt that we are the ones who deserve your protection from these corporate hooligans, and not vice versa."

What Kauders did not know is that in the months before the media company's sale to private equity billionaire Zell, inside the offices at Citigroup and

Merrill Lynch, some were concerned about the leveraged buyout agreement that saddled Tribune with so much debt that it had nowhere to go but down. Standard & Poor's also said months before the sale was finalized that if it was allowed to proceed, Tribune would be bankrupt within two years. In an August 2013 lawsuit filed against Citigroup and Merrill, a group of unsecured creditors called Tribune Litigation Trust articulated these boardroom fears:

> This lawsuit arises out of the destruction of Tribune Company by greed, fraud, and financial chicanery. The facts of this case show how two Wall Street financial advisors, defendants Citigroup Global Markets Inc. ("Citigroup") and Merrill, Lynch, Pierce, Fenner & Smith Incorporated ("Merrill"), lured by the prospect of huge fees, were willing to set aside their serious reservations and assist a reckless leveraged buyout that funneled more than $8 billion to Tribune's shareholders while saddling the Company with massive debt—debt that quickly led to the bankruptcy of one of America's most venerable media companies.[4]

Tribune's bankruptcy case stretched out for years.

This chapter highlights another feature of the private investment era: the debt. Across the newspaper industry, as the internet threat loomed and hit, head-scratching acquisitions brought debt. Mergers brought even more, despite reporters and editors I spoke with from large newsrooms in Detroit, San Francisco, and St. Louis to smaller ones in Beaver County, Pennsylvania, Boulder, Colorado, and Greensboro, North Carolina, pushing for a deeper engagement with digital as the strategy to engage readers online and build revenues there. Their pleas went ignored, seen as too expensive to enact, as institutional investors wanted more. In some cases, like at MediaNews Group, the investment funds entered after debt accumulation, but at other chains, private investment funds were acutely involved in the runup of the debt. By 2011 the *Wall Street Journal* called the market for newspaper debt "roaring."[5]

The debt in the US newspaper industry fascinated me because of the way private investment funds were involved in both the accumulation of it and the profiting off of it.[6] The Great Recession and advertising revenue losses hit newspapers hard. There is little to debate there. But before and after the recession, investment firms and the private equity divisions of Wall Street banks created conditions that left newspaper chains hamstrung and in debt for billions of dollars after a wave of acquisitions and consolidations. Different private firms then profited off newspaper bankruptcies or debt financing in a process authors Robert Kuttner and Hildy Zenger called "nothing if not bad faith."[7] Tribune's private equity involvement and its debt form a notable case study in Wall Street financial engineering that brought down a company and helped fuel a boom in distressed debt investing. At McClatchy, Chatham Asset Management converted $275 million in unsecured debt into secured debt, giving it an unfair advantage in bankruptcy restructuring, according to a claim filed on Valentine's Day 2020 in US Bankruptcy Court for the Southern District of New York. That claim was eventually thrown out.[8]

It would oversimplify the newspaper crisis to say that it was brought about and worsened just by the debt in a similar way that it oversimplifies the crisis to say it only was brought about by the loss of advertising revenue to free internet sites. In essence, the two issues combined to create corporate newspapers' perfect storm. In 2018 Craigslist founder Craig Newmark gave $20 million through Craig Newmark Philanthropies to the City University of New York Graduate School of Journalism to make up for his company's role in exacerbating the newspaper crisis.[9] Through an in-depth examination of several chains, this chapter explains why Wall Street financial firms and private investment funds might want to ante up, seeing that their actions were the first part of the one-two punch that knocked newspapers down. As some investment funds profited off the debt or the cuts made after mergers and acquisitions (M&A), they set a vector for some of the country's most notable newspaper chains to end up in hedge fund portfolios. I start with a discussion of debt in the US economy before moving to a discussion of debt in the newspaper sector specifically and then focusing on its impacts at Tribune, Journal Register, MediaNews Group, and GateHouse.

"Ready to Draw Its First Blood"

Looking at the US economy broadly, historian and former Republican strategist Kevin Phillips explained in his book *Bad Money* that the last few decades have been marked not by manufacturing but by debt accumulation. Entire industries were built around the debt, another part of the financialization of the American economy: "These are not circumstances in which a nation should put faith in an overgrown and overextended financial services sector, with its bankrupt mortgage lenders, hotshot hedge funds, and reckless megabanks, several of which (fined years back for colluding with a scheming Enron) wouldn't know a civic obligation from a parking ticket." Despite this incredible growth of debt in private sector economies, Phillips wrote that neither economists nor historians have given the subject its due. In writing about the loss of manufacturing, Phillips also explained that leveraged buyouts and debt accelerated the losses in 2008: "If more attention had been paid to private debt back during the S&L playpen years and in the early 1990s, the critical mass reached in 2007 might have been kept smaller and possibly manageable."[10] Phillips wasn't talk-ing about newspaper debt specifically, but its parallels to the risks of its usage in the overall US economy reveal several of the same issues. More articles on the subject have emerged in recent years, but the reliance on debt as a profit tool, especially in a period of relatively low interest rates, has only accelerated since the 2008 recession.[11]

Both M&A and debt have gotten more scrutiny this last decade, including from a powerful US Senate committee that has addressed the subject numer-ous times. By May 2016 the US Senate's Committee on Finance had convened, once again, to discuss corporate issues related to debt and tax reform. The committee's seventy-nine-page transcript from that hearing noted that most US businesses pay a tax rate of 37 percent on equity financing, which entails a sale of a company's shares.[12] Yet the tax rate on debt financing, which uses bonds, is negative. Former US senator Orrin Hatch, a Utah Republican who died in April 2022, explained during the hearing: "That is right: negative. The tax code actually gives a subsidy to corporations for debt financing and that, in turn, may lead to financial distress especially in times of economic downswings. Experts and policymakers across the ideological spectrum have acknowledged that this is a problem." John McDonald, a partner in the Chicago firm Baker and McKenzie who testified that day, shared that debt-financed profits do not face tax penalties. Harvard Law School professor Alvin Warren Jr. also addressed the Senate committee, noting that differences in how corporate debt and equity are treated in the tax code also mean differences in how corporate executives pay dividends, which are discretionary, and whether corporations decide to reinvest in their businesses. Jody Lurie, a vice president and corporate bond research analyst in Philadelphia, told the committee: "Rather than invest in new projects that may take years before realizing a return, companies are looking at share buybacks, dividends, M&As, and tax minimization to bolster share-holder returns."[13] The differences also mean that companies can use Chapter 11 to renegotiate debt, which US bankruptcy courts describe as a "reorganiza-tion" bankruptcy.[14] With court approval, the company may borrow new money, even paying its executives lucrative fees in the restructuring process. Tax law also reveals discrepancies in how companies may use debt compared to equity, another factor that contributes to M&A and leads to "distortions" in policy, Hatch said at the hearing.[15] Debt investments do not face the same regulatory burdens as equity transactions, and their use in the last two decades has also taken off.[16]

Distressed debt investing came into its own right in the decade between 2001 and 2011, with investors seeing new opportunities.[17] By 2014 Edward Altman, who created an index to examine debt and bonds, explained that more than two hundred financial institutions had as much as $450 billion invested in the US distressed debt market. Three types of control can emerge from distressed debt investing, including what Altman calls "Active-Control," which means the debtors can take a significant portion of the restructured company and even name executive leadership, including a chief executive.[18] In a chapter on distressed debt investing in the edited collection *Private Equity: Opportunities and Risks,* Stephen G. Moyer and John D. Martin described other techniques private investors use to pick up distressed companies. In one type of distressed debt investing—loan-to-own—the asset manager may buy the debt, then restructure it with a different loan, possibly returning the company in some way back to its shareholders. The private equity firm receives a 15 percent or higher "return for very little work."[19] There's power for the firm if the business doesn't turn around, too, when the firm can force a reorganization or take the business over completely. Dividend recapitalization is one type of exit along with others that may include an initial public offering, which sells shares on public stock markets.[20] Irina Fox, in a 2020 article for the *Delaware Journal of Corporate Law,* explained that dividend recapitalization happens "when a company changes its capital structure by using debt to pay a special dividend to its stockholders." Fox continued: "A large amount of the retailers that filed for bankruptcy within the past few years carried debt loads remaining from leveraged buyouts by private equity firms."[21]

Michelle M. Harner, a former University of Maryland law professor who is now a US Court of Appeals bankruptcy judge, has focused research on debt and private equity in the newspaper market. She explained that Chapter 11 filings allowed shareholders' interest to be "extinguished" and played a role in debt holders' "loan-to-own scenario." In a 2011 *Washington University Law Review* article, Harner asked if activist distressed debt holders were the "new barbarians at the gate," explaining that prior to the 1980s, buyouts were done using equity. That shifted to the use of debt as a profit-motivated strategy, and Harner explained that debt purchases lack transparency and fly under the proverbial radar of other SEC policies dealing with equity takeovers. In studying the newspaper industry, she showed "the potential of the gamesmanship and abuse in debt-based takeovers." Harner applied this examination of debt-based buyouts to several media companies, including Avista's takeover of the *Star Tribune* and Tribune's disastrous leveraged sale to Zell in 2007. Avista took the Minnesota newspaper into Chapter 11 bankruptcy in 2009, two years after buying it from McClatchy. Avista's leveraged sale of the company meant that other private investment firms ultimately bought the debt, then swapped it for ownership.[22]

By 2008, with private equity investment locked in at major newspaper chains, the debt started to take its toll on day-to-day operations alongside the financial crash and online revenue losses. Dan Beighley reported in the *Orange County Business Journal* that companies backed by private equity investment and in debt would face fallout. Even then, Beighley reported that returns on investment for those newspapers still reached 15 to 20 percent, dropping from 30 percent.[23] By then, M&A and debt had plundered the newspaper industry, but it still boosted private equity's bottom line, often through the use of tax loopholes. Kuttner, a Brandeis University professor, and Zenger explained:

> The second loophole exploited by private equity is the unlimited tax deductibility of borrowed money. That allows private equity managers to borrow massively against the companies that they buy and sell, and use some of the debt to pay themselves. This seems like a conflict of interest, but as owners, the managers are free to do whatever they like. Many critics have argued that unlimited tax deductibility for borrowed money is bad policy—it promotes over-leveraging and hidden liabilities of the sort that crashed the economy in 2008—and the abuse of debt by private equity managers is an extreme case. An aggressive SEC could crack down on these practices, especially when private equity managers prosper at the expense of their own investors or limited partners.[24]

Mergers and acquisitions across the newspaper sector, often backed by private investment funds, also led newspaper industry publications to question what was really going on behind the stock tickers. An *Editor & Publisher* article from June 2008 explained that industrywide, newspaper dividends grew at a compound annual rate of 8 percent as the ratio of payouts spiked, sometimes as the stock price fell: "Of all the reasons newspaper companies are suffering through industry recession, debt may be the most powerful force upending the business, from the newsroom to the loading dock and everywhere in between. And now debt looks ready to draw its first blood."[25] Alongside the debt, companies still had no real digital plan, though people will make quips about being told to "stack digital dimes" as print dollars evaporated.[26] Inside newsrooms, as chapter 4 explained, few plans took hold, often because of the cost.

The advertising revenue crash of the mid-2000s changed—but in many ways strengthened—larger private equity firms' and hedge funds' positions in the marketplace. In 2009 print advertising revenue reached an astounding $24.4 billion. But institutional investors spiraled, looking at the numbers and downward trends. As they looked for sell-offs, others looked to scoop up the debt. Harner explained that certain private equity firms and hedge funds target distressed sectors specifically: "Some investors choose to concentrate their efforts in certain industries. Angelo, Gordon & Co. (Angelo Gordon), Alden Global Capital, Avenue Capital, and Oaktree Capital Management (Oaktree), among others, selected the newspaper industry."[27] Yet distressed doesn't necessarily mean broke. Firms enter sectors when they are shown that profit still exists or when the debt can be transformed into ownership.[28] An industry in crisis may offer just the bargains—and the assets plus the debt remaining—that some hedge funds and private equity firms seek. The Chapter 11 reorganization plan at Freedom allowed Angelo, Gordon, Alden, and Luxor, along with JPMorgan Chase, to exchange nearly $450 million in debt for new common stock, which essentially put those firms in control of Freedom's assets.[29] *Editor & Publisher* reported that JPMorgan Chase, described as being among the fallout's "accidental publishers," ended up with a chunk of newspaper company assets cast off by the bankruptcies.[30]

The Great Recession is notable for its impact on many industries, not just newspapers.[31] But understanding the conditions that existed in the market leading up to 2008 and the wave of bankruptcies that followed gives a more complete picture of the way newspaper companies responded to a confluence of crises, often crises created through the influence of private investment funds. Corporate newspaper management, including that influenced by fund managers, deserves more scrutiny for its role in our newspaper crisis, specifically decision-making that led to debt, while other investment funds have profited from it.

Newspaper company annual reports called 10-Ks filed with the US Securities and Exchange Commission complement bankruptcy filings and allow a mapping of the funds' problematic influence over entire chains. The housing market crashed as digital became more important, and many legacy newspaper companies were without an effective strategy to transform to the internet, to engage communities online, to turn into a news platform, or to handle the classified revenue losses that arrived. They were beholden instead to institutional investors and then debt. It's hard to steer yourself through the chop when you aren't at the helm and even harder under the leadership of people like Zell. In her book *The Vulture Investors*, Hilary Rosenberg described Zell as both a vulture and a financial "grave dancer" who was quoted once saying, "I like what I do, and society rewards it very highly."[32] By the time Zell bought Tribune, he'd had years of practice in the distressed market.

"Truly Amazing Financing Engineering"

In 2021 hedge fund Alden Global Capital took over Tribune. Fourteen years before Alden's ownership, private equity divisions of some of the world's largest banks provided financing for the budget-busting Tribune sale to Zell.

Bankruptcy court filings and exhibits that include executives' depositions and confidential company records, including emails, tell a more complete picture and history about what happened at both Tribune and the banks, which both advised on the $8 billion leveraged deal and financed some of the debt. Andrew Ross Sorkin, writing for the *New York Times*, called this advising-financing relationship "Wall Street's version of vendor financing—or, potentially, conflict-ridden double dipping." Sorkin reported that the relationship between the Chicago billionaire and the banks may have factored into Tribune's board favoring Zell's takeover bid over others, including one from another billionaire, Los Angeles–based philanthropist Eli Broad.[33]

The leveraged deal was never about journalism and always about money, revealed through the court battles that went on for years even after Tribune officially emerged from bankruptcy in 2012. A 120-page complaint dated November 1, 2010, filed on behalf of Tribune's unsecured creditors against Zell and other Tribune dealmakers, including Citigroup Global Markets, Merrill Lynch, and Morgan Stanley Capital Services, lashes out at the dealings that led to Zell's takeover, noting the sale was "tainted from start to finish." It refers to the leveraged buyout (LBO): "The LBO was designed to cash out the large shareholders of Tribune, and to line the pockets of defendant Sam Zell and Tribune's directors and officers. Faced with a severe decline in Tribune's stock price, starting in 2005, and continuing through the relevant time period, certain large shareholders of Tribune that collectively owned 33% of its shares began exerting extreme pressure on the Company to take prompt action to maximize the value of their investment."[34] A bankruptcy exhibit marked "highly confidential attorneys' eyes only" includes former senior vice president Todd Kaplan of Merrill Lynch's Global Leveraged Finance Unit saying in February 2007 that the struggle to convince the newspaper company leadership to take on the billion-dollar debt "is like wrestling an octopus." Michael R. Costa, managing director of Merrill Lynch's Mergers & Acquisitions Unit, emailed back: "Which one of those 8 arms represents our CEO now saying its [*sic*] too much debt. Not kidding." Two months later, Chris Cormier emailed Costa and Kaplan to say: "Guys—truly amazing financing engineering." Cormier wrote that a "decent amount of investment grade debt" from the deal could actually be transformed into equity. That "amazing financing engineering" left others, among them Citigroup's Julie Persily, concerned, according to emails included as part of the record. Persily emailed a colleague: "I am still extremely uncomfortable with Zell." In another, she said: "I am beside myself. Just sick over this. Don't know what to do." She had emailed that on March 28, 2007, in response to Michael Canmann, who wrote, "Chandler called me and said that Merrill was very positive on the ratings news. Morgan was more guarded. Said Zell was positive as well." Once in the courts, the deal's structure and the banks' fees to create it became fundamental issues.

Carey, the former chief judge, wrote a 128-page document dated October 21, 2011, called an "Opinion on Confirmation for the U.S. Bankruptcy Court for the District of Delaware." The document reviewed the core details up to that point in the nearly three-year-old case, and Carey started it with the parable of the scorpion and the fox crossing a river. Carey, apparently frustrated by copious actions in the case, wrote: "There is no moral to this story. Its meaning lies in the exposition of an inescapable facet of human character: the willingness to visit harm upon others, even at one's own peril."[35] In June 2006 Tribune had borrowed $1.5 billion as a way both to refinance earlier debt and to repurchase Tribune shares. This money, called the 2006 Credit Agreement, with a $1.5 billion Bridge Agreement later that year, is debt taken on before the leveraged buyout. It also is what led Tribune's board of directors to consider a number of options on the media company's future. The board settled on Zell, and in doing so it "approved a series of transactions with a newly formed Tribune Employee Stock Ownership Plan," referred to as the ESOP.

Zell's leveraged buyout was financed in two parts, also referred to as steps. At step 1, the ESOP bought 8.9 million shares at twenty-eight dollars a share. Putting the money into an ESOP also was a feature of financial engineering that allowed Tribune to avoid paying federal income taxes.[36] Carey's document charted Tribune's step 1 payments to shareholders, which it noted reached more than $4.2 billion. Also, under step 1 payments Carey listed the following: Merrill Entities were slated for $34.9 million, and slightly less than that was set aside for Citigroup Entities. ("Entities" refers to the companies involved in the deal.) Bank of America was set to make $18 million from the step 1 financing, which for Wall Street firms and banks together totaled $134 million. Step 2 was the final consummation of the deal, when Tribune was bought out by the ESOP for $8 billion. The leveraged buyout ultimately more than doubled Tribune's debt to $13 billion, piling on what already was left over from its 2000 acquisition of Times Mirror Company.[37] Within weeks of the Zell purchase, Tribune's publishing sector laid off 5 percent of its workforce to begin coping with the debt.[38]

In May 2010 the US Bankruptcy Court for the District of Delaware tapped Kenneth N. Klee to investigate the case, including the ratings, debt steps, and revenue projections used for the 2007 leveraged sale. Klee, an emeritus professor of law at UCLA, is credited with drafting the US Bankruptcy Code.[39] In the course of this three-month investigation, which cost more than $12 million, Klee generated more than twenty-one thousand pages of exhibits.[40] While

Klee's findings were not binding, they were influential. His report stretched to more than fifteen hundred pages in multiple volumes, and it targets both Tribune and the banks involved. Klee stated: "In other words—and this is critical for purposes of analyzing the intentional fraudulent transfer issues at Step Two—by design, a direct causal nexus existed between, on the one hand, the obligations incurred and transfers made at Step Two and, on the other hand, the procurement and issuance of the solvency opinion and solvency certificates and the making of solvency representations." Klee's investigation found that it was "reasonably likely" at step 1 and "somewhat likely" at step 2 that Tribune executives were part of an intentional fraudulent transaction.[41] Klee's findings note that at the end of the two-step transaction to finance Zell's deal, Tribune was "rendered insolvent."[42] In his investigation of the case, Klee determined that bond markets, ready to profit off the debt, responded favorably.

No one faced penalties for the transactions and insolvency as Wall Street banks and other private equity firms fought out who would get what for years in the courts. News reports noted: "Holders of roughly $2.3 billion of senior secured debt have protested Tribune's proposed plan because it lets Zell and the banks that underwrote the debt (and wound up holding onto a large portion of the debt) off the hook too easy for engineering Tribune's massive debt load."[43] Private investment firms faced off over what was left.

As the years stretched on, Tribune's bankruptcy files in part read like a *Goliath v. Goliath* Wall Street battle, with Bank of America, Citicorp, JPMorgan, Merrill Lynch, and Oaktree Capital on one side and Aurelius Capital Management and Alden Global Capital separately on the other.[44] Numerous plans shuttled between them until the court eventually was forced to appoint a mediator.[45] Aurelius, a hedge fund that specializes in distressed debt, bought $2 billion of Tribune's pre-LBO debt from the 2006 Credit Agreement and factored heavily in the case.[46] A *Wall Street Journal* article from March 2019 quoted a distressed debt researcher, who said this about Aurelius: "They just care about making money on events."[47] In court documents, Aurelius's attorneys defended its protracted battle with Oaktree and the banks: "Aurelius objected because it believes the LBO-Related Causes of Action are worth far more than the examiner or Bankruptcy Court thought and that it can get a great deal more money in litigation than it got under the Settlement."[48] In news reports Aurelius was called the "hedge fund keeping Tribune in bankruptcy."[49] The fight between Aurelius and Oaktree over Tribune's debt became a fight over who would emerge with control.

In 2013 Michael Oneal and Steve Mills wrote a series on the case for the *Chicago Tribune*. In one piece, Oneal wrote that the bankruptcy case showed the intricacies of leveraged buyouts and the fallout potential of deals like these. More notable is what the case revealed about federal bankruptcy and private firms that profit off the debt: "The Chicago-based media company's lengthy journey through Chapter 11 exposed a powerful but little-known industry thriving in the midst of the American bankruptcy court system. It's a business built on the bewildering complexity of the global markets, and it attracts some of the brightest minds in law and finance. They are members of a clubby group of specialist investors who buy up a troubled company's 'distressed debt' and other securities for pennies on the dollar." The years-long battle would leave Tribune unable to shift at a pivotal time for newspapers in an online world. It also left Oaktree and Angelo, Gordon and Co. in control of Tribune's assets. Oneal wrote of these private investment firms: "Many succeeded brilliantly, most notably Oaktree and Angelo Gordon, which emerged from the fray in control of a much healthier company with an array of iconic media assets, including the Chicago Tribune and the Los Angeles Times."[50] According to Harner's debt research, these firms also put Tribune into a protracted bankruptcy case that lingered for years, making the media company vulnerable to later hedge fund ownership. Tribune spent, according to court documents, upward of $400 million in fees related to the bankruptcy.[51] Imagine that money reinvested in journalism.

The financial executives' and funds' play for the venerable newspaper company show a Wall Street financial sector intent on maximizing revenue with little concern for either newspaper employees or Tribune's role as a leading institution of the US press. Offshoots of the case lingered for more than a decade as creditors, including former Times Mirror workers, sought restitution.[52] After Tribune filed for bankruptcy in 2008, it allegedly left retirees held over from the Times Mirror acquisition in the hole by tens of millions of dollars. The fight for those workers, referred to in legal documents as TM Retirees, has lasted for years in the courts. Attorneys for a group of 200 TM retirees wrote in January 2019: "The TM Retirees are people, not faceless Class 1F Creditors. Unlike Aurelius and other Senior Noteholders, the TM Retirees did not secretly acquire bankruptcy claims to speculate on the outcome of Tribune's Chapter 11 cases. The TM Retirees earned every dollar of their claims against Tribune."[53] Their wages and retirement compensation were devalued by two-thirds. Over the decade while trying to be made whole, nineteen of the retirees died.

Tribune fell into Alden's hedge fund portfolio in May 2021. In 2018 billionaire Patrick Soon-Shiong paid Tronc, a short-lived Tribune rebrand, $500 million for the Los Angeles Times and the San Diego Union-Tribune. That took those newspapers out of the publicly held Tribune portfolio, providing a major money infusion to the company, and making those two newspapers privately held.

Soon-Shiong held a 24 percent stake in Tribune, and a Manhattan Institute article on news deserts classifies his ownership of the *Los Angeles Times* this way: "But while Soon-Shiong has said that he wants to run the Times like a business, his stated devotion to print journalism makes clear that return on investment isn't his priority, given the high cost of publishing a daily print paper."[54] In May 2021 Soon-Shiong was criticized for abstaining from a shareholder vote that sold the remaining parts of Tribune Publishing to Alden for $633 million.[55] Keith J. Kelly, the now-retired *New York Post* media columnist, at the time called Soon-Shiong, a billionaire founder of a cancer drug, "despised" after his decision, which essentially put Alden in control of yet another newspaper chain.[56] More than eight out of ten Tribune shareholders voted for the sale despite well-documented concerns from industry watchers, free press advocates, journalists, and researchers. In the terms of the 2021 deal, Alden got control of both Tribune's $250 million cash on hand and its assets. A May 2021 SEC filing for the first quarter of that year showed Tribune in control of $534 million in total assets.[57]

Using the Debt

As of March 1, 2023, Alden Global Capital controls Digital First Media and Tribune, but its real power in the media industry started in July 2011, when it bought the Journal Register Company, which was deeply in debt. Journal Register's CEO John Paton wrote this on his blog at the time: "Alden has been an investor in our company for some time and they have had a courtside seat to the Journal Register Company's radical makeover following our Digital First strategy. They know what we do, they like what we do, and today they are putting their money behind our efforts."[58] Journal Register filed for bankruptcy twice, its first following what an industry publication called "an acquisition spree."[59] Consider that at the time of its 2009 bankruptcy filing, Journal Register maintained a 19.3 percent operating profit, which, as Alan D. Mutter explained, surpassed profit margins of other publicly traded companies, including Chevron, General Motors, and Wal-Mart.[60] The *Philadelphia Inquirer* reported at the time: "Under a proposal filed as part of the bankruptcy case, the company has asked for permission to pay as much as $1.7 million in bonuses to 30 top officers and key employees, should the Journal Register meet certain reorganization goals, including closing more papers and eliminating more employees."[61] When Journal Register, former publisher of the *New Haven Register*, filed Chapter 11 bankruptcy again in 2012, it was at the time "loaded" with debt and by then was owned outright by Alden. At the time of its second bankruptcy filing, Journal Register was

$692 million in debt. In reality, Alden had been both Journal Register's owner and its lender.[62] Both private equity firms and hedge funds have had different strategies in the newspaper marketplace, some that have accumulated debt and then used it as leverage.

While Alden's tactics have faced scrutiny, Fortress Investment Group, a private equity firm, was for years the largest newspaper owner in the United States. Through its GateHouse chain and later New Media, Fortress also has had the longest history during this era, operating as a manager, a shareholder, and a lender, and its market strategies have harmed newspapers nationwide. In its Form 10-K for the fiscal year that ended December 30, 2012, Fortress's Gate-House explained that it owned seventy-eight daily newspapers with a combined circulation of 597,000.[63] It also owned more than two hundred weekly publications and ninety-one "shoppers." It owned newspapers its financial documents classified as being in communities with more than thirty-five thousand people who lived more than fifty miles from major metropolitan areas, giving them a near monopoly on advertising revenue. This included the *Peoria Journal Star*, with a paid daily circulation of 58,319. These newspapers, GateHouse's annual report noted, faced less turmoil from the downswings in advertising revenue. The Form 10-K explained: "We believe that local advertising tends to be less sensitive to economic cycles than national advertising because local businesses generally have fewer effective advertising channels through which they may reach their customers."[64]

After a mind-boggling string of acquisitions, GateHouse's debt proved significant but didn't stop executive payouts as staff lost jobs. Despite the debt accumulating, GateHouse's 2007 annual report showed that its dividend payments to shareholders rose from $9.3 million in 2006 to $23.1 million that year, with Fortress in control of 42 percent of its stock.[65] Jody Lurie told the aforementioned US Senate Committee on Finance that dividend payments are part of the problem in tax code: "For the debt side, increasing dividends or share buybacks are both negative events. Cash is not going towards debt repayment or long-term growth initiatives." She added later in the same testimony: "Industry cyclicality is, perhaps, inevitable, but what is not is a tax policy that favors companies paying out most of their cash so that they do not have the cushion necessary to weather a down market."[66] As GateHouse was paying those dividends, which are cash payments awarded for each share owned, it also faced the debt. GateHouse revenues at the end of 2005 hit $384.9 million, climbing to $661.8 million two years later. But GateHouse's acquisitions meant that the interest on its debt doubled in that period, too. By December 31, 2007,

GateHouse was $1.2 billion in debt.[67] At the end of 2007 it was paying $96 million in loan interest, down to a still-staggering $60 million in 2010.[68]

As 2012 closed, Fortress owned 40 percent of GateHouse stock, and the newspaper company was $1.2 billion in debt with an interest expense that calendar year of $57.9 million. The debt got GateHouse a "below-investment grade" rating from Moody's Investors Service. Months later, GateHouse filed for Chapter 11 bankruptcy, and a new media company was formed again with Fortress as both the newspaper chain owner and the lender.[69] Its march to Chapter 11 allowed GateHouse to emerge from Chapter 11 with debt canceled and "a 40% cash distribution."[70] In September 2013 another Fortress holding company, called Newcastle Investment Corp., bought the Dow Jones Local Media Group from News Corp. for $87 million, and Fortress acquired the Dow chain through the bankruptcy terms.[71]

Across the industry, executives in 2007 and 2008 faced the fallout over the accumulation of debt spurred by a mergers-and-acquisition frenzy from the years prior. GateHouse's debt was extinguished in exchange for a new company helmed by the same leadership team. A GateHouse document filed with the US Securities and Exchange Commission after its 2013 bankruptcy noted: "The Reorganized New Media Group may enter into such transaction and may take such action as may be necessary or appropriate to effect a corporate restructuring, including one or more mergers, consolidations, restructurings, transporters, dispositions, spinoffs, liquidations."[72] After it filed Chapter 11 bankruptcy, its restructuring under the New Media moniker noted that its plan to eliminate debt also included plans to further acquire and consolidate, which is part of how it had accumulated its heavy debt load in the first place. At the time of its Chapter 11 filing, CEO Michael E. Reed was quoted as saying, "We have complied with and are current with all our obligations, but with the challenges facing our industry and the impending maturity of our secured debt next year, we needed to be proactive in exploring options to restructure our debt, recapitalize, and position ourselves for future growth. The prepackaged plan proposes a 'balance-sheet restructuring,' by which GateHouse will emerge from bankruptcy with much less debt on its balance sheet, but with its business operations completely intact."[73] Reed is now Gannett's CEO.

By 2019 Gannett and GateHouse had merged in a deal worth $1.3 billion, buoyed by private equity firm Apollo Global Management's financing.[74] While the Gannett name still is in play, the company is under the leadership of long-time GateHouse executive Reed, who will earn $900,000 a year, with a targeted annual bonus worth 110 percent of his base salary.[75] GateHouse and Gannett put 30 percent of America's daily newspapers under one company's masthead.[76] At the time of Gannett's filing of its 2020 Form 10-K annual report to the SEC, Fortress owned 4 percent of Gannett stock. As part of its sendoff, FIG LLC earned from Gannett a $30.4 million "cash payment."[77] Throughout 2020, FIG LLC extracted management fees and what Gannett's annual report that year called an "incentive fee."[78] It also means that the whopping 2019 merger and million-dollar payments have accumulated to put Gannett $1.545 billion in debt. In its year-end SEC filing for 2020, Gannett wrote, "Our substantial indebtedness could materially and adversely affect our business or financial condition."[79]

Today, many of its newspapers are zombies, relegated to industrial parks or strip malls on the edge of town and staffed by a few overworked reporters who have hung on, watching their colleagues get laid off year after year. Those are the lucky ones. Newspapers in Allentown, Annapolis, Boise, Hartford, and Miami under other private fund influence no longer have central newsrooms, perhaps the best metaphor we have for the connections hedge funds and private equity feel newspapers should have to the communities they supposedly cover.[80] Yet again, because of the debt and the utter disregard for newspapers' role in civic and political life, we're likely to see an asset sell-off as a stopgap before an inevitable bankruptcy that will see other private equity firms jockeying for the junk bonds left over as more journalists lose their jobs. Rosenberg wrote about hedge funds and bankruptcies three decades ago: "Hopefully, these accounts will serve as keyholes into the world of bankruptcy where technicalities of law and finance lock most people out."[81] It is both maddening and frustrating to see how these last twenty years have all played out, as the internet has been blamed for so many problems that are functions of corporate profit-making. What we're also likely to see continue are huge layoffs at those companies, another reality of the private investment era that is discussed in the next chapter. To form a more complete picture of these last two decades, I talked to more than three dozen reporters and editors about how layoffs and labor conditions influence everything from newsroom morale to their functions as government watchdogs. Chapter 6 tells their stories.

Chapter 6

Layoffs

The last layoff Kristen Doerschner made was her own. Like that of many journalists I interviewed, Doerschner's draw to the field started young. She asked for a typewriter when she was eight, and she wrote for her high school newspaper before studying communications at John Carroll University in Ohio. She sold newspapers from a kiosk and freelanced before landing her first full-time reporting gig in 1999. In June 2005 she went to the family-owned *Beaver County Times* in western Pennsylvania to cover a regional beat that included education, city government, and sewage authority meetings. She also covered courts and police, a beat that requires reporters to cover a community's criminal justice apparatus, networking and sourcing everyone from aides and secretaries to clerks and cops.[1] The staff felt supported, and it was doing crucial accountability work in the community of 170,000 people thirty miles northwest of Pittsburgh. Doerschner remembers pooling money with colleagues to buy lottery tickets. "Even if we had hit the lottery for fifty million dollars, I would still have come to work," she said.

Scholars can debate what local journalism means to a community, but Doerschner defined and represented the best of it. In December 2011 she reported on registered sex offenders working at local churches.[2] She covered arrests, hearings, and trials, a lot of it day-to-day grunt work that spiked her curiosity about the county's functions. In that time on the beat, Doerschner noticed that one public defender rarely appeared at the courthouse. His assigned parking space often was empty. He missed court hearings. She connected his absences to other problems, she remembered, determining that funds from a trust account called an IOLTA (Interest on Lawyers' Trust Accounts) had not been appropriately distributed.[3] Her pursuit of the story helped return funds to victims' families, and the newspaper in 2016 earned recognition from Pennsylvania's Keystone Media Awards for its freedom of information efforts.[4]

Doerschner eventually worked her way up to the post of managing editor. Fortress Investment Group's GateHouse purchased the paper in June 2017, and Fortress, as it had in prior years, took a 1.5 percent management fee based on the chain's total equity.[5] Within weeks, copy desk work had been outsourced to Texas and designers had been laid off. Eventually, the layoffs and buyouts reached the core reporting staff, forcing Doerschner to make decisions about which beats could get covered and leaving entire sections of the news building dark. Photographers and videographers were laid off later. Covering meetings represents a local newspaper's core responsibility, as community members seek out information from the county commission, the school board, and the other elected boards that set sewer fees and decide trash collection schedules. Newsroom layoffs meant reductions in coverage. Doerschner, a mother of two who describes herself as a "human Swiss Army knife of skills," said meeting coverage was cut and police and courts coverage was diminished. Work was transferred, piled on, or given up out of necessity. "My phone would ring at 6 a.m., at midnight, during Thanksgiving dinner, you name it," she remembered. "There were always problems and not enough people to handle them." Eventually, readers started calling in, angry about the coverage cuts and upset with the staff: "Nobody in our building had control over it. All I could say was 'I'm so sorry.'" She said her hair began falling out from the stress, and she cried every day on the drive home.[6]

After GateHouse bought the newspaper, layoffs made both the day-to-day and the long-term investigative work harder, but the cuts boosted Fortress's fees, which are based on profits. With every cut, the newsroom reacted, knowing what their job losses meant for GateHouse corporate and Fortress. "It makes me so angry that these people have so much money," Doerschner said. "Take somebody making thirty-eight thousand dollars and lay them off so some rich person can get a few more dollars. They gutted us to make somebody else richer. And we knew it. We would say, 'I guess the shareholders are getting another payday.'" Fortress managers earned from the newspaper chain $10.7 million, $10.6 million, and $9.8 million in management fees for the years 2018, 2017, and 2016 respectively. Fortress executives took an additional incentive fee in those years worth more than $28 million.[7] Between 2014 and 2018, Fortress's New

Media also paid $298 million in dividends.[8] Yet the cuts to the reporting corps continued.

When in October 2018 GateHouse executives wanted one more cut, Doerschner said it was time for her to go. "We were waiting to adjust to whatever this new situation was," Doerschner remembered. "It was one indignity after the next. We never hit bottom. It was why I ultimately left. I couldn't keep falling anymore. I couldn't do it anymore, and I said, 'Lay me off.'" She quit without another job lined up.[9]

"An Existential Threat"

This chapter features the fourth component of the private investment era: layoffs. In this chapter I not only document how it feels to work in newsrooms with private investment fund owners such as Alden, Chatham, and Fortress but also share stories generated from interviews with more than three dozen reporters and editors about how accountability journalism has changed over this twenty-year period. Whenever we look back at the history of journalism, there is the threat of nostalgia. Yet in my own experience and in talking to the journalists for this chapter, I can say that our nostalgia is not for some inflated sense of what the good old days meant but rather for a time when reporters were hired and empowered in local newsrooms to do critical accountability work by attending meetings, building sources, and covering issues from education to zoning.

I specifically targeted journalists from the chains under review, and the sample includes reporters and editors—some still working, others retired or transitioned to other fields—from Gannett, GateHouse, Digital First Media, Lee Enterprises, McClatchy, MediaNews Group, and Tribune. All but one interview was by telephone between September 2020 and December 2021. My hour-long interview with Jon Schleuss, president of the NewsGuild–Communication Workers of America, was done by Zoom. It was my thirty-eighth interview for this chapter and the final interview of 124 done overall. The interviews for this section generated more than thirty-five hours of material, and I contacted and found subjects in a variety of ways. I saw some on Twitter, and I sent direct messages. I read others' work online, and I sent direct messages or emails. I found four through my October 2021 post to the Facebook page called "What's Your Plan B?," a site dedicated to journalists in transition. These conversations are a complement to countless others I've had informally over the years with friends, former colleagues, and students who went on to work in newsrooms nationwide that were impacted by these profit-motivated funds. Through the formal interviews, I sought to understand what private equity and hedge fund influence meant for those who staffed the shrinking newsrooms, who took on extra beats, and who handled complaints from citizens who watched as their newspapers faded.

The interviews are complemented by a review of US Securities and Exchange Commission filings, trade reports, union documents, and US Department of Labor records obtained through the Freedom of Information Act. These documents together reveal how private investment funds pose new labor challenges as layoffs continue to threaten the role of newspapers in communities. As hedge funds circle, this period's labor issues are also marked by reporters publicly unionizing and unsuccessfully trying to find new owners, among them the Save Our Courant campaign in Connecticut.[10] Once hedge funds take over, a new cry for help emerges from reporters remaining in the newsrooms, that is, if the newsrooms have not yet been sold off. Journalists from the *Loveland Reporter-Herald* in Colorado circulated a petition in November 2021 calling for the Alden-owned MediaNews Group to stop cutting jobs, explaining that "further cuts would pose an existential threat."[11]

Executives at all corporate newspaper companies widely influenced by private investment funds reach for layoffs as a favorite playbook, sometimes to boost profits or sometimes to make balance sheets look better before an eventual sale. GateHouse, which before it merged with Gannett in 2019 was run by private equity fund Fortress Investment Group, cut jobs as it acquired newspapers nationwide to become the country's largest chain. In 2011 GateHouse laid off seven staffers from its *Norwich Bulletin* newsroom in Connecticut one year after CEO Michael Reed took home a $750,000 bonus.[12] In 2019, a few months before its merger with Gannett and after a period during which it snapped up $30 million in acquisitions, GateHouse cut more than two hundred jobs.[13] After the merger, the new megachain cut another 215 employees.[14] McClatchy, facing the debt from its $4.5 billion purchase of Knight Ridder, in 2008 laid off 10 percent of its staff, meaning fourteen hundred lost jobs.[15] At Tribune in 2009, the year after it filed for bankruptcy, reporters were "outraged that even as the company fell into bankruptcy, top managers awarded themselves $57.3 million in court-approved bonuses while 4,200 people lost their jobs."[16] In May 2015 Tribune's *San Diego Union-Tribune* laid off 178 of its 603 staffers not long after acquiring the newspaper from MLIM LLC.[17] In 2018, after taking over the *Boston Herald*, Digital First "immediately" laid off 27 percent of the staff.[18]

In 2018 Digital First Media's parent, Alden, also owned the *Denver Post*, long considered one of the country's great regional newspapers. It had earned accolades over the years for its work, earning the Public Service Pulitzer Prize in 1986 for its coverage of missing children and trumped-up federal statistics.[19] The decades between that Pulitzer win and its Alden ownership have not been kind to the Denver daily or other Alden papers. Between 2012 and 2017 Digital First Media cut more than half its newspapers' staff, slashing positions at the *Post*.[20] In March 2018 Alden cut thirty newsroom positions in Denver, roughly 30 percent of its remaining staff. The cuts put the newspaper's staffing at 25 percent of what it had been at its peak.[21] In April 2018 the *Denver Post*'s editorial staff put those cuts into sharp focus, printing a color photograph on the front page that compared its full-time staff in 2018 to its staff five years prior. Under the headline "As Vultures Circle, the Denver Post Must Be Saved," the photograph blackened the cutouts of those journalists who had lost their jobs.[22] It was a jarring depiction of what staffing losses look like at an award-winning news organization, and the fact that editors would use the pages of the newspaper to call out their hedge fund owners also made news.[23]

Cuts at smaller newspapers get less attention, and chain layoffs are often grouped together in financial publications' reporting as mere statistics in the corporate newspaper game. Meanwhile, private investment funds are never far behind. Private Capital Management, which pushed for mergers at other chains where it owned shares, had quadrupled its investment in Gannett between 2003 and 2006.[24] Gannett is not the only newspaper company influenced by private equity and hedge funds, but over the last two decades it regularly has chosen layoffs as a way to boost the bottom line, earning it the ignoble nickname the "Rembrandt of cost cutters."[25] In 2016 380 people lost their jobs.[26] Newsroom cuts over the years happened as Gannett executives like Craig Dubow, who took over as its president and CEO in July 2005, earned big money. In 2007 Dubow took home $7.5 million in total compensation, dropping to $3.1 million the following year.[27] In 2009, despite telling shareholders in Gannett's annual report that employees needed to be furloughed, Dubow's take-home salary, pension, and stock compensation hit $4.69 million, his second highest annual payout in a three-year period that saw layoffs so deep, reporters and media insiders called it a "bloodbath."[28] Not once, and not twice, but at least four times the bloodbath moniker has been used to describe Gannett layoffs. Gannett reporters endured the bloodbath in 2008, 2014, 2017, and 2019, which is the year it merged with GateHouse.[29]

Since that merger, core newsroom cuts have continued as executives have received huge windfalls. Michael Reed, Gannett's chief executive, who once ran GateHouse for Fortress Investment Group, received compensation including stock awards worth more than $7.7 million, according to the company's April 27, 2022, notice to shareholders.[30] Former Gannett CEO Paul J. Bascobert had total compensation in 2020 worth $4.1 million, according to Gannett's Form 14A proxy statement filed in April 2021. But in a two-month period following its merger with GateHouse, Gannett laid off hundreds.[31] By March 2023 Gannett had cut half its workforce in less than four years.[32]

Between 2008 and 2020 the Pew Research Center documented a 26 percent drop in newsroom employment.[33] In 2018 newsroom jobs plummeted by 25 percent, and the majority of those positions were at newspapers.[34] That followed a pattern of cuts and newspaper consolidations, with 2014 representing the largest loss since 2009, according to Pew's 2016 "State of the News Media" report.[35] Newsroom cuts have been so bad as to warrant studies addressing newsroom labor under the classification called "layoff survivors," those who kept their jobs feeling guilt, not to mention the burden of working the jobs of multiple people.[36] Those who remained often experienced what Scott Reinardy called "a decline in trust, satisfaction and commitment" and exhibited feelings that their newspapers were "creating production-line journalism that is seen as void of purpose and function."[37] Carla Murphy sought to understand more about why journalists of color leave journalism, including newspapers and television. She called her work "The 'Leavers' Survey," an engagement with 101 former journalists that revealed that nearly two-thirds of them left due to workplace stress, while 60 percent noted low pay as another top factor.[38] Dominant themes from Murphy's work, conducted in early 2020, also showed "unethical management" that "doesn't practice journalism in the public service."

Alex Putterman worked at Tribune's *Hartford Courant* for years before Hearst poached him in April 2022. When we first talked in December 2020, Putterman was a twenty-seven-year-old Northwestern University graduate and Connecticut native unsure about returning to his home state. Years before, the newspaper had gutted its coverage of professional sports teams, including the New York Yankees and the New England Patriots, and Putterman wanted to cover sports. But he accepted a full-time reporting position in 2018. Less than two years later, Putterman went from sports reporter to pandemic reporter, covering COVID-19 out of necessity. To hear him list the newsroom departures in the few years he worked there is like listening to a Beatles fan list the band's number 1 hits. The list goes on and on. There was the environmental reporter, then the dedicated health reporter. A dozen cuts through buyouts came in late 2018. Then in 2019 it seemed like things were turning around. "Then Alden," he said. "When I heard 'Alden Global Capital was the largest shareholder' it meant nothing to me. But immediately there was this sense of fear, and all you had to do was Google them. I went from never having heard of Alden to fearing Alden."[39] Putterman and those who remained in February 2019 formed the

Courant Guild, part of the larger NewsGuild–Communication Workers of America union. His work covering the pandemic was then complemented by his work with the Save Our Courant campaign, which was actively trying to find a new owner to insulate the paper against what seemed inevitable: Alden's complete takeover of Tribune. Eighteen reporters left the *Courant* in 2020, a loss so large that Hartford City Council members introduced a resolution in support of the union's efforts to find new owners. A new owner never materialized, and the *Courant* went into Alden's portfolio, just as the *Denver Post*, the *Daily Camera*, and the *East Bay Times* had done before it.

The working conditions created by private investment funds delivered an industry untenable for many journalists. Many have stayed, feeling like they are the last democratic line of defense for communities nationwide. George Kelly, a fifty-year-old journalist with twenty-five years of experience, works as a breaking news reporter at the *East Bay Times* in Oakland, California. Kelly has had colleagues forced to take second and third jobs to stay working at the newspaper, which is also part of Alden's portfolio. One rented a backyard shed to live in as a way to get around the Bay Area's high housing costs. As reporters leave, their positions remain unfilled. "Working here means knowing that there are issues that aren't getting covered," Kelly told me. One issue the newspaper staff managed was its extensive coverage of the December 2016 Ghost Ship fire, which ripped through an Oakland warehouse, killing thirty-six.[40] Newspaper staff writers covered the initial tragedy, and reporters followed with stories about local government failure—lax enforcement, missed inspections, and overlooked code violations. Kelly remembers feeling the need to document the fire's aftermath, but he also explained the need to hold officials accountable for what went wrong.[41]

Covering the deadly fire at the warehouse, which had been used as artists' studios, a music venue, and living quarters, culminated in the newspaper's legal fight to obtain city records, and the staff won a Pulitzer Prize for breaking news reporting.[42] The Pulitzer announcement came in April 2017, and layoffs followed two weeks later.[43] Kelly remembered: "Nobody could believe that we managed to hit this pinnacle and then, you know, less than two weeks later, the crew that won the Pulitzer isn't literally worth keeping together." He continued: "The awareness was this was never about some budgetary constraint; this was clearly about a detachment from community needs." One year later, more layoffs hit the newspaper.[44] Kelly has been a vocal critic of Alden, and I asked him if he fears retribution. He doesn't, telling me in November 2021: "Editors know I speak the truth. My publisher knows where I'm coming from. All I have done is insist on the dignity of the people who do the work. That they deserve better. The community deserves better." Between 2012 and September 2021 the *East Bay Times* lost 91.2 percent of its staff represented by its local bargaining unit, according to figures provided by the NewsGuild. Those figures also show the impacts of layoffs at other newspapers. The *Monterey Herald* has seven employees, down from sixty-two in the same time period. At the *Norristown Times-Herald*, four staff members are left, a 91.1 percent drop.

Nobody to "Keep Us in Line"

Reporters hold governments accountable, monitoring them and documenting their activities for a public audience. In tracking layoffs, this chapter also looks to gauge the loss of local accountability journalism, a loss that academics have found is difficult to measure. James T. Hamilton in *Democracy's Detectives* explained: "Regardless of the incentives that generate resources for investigation, stories only get told when those resources are translated into support for the people who discover, construct, and distribute investigative work."[45] Stephanie Mills, thirty-nine at the time of our interview, covered police, water issues, and the Tuscarawas County Board of Engineering for the *Times-Reporter*, which, before she left in 2006, was a daily with a circulation of eighteen thousand readers in northeastern Ohio. She told me in an October 2020 interview: "I would put in information requests, and that prevented situations from becoming a disaster. Without enough of that, society is missing something that keeps it from falling apart. I can see a demise in journalism and watchdoggedness and how divisive our politics have gotten." She described local political leaders: "I felt they were honorable and good people, but I think power corrupts, and without local journalism there would be a creep of people who were in it for the wrong reasons." Mills left in 2006 for a trade publication, one year before GateHouse bought the newspaper. "Since I left, it's been gutted," Mills said.[46] The losses mean an increase in government unchecked.

While scholars have fairly critiqued whether news historically has operated in the public interest of all citizens in a democracy, a robust reporting corps in local communities can strengthen both community connection and watchdog reporting.[47] In 2009 David Simon, creator of HBO's *The Wire* and a former *Baltimore Sun* reporter, testified about the future of journalism to the US Senate Commerce Committee: "I am offended to think that anyone, anywhere believes American institutions as insulated, self-preserving and self-justifying as police departments, school systems, legislatures and chief executives can be held to gathered facts by amateurs pursuing the task without compensation, training, or for that matter, sufficient standing to make public officials even care to whom it is they are lying or from whom they are withholding information."[48] What strikes me about Simon's statement is how difficult it is to measure what the layoffs—not to mention the objectively terrible working conditions—mean for local communities that no longer know or see reporters and that cannot benefit from the knowledge generated by their work about local government and industry. Like Simon, I know this because as a local reporter I uncovered local political corruption, which is intended to be hidden from public view. In many ways, measuring corruption's existence means tracking something that isn't there.

Scholarship that explains what the loss of news coverage means for polarization and municipal finances is emerging. Researchers in 2018 published a study showing that newspaper closures impact public finance. Pengjie Gao, Chang Lee, and Dermot Murphy determined that there was a causal effect between newspaper closures and municipal borrowing increases: "Overall, our results indicate that local newspapers hold their governments accountable, keeping municipal borrowing costs low and ultimately saving local taxpayers money."[49] Joshua P. Darr, Matthew P. Hitt, and Johanna L. Dunaway determined that vibrant and local opinion pages in newspapers slowed polarization, a finding that they outlined in their 2021 book *Home Style Opinion: How Local Newspapers Can Slow Polarization*.[50] Others have sought to measure how newspaper cuts have impacted coverage, including Lindsey Meeks's content analysis, which looks at the role of county newspapers and the comprehensiveness of coverage. She noted that there is a gap in covering sheriffs that is often due to resource differences between larger and smaller newspapers.[51]

In Boulder, Gabi Boerkircher studied journalism and then worked at the *Daily Camera*, part of Alden Global Capital's portfolio after its takeover of MediaNews Group. Boerkircher was laid off in February 2013 from her $23,000-a-year job as a designer. Her responsibilities were given to an unpaid intern, and she still knows reporters in their forties and fifties there who face little retirement savings or options to shift careers. Since she was laid off, Boerkircher has been a communications director in two different Boulder County municipalities. When we talked in October 2021, Boerkircher said she had enjoyed working in the news business, noting that she "believed in public service." She choked up over the idea of the mission newspapers are supposed to play in a democratic society. Now, from her position as a government official, she tries to bring that public service mission into her direct communications with constituents. She has to. No reporters call her. None try to work her as a source. And few are left to report on, let alone investigate, any of the area's officials and their actions, which she knows from talking with other municipal communications directors, who say they also never hear from reporters.

It's an observation supported by a national trend reported by trade industry publications, which in 2018 noted that PR workers outnumber journalists by a ratio of six to one.[52] Boerkircher has seen those figures come to life and knows that the numbers also represent the erosion of the newspaper's watchdog function. "Knowing what I know now that journalism is supposed to do and be a watchdog, I haven't had a reporter call or talk to me in weeks or months," Boerkircher said. Reporters are missing stories that should be tackled, newsworthy items Boerkircher said would be "of the public interest" and "keep us in line." She continued: "It's just not happening."[53] The layoffs as a profit-motivation strategy on their own are concerning, but Alden is forging new paths to exploit employee labor that appear to have an impact on its reputation but not its power.

"Forces Unleashed"

On June 27, 2016, the US Department of Labor's Employee Benefits Security Administration opened an investigation of Alden Global Capital's alleged use of its employees' pension plans and master trust in offshore vehicles it operated. Documents I obtained through the FOIA noted that the investigation focused on whether Alden had met financial compliance requirements in its investment of those employee funds. The investigation document reads, "As stated above, our investigation identified that from August 2013 forward, the Plans invested in two Alden-sponsored vehicles: the Adfero Fund and the CRE Fund." The investigation, which saw subpoenas over the years issued to Goldman Sachs, JPMorgan Chase Bank, and MNG, showed $180 million invested in Adfero and $15 million in the CRE Fund. The US Labor Department document, summarizing its findings, explained: "It appears that the Plans' Alden investments, as well as the investment strategy of the Adfero Fund, which, as noted earlier, often acquired securities alongside other Alden vehicles, were part of a broader overall arrangement designed to benefit Alden." The investigation report, dated December 5, 2019, also stated: "It appears that the committee's investment selections did not comply with applicable plan provisions and fund investor restrictions, and steps were not taken to ensure that the interests of the Plans would be separately and distinctly represented in the transactions." The report explained further: "The Plans' investments in the Adfero Fund and the

CRE Fund, however, represented non-exempt prohibited transactions in violation of ERISA sections." ERISA is the Employee Retirement Income Security Act of 1974, which is designed to protect individuals invested in retirement and health plans. The Labor Department's report continued: "After we advised MNG's outside counsel of our concerns regarding the Plans' investments in the Adfero Fund and the CRE Fund, the Plans' interests in these funds were liquidated." The document said that Alden took voluntary measures to "resolve the alleged violations."[54] I filed a second FOIA request in June 2022, and I received a second round of documents in September 2022. Aside from the prohibited documents and the use of employee pension funds, what strikes me most about these records is that federal officials knew for years about Alden Global Capital's business practices and did nothing to stop the hedge fund's growth.

In November 2021 Alden announced a twenty-four-dollar-per-share play for Lee Enterprises, which was expected, given that Alden and MNG had acquired shares of the still (as of February 2023) publicly traded company. Sabrina Moreno, then a reporter for the *Richmond Times-Dispatch*, tweeted after that November news broke: "Alden stripped the Virginian-Pilot down so much that the Richmond Times-Dispatch became the largest paper in Virginia." Using the abbreviation for Richmond's daily, she noted, "Now it's coming not only for RTD" but also for two other Lee-owned newspapers in the commonwealth.[55] Moreno's Twitter bio at the time read: "Unionize." And that's just what newspaper staffers have been doing nationwide. As cuts have deepened, per capita union membership is up, with the NewsGuild representing 18,707 workers in 2021, according to figures provided by its president.[56]

Organized labor and modern newspapers have long had a tenuous relationship.[57] Walter Brasch explained that corporate firms in the pursuit of wealth will exploit employees, a fact lost on many journalists who are from educated and higher-income households and who pursue white-collar jobs in the field: "However, with the increase of ponderous organizational structures—results of mergers and buy-outs—that emphasize the lack of individuality, the white collar workers, no matter how well management pretends to stroke them, have begun to realize that they, like the skilled worker, are still laborers, subject to the same set of arbitrary and capricious actions of any employer, no matter how benign, no matter how caring."[58] In the mass market era and into the twenty-first century, there has been a two-pronged issue of the flawed ways by which newspapers have traditionally covered labor unions, as well as how little newspaper management has been willing to tolerate unions in their newsrooms, in part due to modern objectivity standards.[59] Allowing newsrooms to unionize was seen as a signal of bias toward unions. William J. Puette's *Through Jaundiced Eyes* laid bare the notion of liberal media bias in covering unions, finding instead outright discrimination against the working class.[60]

Studying the first decade of the 2000s as commercial motivations at newspapers became the norm, Wendy M. Weinhold used ethnographic methods to examine tensions between the journalistic mission and business obligations at a community newspaper in Illinois, filling a crucial gap outside of national newspapers and survey coverage.[61] More than a decade after Weinhold's study, unionization is up nationwide, as much about survival and ethics than anything else. In 2021 Jennifer Proffitt published an analysis of two Florida newsrooms' unionization efforts, finding that "the main motivation was having a voice in the workplace."[62] In an interview published in *New Labor Forum*, Schleuss, a former data reporter at the *Los Angeles Times* who is now president of the News-Guild–Communication Workers of America, discussed the need to empower journalists through unions. For Schleuss, journalists' labor is tied directly to the foundations of democracy: "It's really about what type of government do we want. Do we want fascism or democracy? Our founders realized that you can't have a free people and a free country without a free press."[63] I spoke with Schleuss, who was thirty-four at the time, in December 2021 about the uptick in unionization and union support. He linked the rise of labor participation to conditions in newsrooms, noting that job security and a lack of benefits have become the industry norm. These features are also part of broader financialization conditions that reveal increases in productivity but slowdowns in wage growth.[64] Schleuss told me: "The free market has been allowed to destroy all of these amazing community newsrooms." He's trying to help build them back, but Schleuss knows that to save local journalism, you need to get rid of the hedge funds. He described their ownership as being "in complete opposition" to the ideals and values of a free press.

In January 2019 Alden made an unsuccessful push for Gannett, owner of *USA Today* and the *Arizona Republic*, where Rebekah Sanders was until 2022 a reporter and president of its guild. We talked in November 2021 about her push to unionize, which started after the threat of an Alden takeover. "I was terrified by that," Sanders told me. She had followed the *Los Angeles Times*' unionization efforts closely, and she reached out to guild members there, asking how her team in Phoenix could protect themselves. Their advice: form a union.

There is a certain irony in forming a union in solidarity against Alden only to brace for the GateHouse-Gannett merger that materialized. Sanders understands that GateHouse may not generate the headlines Alden does, but she knows it has slashed and burned newsrooms across the country, too. "For me the goal of unionizing was always to protect our newsroom and to protect the journalists in it and to protect the anchor news source in our community for as long as we can from these forces unleashed by these private equity and hedge funds on our industry," said Sanders, thirty-seven. "Our slogan during our organizing campaign was 'Protect Local Journalism. Preserve Our Republic,'" Sanders said, noting the play on words of the newspaper's name. "The free press is a cornerstone of ensuring a free society." The labor of forming a union or seeking alternative funding sources requires time and energy, as reporters already are working more, with other newsroom positions having been cut.[65] Sanders considered the period covering local and national issues alongside the work to unionize to be like holding down two full-time jobs, and it impacted both her health and her personal life.

That Sanders was able to form a collective bargaining unit in October 2019—before that Gannett-GateHouse merger—proved powerful in protecting against Gannett's cost-cutting strategy related to its workforce. In a flyer titled "Key Contract Victories So Far," the Arizona guild noted its successful efforts to fight against health care cost increases, as it was able to secure access to vaccines and personal protective gear during the pandemic. It also noted its effort to protect "journalistic integrity," fighting against Gannett's use of "advertorials." Job security, too, was also listed as a key victory. "We have not had layoffs in three years, and that is unheard of in our industry," Sanders said, noting that voluntary buyouts did hit the paper, but she said that those come without the emotional trauma of layoffs. Gannett also eliminated at other newspapers a 401(k) match during the pandemic, but because the newly formed union had what is called in labor law "status quo," Gannett could not eliminate its retirement match at the *Republic*, a move Sanders estimates saved the employees in the Arizona newsroom upward of $300,000. Gannett refused to provide health benefits or paid sick leave to its fellows—at the start of a global pandemic—and also sought to furlough web producers, who tend to earn less, in a second round of cost-cutting measures. "We just found that repugnant," Sanders said of the targets to one department. "We were all in this together, and we were not going to let our colleagues be singled out." Because they are a union, the guild forced Gannett to the bargaining table. Sanders suggested that the media company ask across departments who might be willing to take voluntary furloughs, which is unpaid time off. More people volunteered than expected, and because some of the higher-paid staff took them, the furloughs needed to meet Gannett's targets were shorter and impacted fewer people. To Sanders, that meant that more journalism got done at a crucial time, covering the 2020 election upswing as COVID-19 raged.

Moving ahead toward what Sanders hopes will be the newsroom's first union contract, the Arizona guild wants to ensure local creation and production of the newspaper, noting that Gannett has replaced reporting staff with interns. The flyer says of the work remaining: "No Outsourcing: Gannett must keep our journalists in our newsroom. We know our community best." As Sanders and others across Gannett fought in 2020 to keep basic benefits, Gannett that year paid its lenders $116.6 million in fees and $217.5 million in interest. It also paid Fortress Investment Group, which is listed as its manager, a "one-time cash payment" of $30.4 million.[66]

I am encouraged by the people I spoke with for this chapter, but I also am realistic about the power hedge funds and corporate chains influenced by private equity have and the resources at their disposal to fight workers uniting against their influence and profit-motivation tactics. Alden, the same hedge fund that allegedly extracted pension funds for its gain, has fought through the National Labor Relations Board process the efforts of several unions to unite in solidarity against its ownership.[67] Alden also has been willing to fight organized labor in the courts. After Alden took over Journal Register in 2011, two unions objected after the hedge fund eliminated long-standing collective bargaining agreements under federal Bankruptcy Code Section 1113.[68] The US Bankruptcy Court for the Southern District of New York rejected the unions' claims. How rising union power since then can counter hedge fund owners remains to be seen, but empowering workers is one tool as these funds cut deeper, severing important community connections.

I was interested, absent of a model by which to address corruption and the loss of both public service mission and accountability reporting, to document through the narrative experience of those journalists forced out or left behind what layoffs mean for governments going unchecked, and that has consequences. Hamilton devotes a chapter in *Democracy's Detectives* to Pat Stith, the respected and decorated investigative reporter who retired from the *News & Observer* in 2008. Hamilton showed how even one reporter like Stith, who at one point averaged ten stories per year, conducted public-interest work with impacts. Hamilton's coding of 314 Stith stories showed that he mostly covered North Carolina state issues, with local reporting next. More than one hundred of those stories produced what Hamilton called "deliberative impacts," with nearly four dozen resignations or removals, including firings or demotions attributed to Stith's investigative work. "Findings of corruption often triggered new regulation, audits or new leadership," Hamilton wrote.[69] Over a thirty-six-year span, Stith's reporting led to thirty-one new laws. It's hard to imagine that scope today, not because dedicated reporters like Stith aren't out there but because the conditions imposed by private investment funds are making it harder to do. The *News & Observer* is now part of Chatham Asset Management's McClatchy portfolio. A *News & Observer* subscriber in 2020 told me: "I still think that the *News and Observer* is an important resource for information that I want and I need about the community and the world around me. I don't think it's as good of a resource as it used to be."[70]

There are wider impacts of these losses that reach to the highest echelons of power in our democratic society. I believe these issues of ownership and press freedom transcend politics, but when Donald Trump calls reporters an "enemy of the people" I believe it is easier for people to consider that journalists really are the nation's monsters if people don't ever meet, read, or see one.[71] Once you know someone like Doerschner is making sure your places of worship are safe from predators or Sanders is helping you recoup money lost to scams, it's harder to see them as enemies. You start to see them as what they are: a critical part of a community's social fabric and democratic infrastructure. But left with fewer reporters and less news to report, local newspapers have seen an exodus of their readers over the last twenty years. Chapter 7 explains more about the audiences who turned away, seeing little left to keep them engaged and paying.

Chapter 7

Neglected Audiences

For Jenny Breen, subscribing to a newspaper was just something adults did.[1] You paid rent. You did your own laundry. And you subscribed to the newspaper. Breen, forty, grew up in a household with a print subscription to the *Florida Times-Union*, a Jacksonville daily owned by Morris Communications for decades. GateHouse bought it in 2017, and it's now a piece of the Gannett chain. Newspapers throughout American history have provided subscribers a window onto their communities, a kind of connection to both local politics and civic life, with space for features and entertainment. Breen respected that connection, and she sought it out. As a University of North Carolina Chapel Hill undergraduate, she and her housemates paid for a *News & Observer* subscription. By 2005 she and her husband had moved to Ithaca, New York, and the couple took a subscription to the *Ithaca Journal*, a newspaper with such a long history in the region that its early nineteenth-century leaders reminded subscribers to pay with cash, not vegetables.[2] Less than one hundred years after its founding, the newspaper caught the attention of Cornell University graduate Frank Gannett. He bought the *Ithaca Journal* in 1912, and it became the second newspaper in what eventually would become a national media empire.

When Breen signed up for her subscription, Gannett had a combined nationwide paid circulation of 7.3 million.[3] "At the end of 2005, the company operated 91 U.S. daily newspapers, including USA Today, and nearly 1,000 non-daily local publications in 36 states and Guam," its annual report showed.

Gannett employed 39,700 full- and part-time staff, and that year local advertising revenue from its local newspapers jumped 8 percent, to $163 million. Its publishing revenues were up 6.2 percent over 2004, bringing its total revenue companywide to $6.9 billion. Yet despite those robust revenues and three years before the Great Recession, executives revealed concerns on the horizon about rising costs, most notably, "employee benefit costs."[4] Gannett, like other publicly traded newspaper companies, has long looked for ways to maximize profits, and cutting staff even in years of hefty profitability has been one of those ways. In 2006 Gannett laid people off at the *Livonia Observer & Eccentric* a year after acquiring the Michigan daily.[5] The next few years would be a bloodbath for Gannett staff and reporters at daily newspapers nationwide. "In SEC documents covering those years, they cited a long list of accomplishments that specifically included whacking 11,000 jobs," former Gannett editor and reporter Jim Hopkins wrote in a 2013 blog post.[6] As layoffs accelerated, local news stopped getting produced, and wire service and national content took its place.

On visits home to Jacksonville, Breen remembered asking her parents why they still subscribed, noting that the *Florida Times-Union* was filled with advertisements and wire content, and she believed it offered little connection to the community she remembered. "'This is garbage,' I said to them. I asked them, 'How can you pay for that?'" Breen remembered. She started to feel that way about the Ithaca paper, too. One night, Breen and her husband flipped through television channels, and they stopped at a meeting broadcast on public access television. It seemed heated, but they had missed the beginning and, therefore, the debate's core. The next morning's newspaper covered nothing. Breen called the *Ithaca Journal*, and someone told her that no reporter had attended because the paper didn't have the staff. "That's why I'm paying," Breen said, "to have them attend public meetings and report on them. I do not need Gannett copy on Syria or the Russia investigation. That is worthless to me in a local paper. The thing that I would pay for would be news about Ithaca, New York." Breen canceled her subscription.

Cuts, layoffs, and profit targets influencing the newspaper as a product take us to the final feature of the private investment era: its neglected audiences. Substitute Gannett with other publicly traded newspaper companies influenced by private equity or others now in the hands of hedge funds, and the story is the same: reporter job cuts, for-profit motivation prioritizing surface coverage, consolidation, a diminished watchdog role, and dissatisfied subscribers who have turned away from local newspapers. Facing pressure to maintain once-stratospheric profits as advertising revenue began its decline, corporate newspaper organizations in the 2000s started cutting staff, consolidating beats after mergers and acquisitions, closing bureaus, and selling off landmark buildings that communities had recognized for decades. Corporate chains that had long treated news as a product also stopped generating something audiences in small towns and cities nationwide wanted to pay for. It's no shock that readers like Breen, fed up with a loss of local news, turned away, and it wasn't only because of the internet. Readers watched as stories about their children's schools, crime, local commissions, and elected boards disappeared from print and digital pages. Corporate newspapers left readers. And readers paid attention.

The Audience Exodus

Breen is part of a well-documented reader exodus, yet the reasons behind the subscription stoppages are not as well known. Amy Mitchell and Jesse Holcomb's research for the Pew Research Center showed that circulation declines in 2015 were the worst since 2010.[7] Between 2018 and 2020 print circulation dropped five million.[8] Research showed a positive relationship between newsroom investment and circulation growth.[9] But what about the reverse? What happens when cuts leave local newspapers with little local news, the very product that is promised? Longitudinal research published in 2018 showed that the decline of local news is tied to a reduction in citizen engagement.[10] Yet few studies have addressed why readers leave, start, or stay, and that means that the connections between private investment fund influence, slashed coverage, and citizen audiences' decision-making are missing. In this chapter I explore more about what current and former subscribers understood about their local newspapers. I spent much of the summer of 2020 talking to people in two dozen states. Ultimately, by February 2021 I had interviewed eighty-five people from Hawaii to Maine.

Previous chapters documented how a new private fund oligarchy plundered newspapers and how executives influenced by private investment funds reached for mergers and acquisitions as a playbook to address the digital transition. When that didn't work, layoffs were seen as one way to boost the bottom line. At publicly traded newspaper companies with profit margins above 25 percent, staffing cuts accelerated often as competition declined.[11] Many raised subscription prices as they slashed local coverage until audiences stopped seeing value.[12] Before he bailed from local newspaper ownership, Warren Buffett understood this. In his March 1, 2013, letter to Berkshire Hathaway shareholders, Buffett wrote: "We do not believe that success will come from cutting either the news content or frequency of publication. Indeed, skimpy news coverage will almost certainly lead to skimpy readership."[13] This chapter addresses through in-depth interviews why subscribers leave and stay as it attempts to place their concerns as a core part of our newspaper crisis and a threat to democracy.

In both applied and theoretical research, audiences are receiving increased attention as views are changing on news media's relationship to the public.[14] Robust scholarship reconceptualizing audiences and the impacts of the digital transition has also brought more nuance to who the audience is, what it needs and wants, and how news organizations seek to engage and to monetize it.[15] Philip Napoli, focused on the institutional concept of the audience, called this turn an "audience evolution."[16] Chris W. Anderson's ethnographic work in newsrooms noted that the "agenda of the audience" drives the field despite quite paradoxically being a term that has multiple and sometimes conflicting meanings.[17] Tim Vos, Martin Eichholz, and Tatsiana Karaliova considered that audiences have renewed importance in part because so many have turned away and taken their attention and their dollars with them.[18] Irene Costera Meijer has examined issues of valuable journalism, writing that if news is to be effective in a democracy, it should be as widely used as possible and relevant to citizens' lives.[19] Chris Peters and Tamara Witschge interrogated the concept of democracy and the "grand narratives" of journalism's links to it, finding in the digital sphere concepts of the user and audience mostly linked to their ability to click rather than engage as citizens.[20] Magda Konieczna and Elia Powers found that the nonprofit International Consortium of Investigative Journalists' focus on purposely and explicitly producing work that powered democracy actually separated it from traditional news entities.[21]

Engagement, analytics, and the study of the audience have become, especially in the last decade, a crucial point of inquiry focused on learning more about how news is used, as well as how audiences influence newsroom decision-making.[22] Studying audiences has fractured into those examining for-profit spaces to others examining nonprofit newsrooms, especially considering that nonprofit digital newsrooms are "praised for their innovations in audience-focused interventions."[23] Rodrigo Zamith called this renewed focus on audience engagement a "third wave period" driven by analytics and metrics but still rooted in technological developments alongside economic and social changes.[24] Meanwhile, at a time when, as Jacob L. Nelson explained in *Imagined Audiences: How Journalists Perceive and Pursue the Public*, more data than ever are available about audiences through analytics, newsrooms remain somewhat ambivalent and skeptical about integrating those data into engagement practices.[25] Nelson's work showed a tension between journalists' conception of the audience, noting that many journalists believe they have expertise over what should be covered, which results in a detachment from the audience. Still, newsrooms have sought to hire engagement editors to help shape and drive an understanding of this volume of available data.[26] Caitlin Petre in *All the News That's Fit to Click* called this "the traffic game," explaining that the use of analytics in newsrooms had journalists competing "to achieve ever-higher metrics of audience attention."[27] Looking at two nonprofit newsrooms, Nelson, Valerie Belair-Gagnon, and Seth Lewis published on audience engagement and community connections using interviews with producers and observation. The authors noted that the coverage of communities and issues may be unique from the audiences that newsrooms reach.[28]

Audience research often frames the issue of newspaper survival or start-up sustainability in different ways, but the crux of these arguments is often how, why, and if users pay.[29] Research pioneered by Iris Chyi has sought to understand more about users' willingness to pay as digital content and paywalls have become the norm.[30] In 2014 Manuel Goyanes used data of 570 US users who were part of a Pew Research Center telephone survey and determined that consumers were unwilling to pay for online news simply to acquire knowledge.[31] One year later, Goyanes published work that examined local newspapers, finding that demographics of age and gender plus news interest were important variables in determining willingness to pay.[32] The 2020 Reuters Institute Digital News Report, focused in part on how and why people pay for online news in 40 markets on six continents. Looking at the United States specifically, the researchers explained a bump in paying for online news after Donald Trump's presidential victory.[33]

This time period may be the closest contemporary example to Stuart Hall's concept of encoding and decoding—a mediated mass communication circuit with profit-motivated producers trying to reach audiences who are desperate for fact-based information sources.[34] Yet that transactional exchange and the limits of it in a system dominated by private investment fund influence remain relatively underexplored. I believe readers could still find value inside the digital or print pages of newspapers if only readers had a nudge toward them and if newspapers did more to cover communities authentically without the influence of advertising dollars.

Structural critiques should and do consider audiences, although combining structural and reception research has been frequently debated, including from both cultural studies theorists and political economists.[35] Dallas Smythe's concept of the "audience commodity" infused the debate on mediated power structures and their relationship to readers who do media labor on behalf of advertisers, often at home in private spaces.[36] Based on Smythe's work, others have expanded critical production perspectives and the audience. Graham

Murdock's critique of commercial broadcasting hinged on undermining citizenry.[37] James S. Ettema and D. Charles Whitney considered that "institutionally effective audiences" are those who are meaningful for their "economic value within the system."[38] Douglas Kellner sought the integration of structural, textual, and audience analyses.[39] Kellner reinforced the integration of a critical media/cultural studies approach, noting that there has never been nor would there ever be in the future one way to approach the variety of problems society offers to study related to its communication systems and power.[40] With Jeff Share, Kellner called on a radical version of media literacy that empowers audiences to understand their place as targets of commercialism in our media system, noting it receives virtually nothing in exchange.[41] Today's private investment fund realities in newspapers bear new fruit for that concept and for Sut Jhally and Bill Livant's decades-old concept of the television audience "watching as working."[42] Indeed, today's newspaper audience through subscribing is trying to do the work of citizenship while overwhelmingly it is laboring to help private funds profit.

Setting aside the theoretical to focus on the practical, certainly news organizations—even nonprofit ones—need to be sustainable. But overwhelmingly, the fact that profit overharvesting is a de facto part of the modern journalism industry seems to be widely accepted as private investment fund control and influence increase. Nelson concluded that separating journalism's economic crisis from its quality crisis could improve both. I believe journalism's economic crisis is its quality crisis, and private investment funds have exacerbated problems with both. We need to frame audience engagement as a by-product of ownership and profit-motivated control. Audiences are active and engaged parts of the news media process, but when newspaper companies treat them as consumers only, their function as citizens is limited. It's no surprise they turn away or never log on at all.

Audiences must be situated within the social and political systems they belong to.[43] Subscribing does nothing more than offer the chance for readers to provide a digital or offline footprint, both of which can be monetized.[44] Approaches derived from applied methods or uses and gratifications may not fully engage with the structural for-profit issues that are so crucial in today's news production. Here, I would argue that the data available today—the clicks or the Chartbeat statistics—do little to explain how a news audience considers a product that has been not just cut but decimated.[45] Scholarship on audience engagement and newspaper usage fails to account for how structure and production are crucial factors influencing the hollowed-out and watered-down newspaper product and the audiences' relationship to it. Furthermore, much of this renewed sense of purpose in audience examination has been done without audience interviews or primary source documents.[46] Whether you view audiences as active or participatory or as engaged or disengaged, the larger question remains unanswered: In the private investment era, what is left for audiences of local newspapers to pay for?[47]

"We Had Had Enough"

During the interviews I conducted, audience power and autonomy were revealed as much in the choice to continue to subscribe as in the choice to cancel subscriptions, but not because user-generated content or even free content was available as an alternative. Canceling a subscription was, quite simply, an action done by newspaper consumers who no longer saw value in the product. Integrating production and audience in this chapter considers citizens' losses and information deficits in their communities that result from massive staff layoffs and mergers that have defined the newspaper landscape of the last two decades. The concept of neglected audiences, therefore, is meant to explain the issues of production and audiences in light of these private investment fund realities. The concept of neglected audiences further recognizes that their relationship to news media also denotes their relationship to community and to civic and government power in those places. In many ways, the increasingly consolidated corporate chain newspaper industry on its own could have provided a rich study of audiences—both those who turned away from newspapers and those who continue subscribing. Hedge fund ownership demands this study.

Writing this book about private investment funds' ties to the loss of local news and democratic impacts without talking to citizens felt misplaced. While I know that eighty-five interviews are by no means representative or generalizable, the similarities shared by those in the sample who talked to me—generating seventy hours of material—are noteworthy. I purposely interviewed people who did once or still do subscribe to local newspapers, broadly defined as any daily newspaper that was not the *New York Times*, the *Wall Street Journal*, or the *Washington Post*. While I did not set out to find people to talk with from the chains influenced by private equity and hedge funds, ultimately that is the sample that I have. Of the eighty-five participants in my sample, sixty-eight do or did subscribe to newspapers in the chains under review influenced by private investment funds and documented in earlier chapters. I sought perspectives from people unconnected to my university campus and without ties to journalism. I allowed people to self-identify their employment category and their race.

There was a nurse in Alabama, a geriatric care manager in California, a dentist in Connecticut, a teacher in upstate New York, a librarian in North Carolina, and an "IT guy" in Cincinnati. There was a pastor in Alabama, a retired judge in Maryland, and a "tech nerd guy" in Delaware. Regardless of interviewees' race, region, or age, my results show that people are active and engaged participants in the financial support of local newspapers, but they will not pay for a product that fails to produce what is promised, which is local news. Studying and conceptualizing audiences as active yet neglected citizens in the process of news consumption addresses a crucial gap in both production and audience studies literature, especially as private investment funds take greater control.

Some of the interviewees included here, like those in chapter 6, offered their names and experiences on the record, while others asked for anonymity. Interviews ranged between twenty-five and ninety minutes. I specifically asked interviewees if they felt connected to and informed about their communities and issues in their communities, and I also asked them whether they believed newspapers did a good job generating accountability journalism, which I did not define. I asked how many years they had subscribed and when they had cancelled, if they had, and how much subscriptions cost. I asked why they subscribe or why they canceled subscriptions. I asked those who still read daily news about their methods of accessing the news, trying to distinguish between print circulation, app usage, or website. I did not ask about bias, but I did ask if people know who owns their newspapers. Interestingly, few did, but many who subscribed to Gannett newspapers understood the connection between their local newspaper and that owner because they recognized similar formatting to *USA Today*. I asked the same question at the end of each interview: "Is there anything about your local newspaper or experience you would like to add?"

At its peak in 1984, daily circulation topped 63.3 million, with newspapers a respected, trusted, and constant part of daily life.[48] They still are today, but as circulation declines, so does newspapers' role in daily life, especially as private investment funds take over. People feel and react to the loss of local news in many ways, but universally there is a sense that the amount and quality of local news coverage are problematic even for those who keep paying. Many stick around for the less measurable connections, too, like the daily crossword over a cup of coffee completed after a quick scan of the obituaries. You don't have to go far to find someone whose parents still have a laminated newspaper article stuck to the refrigerator that describes them playing a high school sport or standing at a microphone struggling with a spelling bee word. Whether it was life or death, the newspaper documented it, and it provided a way both to stay informed and to feel connected. Many people I interviewed for this chapter remembered reading comics while their parents perused political coverage in the next room. I was eager to hear what kept them paying or, more importantly, what turned them away from the dozens of local newspapers that Penelope Muse Abernathy has called "ghost" institutions, objectively dead yet still operating in communities across America, delivering occasional hard-hitting work that should be an expected, daily part of any healthy news organization guarded by the First Amendment.[49]

Fifteen people in the sample were age thirty-five and younger at the time of their interviews, and they offered more comments than older interviewees did on the experience of reading news through a mobile device. Almost all interviewees in the age group eighteen to thirty-five subscribed digitally and accessed content often through a news organization's app or a website home page or via a Twitter feed. A twenty-three-year-old white man living in Bloomington, Illinois, at the time of our July 2020 interview described his digital *Denver Post* subscription when he lived there briefly after graduating from college. He canceled it after just a few months because the experience, he told me, was "nearly impossible." Logging on through a URL on his computer or an app on his phone, he noted that he was subjected to banner advertisements and pop-ups. "I'm paying for this and you're bombarding me with ads," he remembered thinking. "I was just dissatisfied with the experience. It was the general feeling that this was not worth it."[50] Trying to stay engaged and informed online became an act of frustration regardless of age group. A seventy-year-old white woman in southern Ohio said the only reason she takes a print subscription to the *Cincinnati Enquirer* is because "it's almost impossible to read digitally with all of the ads. You're in the middle of a story, and you get a pop-up ad, and it obliterates what you're reading."[51]

Others in the youngest age cohort (age eighteen to thirty-five) were concerned about what the loss of a newspaper's subscription revenue would mean for their community, expressing more collectivist views than those in the sample who were older. A thirty-three-year-old white man in Boulder, Colorado, subscribed to several newspapers digitally, and he was one of the few who knew about the newspapers' owners.[52] He told me: "I'm supporting the reporters. If the reporters said, 'Hey, fuck the *Denver Post*; we're going somewhere else,' I'd follow them, but where are they going? If I don't support it, then no one supports it. Do I like the ownership structure? No. I don't feel good about that." He continued: "The irony is, democracy dies in darkness behind a paywall."[53] A twenty-nine-year-old Black woman from a small town in Florida who works abroad for the US State Department described a similar feeling. She called her subscriptions to five news organizations, including the *Gainesville Sun* and the

Miami Herald, "an investment": "There's news deserts all around the country, and it's really hard for you to get localized coverage. Five dollars a month is not going to make or break me. It certainly feels like I'm doing my part."[54]

Bias was mentioned in only four of the interviews as a point of concern. A fifty-six-year-old white pastor in Montgomery, Alabama, described himself as an Auburn University football fan. He almost canceled a subscription to the Gannett-owned *Montgomery Advertiser* because of what he views as the newspaper's bias in favor of the University of Alabama, Auburn's college football rival. Two others, including a retired Jacksonville teacher, mentioned right-wing bias, though it was not cited as the sole reason anyone turned away, while another expressed concerns about too much progressive and liberal news in his North Carolina daily. A forty-seven-year-old white woman on Hawaii's Big Island who described herself as unemployed due to a disability keeps a digital subscription to the *Honolulu Star Advertiser*, which she canceled once, but she was "lured back" by a five-dollar subscription offer: "We've got all these millennial reporters. The adjectives they use! The bias. The mistakes. It's not just a news piece. Either Left or Right—I'm an independent voter—I don't really care which side it is, it just shouldn't come through. It shouldn't be a liberal paper or a conservative paper, it should just be a paper."[55]

Perhaps most interesting from the interviews was how little bias factored into conversations about local newspapers, but both diminished local opinion pages and community political stories left many readers feeling lost about a range of viewpoints in their towns and cities. People miss reading about others' viewpoints, even if those differ from their own. In October 2022 Alden Global Capital announced that it would stop generating editorials on election coverage, another blow to a community member's search for researched perspectives on key community issues.[56] A variety of viewpoints provided a sense of community connection, and those who still see a range of views in local news look forward to them. A nineteen-year-old white woman in Wayne, New Jersey, who subscribes to the *Wayne Today* said: "The town I live in, my views differ a lot from people in my hometown. Reading the perspectives, it gives me a better idea of what people are thinking. I can get a grasp of how to act without being rude."[57]

People want local news, and even those who cancel their subscriptions would be willing to pay for *something* that helps them stay connected and engaged with their communities and holds elected officials accountable. A loss of local news was most often cited as the reason to cancel, and the interviewees provided a range of responses. Barbara Whellans, of Fort Pierce, Florida, subscribed for fifty-five years to the now Gannett-owned newspaper where I once worked, paying $480 annually for her subscription. In less than three years, the newspaper, published sixty-five miles north of West Palm Beach, had three different owners. It slashed staff. It sold its iconic buildings along the county's main north–south corridor that neighbors knew. It consolidated its operations in locations away from the cities it was meant to serve. The newspaper shrank. The copy desk, outsourced thousands of miles away to Des Moines or Louisville, missed mistakes. Whellans, a retired teacher, noticed all of it, forgiving early changes until eventually, she said, local meeting coverage evaporated. "It just stopped, to me, being a local paper," Whellans, seventy-five, told me about why she finally canceled. "We had had enough."⁵⁸ A Michigan man who identified as both Caucasian and Native American Lakota canceled his subscriptions to newspapers in both Detroit and Vero Beach, Florida—one owned by Alden Global Capital and the other by Gannett—not long before we talked in July 2020, telling me: "There is not enough investigative journalism with corporate newspapers." He had long subscribed to newspapers when he lived in Detroit and later Brevard County, Florida, telling me earlier in our interview: "In general, I have a great appreciation for the press. I don't always agree with them, but I appreciate what they're trying to do. It's a First Amendment right that must not be lost."⁵⁹

A key finding from the interviews of those who stopped subscribing is just how long readers clung to newspapers before canceling, some waiting for a turnaround that would never arrive. For many I spoke with, the decision to cancel was described as "agonizing" after decades as "a loving reader." Several others watched newspapers accumulate around the house and then switched to digital before finding few stories that interested them. A sixty-nine-year-old retired teacher in Jacksonville who identified as Caucasian said she turned to her husband one day in 2018 while reading and said, "I think this is it." She continued: "The local reporting stopped almost entirely. The editorial part of the articles was poorly edited. We noticed an extreme slant to the right. It just felt like we were not reading the news anymore."⁶⁰ A forty-three-year-old white woman in a Cincinnati suburb cut her *Cincinnati Enquirer* subscription more than a decade ago, explaining: "It just felt like it was getting, literally, the paper got smaller and smaller and more and more photography and less and less actual news. I felt like the content online read more like press releases."⁶¹

Those who still subscribe have concurrent feelings of civic obligation, routine, and excitement when an investigative story shows up in print or online that does what readers used to see more often. But almost everyone who keeps subscribing is dissatisfied, suggesting that those who remain have a somewhat precarious paying relationship. Andre Davis, a retired African American judge in Baltimore, has watched the changes at the *Baltimore Sun*, especially in the last decade. When he retrieves the print newspaper in the morning, he jokes that "someone has stolen half of the paper" because it seems so thin. Davis, seventy-one, said the newspaper is "an embarrassment. I think we have good local writers and columnists who do the best they can. The paper's writers have been furloughed. I miss reading what they have to say."[62] Alex Brown, a forty-six-year-old digital subscriber to McClatchy's *Island Packet* in South Carolina who identified as part of the region's African American Gullah community, told me the changes are a point of concern. But Brown keeps paying for a digital subscription: "When you start to really assess the alternative, where there is no alternative, you stay connected. You always want to have a situation where, I guess, leadership at the newspaper may not align directly with your expectations, but in order to have some sense of communication in our small town, the local newspaper is absolutely essential."[63]

Michael Kirk of Coventry, Connecticut, keeps his *Hartford Courant* subscription out of routine and respect for reporters. Kirk began working in Washington, DC, for Democratic congressman John Larson in 2000 when the newspaper had four or five reporters in its Capitol bureau covering both the state's congressional delegation and national affairs. By the time Kirk left that job five years later, the *Courant* had closed its Washington, DC, bureau. Years later, now with a reporting corps forced out of its hometown newsroom and with a fraction of its staff under Alden's ownership, the *Hartford Courant* daily print subscription costs Kirk more than $800 a year.[64] But Kirk still hangs on to his print and digital subscriptions, shelling out hundreds of dollars a year while hoping for a story that would hold a local or state official accountable. He likes to think his subscription helps boost state and local reporters, whose bylines he has come to know over his 6:00 a.m. coffee. But his feeling about the newspaper is anything but optimistic. In July 2020 Kirk told me: "It is absolutely a shadow of its former self. It is a frail, weak, tragic, diminished institution. Just watching it go from what it was to what it is: being taken over by vampire companies with no interest in journalism; they just want to drain all the capital. It has been really difficult to see." Kirk keeps subscribing and periodically thinks, "There's that feeling of 'Wow. I need to know that.'" Kirk shared another view of those who, especially over age forty, keep paying for local newspapers. They hope their subscription revenue will somehow trickle down to the reporters.

I spent three years reviewing financial, corporate, and court documents, and the harsh reality is that subscription revenue will be used to pay down debt, to boost CEO pay, to pay shareholder dividends in good years, or to channel profits to private investment owners and investors. I have seen no evidence in any documents that subscription dollars drive staffing but plenty of evidence that staffing cuts boost bottom lines for private investment fund investors and owners.

Situating the local newspaper crisis as a problem of private equity investors and hedge fund ownership raises alarms about where some readers are turning for information in the void left behind, and that, too, has democratic implications. A sixty-seven-year-old retired nurse outside Birmingham, Alabama, stopped her local newspaper subscription after years of frustration. She told me she had found an alternative outlet online called *Yellowhammer News*, which was the second time an interviewee mentioned the site. In a Winter 2019 piece for the *Columbia Journalism Review*, Lauren Smiley described the site this way: "Yellowhammer is merely a relatively mature example of the attempts to create alternative local news outlets that capitalize on America's media polarization where it dovetails with community news credibility. And as local newsrooms continue to be wiped out, other untested publishers are rushing into the void."[65] Priyanjana Bengani revealed a network of "pink slime" outlets, which are hyperpartisan sites dressed up online to look like reputable local news, although they are funded by dark money, proliferating online and using social media to find readers.[66]

Although few people I interviewed know or understand their local newspaper's ownership, the issues they pinpoint point to ownership as a problem. Although it is different from informational or entertainment texts in film or television and different still from national and international newspaper outlets, there is still an unspoken contract between a local newspaper and its subscribers that they will learn news about their communities. This was a key point overwhelmingly supported by the people I interviewed. Quality news is expensive to produce, and the loss of both quality and quantity of local news due to cuts done to improve a corporation's bottom line is what caused many in my sample to cut ties with their local publication.[67] Newspapers' audiences deserve insights unique to the field, as many pay for print and/or digital subscriptions to help them make decisions about their local leaders and gain knowledge of infrastructure and local government. Studying and conceptualizing active audiences without an engagement with their role in profitability and sustainability therefore leaves out a critical discussion point, one that is of increasing concern, given the current newspaper landscape. Newspapers have offered citizens in markets nationwide less for more.

If we can understand that the focus on profit above all else of the contemporary newspaper's business model is flawed, we can also work to understand how to not only create new production models but also examine how audiences can be part of solutions. Near the end of each interview, I asked people what they knew about nonprofit news outlets and what it would take to get both readers' attention and their financial support. My findings show that, like Whellans, many people still are willing to pay for news, but only three people in this larger sample knew what is available in the nonprofit news space. Whellans has long supported nonprofit public radio, but it had never occurred to her until we spoke in July 2020 that there might be other alternatives to the newspaper that could use her financial support. What both concerned and interested me was that Whellans did nothing to redirect back to news that $480 annually she had spent for the Fort Pierce newspaper. She was unaware of the nonprofit newsrooms available in Florida and nationwide that cover the kinds of stories she likes to read, although none provide the hyperlocal coverage that kept her paying. There was a disconnect there. That also means there is an opportunity, too. With financial support from citizens, more nonprofit and independent newsrooms can thrive, but it's true that the hundreds of nonprofit newsrooms that exist now cannot act as a one-to-one replacement for newspapers.

Cornell Woolridge, a forty-two-year-old working in the education sector in Austin, Texas, canceled his *Austin American-Statesman* subscription, finding that the Gannett-owned daily offered little of the investigative journalism he expected. GateHouse bought the newspaper from Cox in 2018, and it became part of Gannett after the 2019 merger. Woolridge, who identifies as African American, echoed many of the sentiments of other subscribers I've talked to who continued supporting newspapers because they recognize the talent of individual reporters, but as an institution, the news organization was failing. "I know how hard they are fighting, but they are based on a survival foundation," Woolridge said of the *Statesman*. But, different from the majority of others in my sample, Woolridge found an outlet he wanted to support instead. He turned his attention—and his dollars—to the nonprofit *Texas Tribune,* which Woolridge told me felt more like "'Hey, we are one of you. And we're really in it. We're in this together.'" He continued: "With nonprofit news, you can have a greater assurance that they are doing this for the love of news, for the love of their respective community or state depending on the scale. And they're going to do literally the best that they can do. And they are going to squeeze every last penny out of it."[68] Woolridge offered a glimpse of the journalism payer of the future: a person engaged in their community who turned away from their newspaper but saw value in nonprofit news. The reality is that he also has access to one.

Back in Ithaca, Breen has read the nonprofit *Ithaca Voice* for some news, though she has not yet supported it financially. I spoke with Dustin Patte, the

Voice's interim executive director, in October 2020. He said its expansion can be credited to the *Ithaca Journal*'s failings. "The founding of our paper was that void that was really left when the daily paper laid off most of their staff," Patte told me. "People in Ithaca care about local news, and they want local news to survive." At the time of our interview, the nonprofit *Ithaca Voice* had just hired a full-time education reporter, bringing its paid reporting staff up to four. Gannett's newspaper in Ithaca staffs just one full-time reporter.[69]

Conclusion

Ending the Era

Daniel Prude's March 2020 death after a police encounter in Rochester, New York, was revealed publicly months later, and only after lawyers for his family shared law enforcement's bodycam footage they obtained through public records requests.[1] Two months before a Minneapolis police officer murdered George Floyd, several police officers in Rochester responded to a 3:00 a.m. call about Prude, a forty-one-year-old Black man, who was in the midst of "a mental health episode."[2] Prude ignored police demands to stop spitting, and an officer covered his head with a hood. Video shows Prude, hooded but otherwise naked, lying on the pavement in front of the Abundant Life Faith Center Fellowship Hall with his wrists handcuffed behind his back. As light snow fell, Prude tried to stand, and an officer put his knee on Prude's back while another held his head down. Prude gasped, "They're trying to kill me."[3] He eventually lost consciousness. Paramedics tried CPR, but he arrived at the hospital without brain activity and was put on life support. One week later, Prude was dead.[4]

The Prude case is one that a well-staffed newspaper unencumbered by a corporate owner's profit margins should have caught. Reporters—several you met in chapter 6—rely on both sources and bureaucratic paperwork to follow leads, generate tips, and investigate stories. The Prude case offered both across newsroom beats. There was the neighborhood chatter after the incident, the videotaped encounter, an ambulance ride, and a hospital visit, and by April of that year there was an internal police report.[5] The April 16, 2020, autopsy ruled Prude's death a homicide due to "complications of asphyxia in the setting of physical restraint." By July 2020 the case had been turned over to the state attorney general, whose website shows footage from six different body cameras that filmed the incident.[6] Law enforcement, medical personnel, and local and state government officials knew about the case for months. Yet the Gannett-owned *Democrat and Chronicle*, Rochester's newspaper of record, missed the Prude story, having endured round after round of layoffs.[7]

Prude deserved to have his story illuminated by journalists empowered to hold power to account. Had his family not fought for access, the police actions would have remained hidden from public scrutiny. A grand jury did not indict the Rochester officers, but in October 2022 Prude's family reached a $12 million wrongful death settlement with the city. Prude's son said in a statement, "Communities need to know that there will be at least some accountability when police kill people like my dad, whose only crime was needing help."[8]

At a time when government accountability and truth itself are at a crucial nexus, news organizations in the private investment era have failed citizens as these organizations have boosted private investment funds' bottom lines. The public has a right to know how police, elected boards, and governments function using citizens' tax dollars. Newspaper journalism throughout modern history was the system set up to foster that knowledge. As a former local newspaper reporter, as I watched from six different angles Prude naked and dying on that cold Rochester street, what troubled me is how many stories like his remain hidden because our local newspaper system is less equipped to tell them. It is less equipped because of an ownership and investment oligarchy that privileges profit over citizen knowledge in our democracy.

The newspaper industry in Rochester and places across America is not in crisis because its business model changed. The newspaper industry is in crisis because the business models of the powerful private investment funds behind the industry have not changed. Whether you quantify the newspapers by their corporate chain monikers or by the hedge funds and private equity firms shaking out the proverbial piggy banks, the results are the same: structural power and wealth growing in a period of financialization fostered through newsroom job losses with impacts on information quality and quantity. Stephen Lacy and Alan Blanchard's 2003 work showed that profit targets set by publicly traded newspapers were higher than at family-owned newspapers, and that led to smaller newsroom staff.[9] Two decades since, consolidation has increased, and newspaper work is overwhelmingly marked by cuts, furloughs, and layoffs often against a backdrop of extreme private equity wealth. In the private investment era, crucial accountability work is getting harder to do, allowing government agencies, politicians across parties, and industry executives to act without scrutiny.

Through an analysis of bankruptcy and court documents, congressional reports and corporate records, government filings, and trade reports alongside 106 hours of in-depth interviews, this book has charted the modern history and contemporary practices of a small, elite corps of financial firms operating in the newspaper marketplace. It is, like many other political-economic critiques that preceded it, fundamentally a study of influence, money, and power. Political economy of media as a theoretical and methodological tradition has long been concerned with structural power run amok and its impact on audiences and labor. So, too, has watchdog journalism. Critical communications scholarship and normative journalism are united in the ideas and ideals that citizen power needs to be restored. Vincent Mosco has addressed the exploration of media market power as a key feature of the theoretical tradition, one meant to unveil contours of wealth and the inequality it produces and aggravates.[10] I am reminded of Charles Lewis, the founder of both the nonprofit Center for Public Integrity and Investigative Reporting Workshop, who said that a journalist's job is to "investigate the bastards."[11] The theoretical aim of this book has been to provide a lens to address those hierarchies and assess their relationship to the local newspaper crisis. The practical aim has been to show institutional failures and document how money flows to further prop up power as democracy crumbles. The two can and should coexist as a part of scholarship studying private fund power in the newspaper marketplace and beyond it.

This conclusion, therefore, examines through a critical lens and using investigative reporting techniques the campaign finance and lobbying influences that have become barriers constructed in this time period to citizen news access in a democracy. It also examines how an existing antitrust system could be used to thwart this expansion, although I am realistic about its limitations, given fund power over political entities and politicians and a never-ending revolving door between American industry and regulators. As in any case where great challenges exist, the current conditions leave space for opportunities, and perhaps the most notable of all in the private investment era is the innovation coupled with the concern this type of ownership and investment has created. This book ends by elevating the stories of those newsrooms operating to fill the voids left by these funds to show that a return to media operating in the public interest is possible and in demand.

A Newspaper Plutocracy

Hedge fund and private equity investment and ownership over the last twenty years has created a newspaper plutocracy, an elite, wealth-driven oligopoly destabilizing and eroding the constitutionally protected entity entrusted with informing citizens in a democracy. We have known about the threat of corporate newspaper ownership for decades through the work of scholars whose critiques have helped shape our understanding of this profit-above-all-else focus and advertiser influence.[12] Yet the conditions over the last twenty years have only worsened as private investment funds have burrowed deeper into the chain newspaper and television marketplace and as local reporting disappears. While the legal system for years put guardrails on the Federal Communications Commission, which was seemingly intent on relaxing rules meant to protect against consolidation that harms the public interest, recent decisions have eliminated those guardrails. In 2021 the US Supreme Court issued its unanimous verdict in the *FCC v. Prometheus Radio Project* case, agreeing with the regulator's position. Justice Brett Kavanaugh wrote, "The FCC explained that permitting efficient combinations among radio stations, television stations, and newspapers would benefit consumers."[13] That decision, eleven years after the Supreme Court's *Citizens United* ruling gave voice to corporate power, has eroded safeguards enacted to separate broadcast and newspaper ownership so power does not consolidate.

Alden Global Capital now owns two of the country's top chains, Digital First Media and Tribune, putting it in charge of prominent newspapers, among them the *Baltimore Sun*, the *Chicago Tribune*, and the *San Jose Mercury News*. Former MediaNews Group head Dean Singleton said of Alden's *Denver Post* operation: "It's like watching your mother or father go into hospice."[14] Cerberus Capital Management, a private equity firm that manages $55 billion in assets, provided a substantial part of Alden's financing to buy Tribune.[15] Chatham Asset Management, a New Jersey hedge fund, owns McClatchy and its newspapers, including the *Kansas City Star*, which has had five owners since 1977.[16] Fortress Investment Group's ownership of GateHouse and later New Media Investment Group, and the hundreds of newspapers under its private equity umbrella, left communities such as Beaver County, Pennsylvania, with little watchdog coverage after layoffs. Gannett and Lee Enterprises, two publicly traded chains and among the largest in America, have powerful private equity investment. One of Gannett's largest institutional investors is BlackRock, Inc., the private fund with nearly $10 trillion in assets under management. In October 2022 Gannett announced a new round of cuts and furloughs. Apollo Global Management, another private fund with $481 million in assets under management as of September 2021, gained a voice on Gannett's board of directors after financing its 2019 merger with GateHouse at an interest rate of 11.5 percent.[17] In 2022 Apollo, with another fund, sought ownership of Gannett's former television properties in a deal worth more than $8 billion.

These firms have done such tremendous damage to the newspaper marketplace in the name of profit that their actions have raised the alarm of small-town officials and US senators.[18] In 2019 Denver mayor Michael B. Hancock said of Alden's *Denver Post* ownership, "For a New York hedge fund to treat our paper like a mere balance sheet entry and not an institution that is a critical part of our civic fabric, is terribly short-sighted."[19] In November 2019 the US House of Representatives Committee on Financial Services held a hearing called "America for Sale? An Examination of the Practices of Private Funds," and congressional members expressed concerns about the state of the news media under private fund ownership.[20] In a March 12, 2020, letter to Alden's Heath Freeman, Illinois senators Tammy Duckworth and Richard Durbin wrote about the hedge fund's "disturbing history of gutting newspaper's workforce and assets."[21] Freeman's March 27, 2020, response, marked "CONFIDENTIAL," called media coverage of the chain misleading and noted it allows editorial independence.[22] Editorial independence is a funny way to explain syphoning away any resources that would empower journalists to do their jobs. Yet as the cacophony of voices concerned about Alden grew, so, too, did its control.

Political Spending

While individual conflicts of interest pose ethical problems in journalism, institutional conflicts of interest are a far greater threat to democracy, especially when the pressure for profits leads private funds as owners or investors to cut newsroom staff and lobby Congress and other federal agencies, including the US Securities and Exchange Commission, on a range of issues that influence the funds' bottom line.[23] Kevin Phillips, writing about the financial crisis of the 2000s, said: "Far more worrisome is the possibility that neither Washington nor Wall Street is willing to confront the deeper problem—the ascendency of finance in national policymaking."[24] OpenSecrets, the nonpartisan and nonprofit site dedicated to tracking money in politics, says this of the securities and investment sector: "Traditionally, the securities and investment industry's political influence efforts were led by stockbrokers, bond dealers and brokerage houses, but as Wall Street itself has evolved, and likewise Washington's interest in regulating the new frontiers of finance, the industry's Washington money game is now dominated by a new breed: hedge funds and private investment firms."[25] In 2021 the securities and investment sector spent $78.2 million on lobbying, with $104 million spent the year before.

Not all firms classified in that sector have ties to media, but some of the most notable names in the local newspaper and television marketplace spend big. Apollo, BlackRock, Blackstone, and Cerberus all spent more than $1 million on lobbying in 2020, with Oaktree Capital Management also on the list. Those firms appear consistently in other years, including in 2011 alongside Aurelius Capital Management and Ariel Investments, key funds at Tribune before and during its bankruptcy.[26] They spend big in areas related to banking, bankruptcy, and in other areas they invest in, some with public finance or public safety implications that newspapers in a functioning, robust system would cover and investigate.

Increasingly, these firms with influence over newsroom staffing levels are spending tens of millions of dollars annually lobbying for their omnibus business interests. Fortress spent $532,500 on lobbying in 2009, which included expenditures from its Florida East Coast Railway subsidiary.[27] That year, as its GateHouse chain also faced debt from a series of newspaper mergers and acquisitions, one of the top issues Fortress lobbied for was related to bankruptcy.[28] In 2018 Fortress invested more than $3 billion on rail in Florida as public officials raised questions and fought in court about environmental impacts, financing, and the safety of Fortress's plans.[29] In the years since, as Fortress collected millions of fees from Gannett, the newspaper company also laid off dozens in Florida, including staff responsible for covering its rail deals and use of tax-exempt bonds to finance them.[30] What these firms will do for profit seems boundless, and a future that does not include a system of watchdogs and reporters empowered to tell those stories is troubling. Maybe the point isn't to have robust newspaper coverage in the first place but rather to have a news media system that is a lapdog to the funds' growth and power, not to mention to other industries and politicians they pay to influence.

Political Influence

Both major political parties have top-level ties to this newspaper plutocracy. Cerberus's chairman is John Snow, the US Treasury secretary under Republican president George H. W. Bush.[31] Bush's vice president, Dan Quayle, has been Cerberus's chairman and advisor for decades.[32] A US Office of Government Ethics filing shows that a counselor to the former secretary of the US Treasury Department in the Trump administration who was appointed in February 2017 declared a position in two separate Alden funds. More recently, the deputy US Treasury secretary under President Joseph Biden was tapped for that position after serving at the Obama Foundation. Before that, he was at BlackRock.[33]

BlackRock alumni serve as Biden's top economic advisor and Vice President Kamala Harris's chief economic officer, respectively. A fast track between private funds and government is concerning, providing access that an average citizen could never have.

These funds also turn to campaign contributions, spreading money to individual candidates as well as Democratic and Republican party machines, according to an analysis of data on campaign finance between 2006 and 2018 compiled from OpenSecrets.[34] (OpenSecrets is the organization formed from the 2021 merger of the Center for Responsive Politics and the National Institute on Money in Politics that tracks and publishes state and federal campaign finance data.) Fortress, Apollo, Chatham, and Oaktree executives combined to give more than $1.2 million to the Republican National Committee. Without Chatham, that same list of funds gave nearly $1 million in donations in 2012 to the Romney Victory Fund in support of Mitt Romney, a cofounder of private equity firm Bain Capital who ran unsuccessfully for president as the Republican nominee in 2012 and represents Utah in the US Senate.[35] Staffers from Oaktree, which battled for years in the Tribune bankruptcy case and emerged as part owner, also gave to the RNC and in 2010 gave thousands to Orrin Hatch, the Republican senator who had chaired the powerful US Senate Finance Committee, which time and again addressed debt and equity issues in bankruptcy law without action. Between 2013 and 2018 the securities and investment sector gave Hatch $627,700, and that includes payments from Blackstone, JPMorgan, Goldman Sachs, and the National Association of Broadcasters.[36] Employees of Apollo and Fortress combined to give nearly $300,000 to the Obama Victory Fund, while Alden Global Capital's founder, Randall Smith, gave to the National Republican Congressional Committee in 2012, and he gave other donations to the Republican National Committee in other years. Wesley Edens, a Fortress executive, gave to Democratic presidential nominee Hillary Clinton in 2016 alongside other Fortress staff; contributions to Clinton from people who listed their employer as Apollo, Fortress, or Oaktree reached more than $190,000 over the years reviewed.

For funds that unapologetically state that their goal is to boost returns above all else, this money must be an effective strategy to win influence, or else it would be classified as nothing more than fat in the budget. The bigger issue in documenting the political ties to the newspaper plutocracy is how well legislation cultivated in recent years to address the local newspaper crisis can function on behalf of citizens, given this influence.

Craig I. Forman, former McClatchy CEO and president, compiled in October 2021 for Harvard's Shorenstein Center proposals and solutions, among them several bills considered in the 117th Congress.[37] That list included the Local Journalism Sustainability Act. By revising IRS code, the act would have offered tax credits to subscribers, advertisers, and owners, including nonprofit newsrooms and current chains.[38] Rick Edmonds, writing for the Poynter Institute for Media Studies, stated that the act could infuse society with fifty thousand journalism jobs and estimated that the taxpayer impacts of such a push would reach $1 billion, because each job would mean a $20,000 tax credit.[39] The *New York Times*, which would not be eligible for the funds, reported that news outlets could get nearly $1.7 billion under the act. If the act was approved, Gannett could have received $37.5 million in the first year, and both Alden- and Chatham-owned chains also would have been eligible.[40] The private equity industry spends more than $100 million a year lobbying the very institution responsible for creating legislation that leads to bills that empower that industry, which through its newspaper ownership controls a majority of US daily circulation. We need journalists working across America, but to compromise on legislation that benefits the private investment funds, which for years have created conditions responsible for the crisis, seems like handing the keys to the fox guarding the hen house.

Yet one minor change could ensure that hedge fund owners are kept away from the money and still support newspaper jobs. The Local Journalism Sustainability Act states that to be eligible, a newspaper employer must show that "substantially all of the gross receipts of such employer for such calendar quarter are derived from the trade or business of publishing print or digital publications."[41] One way to ensure that the money in that act or any other that manages to make it past a committee incentivizes building jobs and supporting family or independent newspapers would be to treat the hedge funds as the employer rather than the newspaper company. That would limit hedge fund ownership as a qualifying employer because of the funds' investments in fields outside of publishing, outlined in chapter 3. While McClatchy, Digital First, and Tribune would be eligible, their hedge fund owners would not. Any legislative solution that involves private investment owners or chains beholden to institutional investors should require more robust disclosures and oversight of how the money is earmarked as well as harsher policies for violations. If the legislative will exists to create new initiatives to support local journalism, then it should extend to enforcement of the existing US regulatory scheme already operating in the public interest, a scheme that has consistently failed over the last twenty years.

Antitrust: Taming the Oligopoly

When private equity billionaire Sam Zell purchased Tribune, which counted the Chicago Cubs among its holdings, a majority of Major League Baseball owners had to weigh in on the deal.[42] Gilbert Cranberg, a former *Des Moines*

Register editorial page editor, wrote: "It's surreal that an institution so essential to democratic society can fall into the hands of money grubbers with no commitment to a community, even criminal types, while communities are powerless to prevent it." He continued: "It's bizarre—even an outrage—that there are more safeguards over ownership of a baseball team than over who operates the most important First Amendment franchise in town."[43] Yet despite concerns about civic interest, and now fifteen years after that Zell deal, consolidation at the top of the newspaper market has further upended the industry and its public service mission. Taming private investment funds in the newspaper market could happen without new legislation but with existing enforcement of antitrust policy.

Vigorous enforcement of the Clayton Act could rein in these private investment funds that have created an oligopoly and an interdependent relationship among rivals with implications for the US newspaper market and beyond it. The Clayton Act could provide barriers to the small clique of investment funds hovering over the US newspaper market. Passed in 1914, the Clayton Act was designed to strengthen competition and fill gaps in the Sherman Act, the first federal antitrust law.[44] While the Sherman Act was designed to curb monopolistic practices, the Clayton Act addressed cavities, among them interlocking directorates, joint ventures, and mergers that also led to increased and concentrated business power.[45] Section 8 of the Clayton Act prohibits interlocking directorates, which exist when a person on the board of directors or the officer of one company holds the same position for a competitor. For the *Seton Hall Law Review*, Judith Witterschein explained the history of the newer law's aims: "Included among these practices were interlocking directorates, which the President denounced as having the effect of concentrating control of wealth in the hands of a few."[46] The federal government's horizontal merger guidelines also show that it should be possible to prohibit mergers that go beyond simply eliminating competition to address those that "enhance market power by increasing the risk of coordinated, accommodating, or interdependent behavior among rivals."[47]

Concerns about the interpretation of interlocking directorates and corporate connections evading regulation date back decades. Robert Jay Preminger's work on "indirect interlocking directorates" in the *Washington University Law Quarterly* explained that even without shared board seats, firms exert pressure in markets: "The indirect interlock has consequently become a common and invaluable means of achieving anticompetitive intercorporate communication and control."[48] Through board connections, financing, and distressed debt investments, an elite and small group of firms operates in the newspaper marketplace that would be worthy of the scrutiny Preminger argued for and Witterschein articulated. Michelle Harner wrote in a 2016 piece for the *Indiana Law Journal*: "In reality, debt financing can cause management to take excessive risks, limit the company's future operational and restructuring alternatives, and make the company vulnerable to takeover bids by distressed debt investors." Harner said that one way to improve the transparency of debt investors would be to include more shareholder disclosures with the US Securities and Exchange Commission.[49] Building on Harner's work, I showed in chapter 5 that behind the consolidated market and its two hedge fund owners exists a small oligopoly of lenders and traders in distressed debt markets targeting newspapers, and these firms have shared years of deal-making that has been all but ignored in antitrust policy. While I focus here on interlocks and interdependence, Steven Waldman has argued that the federal government could use the Clayton Act and existing FCC policy to address important concerns about the loss of localism in journalism markets after mergers.[50]

Several funds have had quite a run as a small club in the newspaper market, and the longer newspapers stay distressed, the more they become targets of these funds. Cerberus's loan floated hedge fund Alden's purchase of Tribune.[51] Cerberus has ties to other private investment funds stretching back two decades. In 2005 a *Columbia Business Law Review* article called both Oaktree and Cerberus among the world's largest hedge funds at the time, explaining their control of and connections to other firms in distressed debt markets.[52] The other funds outlined in that article will look familiar from the other chapters in this book on mergers and acquisitions and debt: Angelo, Gordon & Co., which with Oaktree and JPMorgan emerged in control of Tribune after its bankruptcy. At the time the article was published, Angelo, Gordon had an $850 million partnership with Fortress. Outside of newspapers, Oaktree and Cerberus jointly owned Formica Corporation, while Apollo and Oaktree shared board seats at NTL Inc. and Spectrasite Holdings. That *Columbia* article also showed that Oaktree held board seats at Sunbeam alongside Bank of America and Morgan Stanley. Cerberus's chairman, John Snow, also has had seats on the boards of Bank of America, US Steel, and Verizon. Over the years, Alden has owned shares in Bank of America, Morgan Stanley, and Oaktree Capital's Oaktree Specialty Lending Co.[53] Anthony Melchiorre, Chatham's head, worked as a banker at both Goldman Sachs and Morgan Stanley.[54] Work published in *Mass Communication and Society* in 2021 outlined connections between boards—interlocks—at more than a dozen newspaper companies and parent companies, including Alden Global Capital, Digital First, Gannett, and Lee Enterprises. The interlocking connections showed that in the five-year period leading up to 2017, the boards had 1,276 connections to 530 organizations. Survey responses from editors at the chains the study reviewed revealed that about one-third experienced pressure from the board of directors or parent company.[55] Essentially, these firms and their executives operating in distressed debt markets or as newspaper owners appear as an interconnected system alongside major US banks that federal law more than one hundred years ago intended to prevent.

These are not impartial connections but those that create what scholars Soontae An and Hyun Seung Jin two decades ago said created "interfirm resource dependence." In their study of thirteen publicly traded newspaper companies, the authors determined that the greater the debt-to-equity ratio, the more involvement financial institutions had on boards.[56] Jennifer Harker, publishing in 2020 on interlocks and explicitly noting the trends in hedge fund ownership, included connections to advertising agencies and financial firms: "Financial interlocks are having long-lasting negative effects on the reshaping of directorships, even inciting directorship wars."[57] While the chains themselves give the appearance of more owners, the reality is that two hedge funds own three of the largest and most influential newspaper chains, and private equity influences others.

In antitrust regulation, this small number represents not a monopoly but an oligopoly, and there is precedent for barring this type of ownership structure, even preemptively. Jeffrey Manns considered that the real problem of regulation is not just monopoly power at places like Amazon, Facebook, and Google but in oligopolies. Manns, writing for the *Indiana Law Journal,* noted that monopoly enforcement also tends to focus on anticompetitive pricing, but federal regulation is meant to stop what he called "collusion among oligopolies" and should limit mergers and acquisitions. Noting the impact on market concentration, Manns wrote: "The problem is often not the market power of any individual oligopolistic actor, but rather the aggregate power of actors in concentrated markets to shape the terms of the marketplace in anticompetitive ways."[58] Moreover, seeing the consolidation and growth of these firms in this period of financialization should lead to expanded definitions of interlocking directorates. The existence of the shared connections is enough to raise concerns, but there also could be a definitional expansion to include financing and industry connections as an expanded view of interlocking directorates in the market.

Outside of the US Justice Department and the SEC, the Federal Trade Commission is clear on its role overseeing mergers and the threat they pose, creating what the agency calls "lower-quality goods": "Merger law is generally forward-looking: it bars mergers that may lead to harmful effects."[59] Speaking of news quality in a democracy, these funds' control has created lower-quality newspapers, and that on its own should trigger blockage of future mergers and acquisitions. Even setting aside that two hedge funds own three top chains—an ownership structure itself veering toward monopoly—both antitrust policy and communications regulation already provide safeguards against mergers and acquisitions that consolidate power and leave chains in debt that threatens their existence, while regulating Big Tech has implications, too. Regulating platforms like Facebook has received important scrutiny (including scrutiny of its draining of advertising revenue away from newspapers), but legislative fixes aimed at curbing their influence actually may help newspapers by looking to stop harmful mergers. Minnesota senator Amy Klobuchar, a Democrat, has proposed legislation seeking to amend the Clayton Act, putting the burden on merging companies to demonstrate that their consolidation would not harm competition.[60] Her bill seeks stronger protection against mergers that lower quality or reduce innovation. The bill's text reads: "Undue market concentration also contributes to the consolidation of political power, undermining the health of democracy in the United States."[61] It could easily apply to newspapers.

"The Point Is to Have the Journalism"

What unites many activists, journalists, and scholars is an understanding that to reinvigorate local democracies, profit harvesting by these elite financial firms must be removed from communities' information ecosystems. While I argue for stronger antitrust enforcement, I also want to address shifting market forces and plans to remove the funds. According to James Fallows, "The same papers that are doomed under private-equity ownership might have a chance in some different economic structure."[62] Waldman, who founded Report for America, a service program focused on placing reporters in newsrooms across the United States, recognizes the dangers of hedge fund ownership, and he charted a plan that would have hedge funds donate their newspapers, thus creating a path back to local ownership.[63] Victor Pickard and Timothy Neff have argued for a media system that is funded publicly.[64] More recently, Robert W. McChesney and John Nichols suggested the need for the Local Journalism Initiative, a government-funded plan that would benefit nonprofit newsrooms to boost local community awareness.[65] What I know, like the others, is that a local news system that removes the locust, vampire, and vulture funds is automatically one that will fight for the communities where it operates, not to exploit those communities but to empower them.

But this book also shows me that no one business or financing model will recapture what has been lost in these last twenty years as social media also has gripped audiences' attention and, with it, concerns about misinformation, hate speech, and rapid political polarization.[66] As such, I close the book looking at news organizations operating in various forms with a public interest mission. I think the power lies there. News organizations today without the extreme influence of hedge fund owners and private equity investors stand in sharp contrast to the chains withering under their weight. Many, including family-owned newspapers, independent sites, and digital nonprofit outlets, do crucial work. Much of that work is not just in the shadow of our crisis but in response to it.

Family-Owned Newspapers

In South Carolina the loss of local news has led to journalistic innovation and new partnerships at the family-owned *Post and Courier* in Charleston. The newspaper staff had been investigating South Carolina sheriffs, several of whom had been indicted. An editor noticed that many of those problems of unchecked law enforcement power occurred in rural parts of the state without daily newspaper coverage—in places described by Penelope Muse Abernathy as "news deserts"—or with weakened coverage upheld by small weeklies without budgets to pay for basics like public records fees and rent. Glenn Smith, a Pulitzer Prize–winning investigations editor at the South Carolina daily, launched a series called "Uncovered."[67] "What if we went into those areas—to news deserts—to try to tell those stories that aren't being told," Smith recalled of the series' origins.[68] In explaining the rationale behind "Uncovered," the newspaper website says, "At the same time, cost-cutting corporate chains and hedge funds scooped up newspapers and axed reporting staffs to squeeze out more profits."[69]

Smith knows reporters and editors at some of those newspapers, and he provided context on an important contrast in profit targets and his ability to do work at a family-owned newspaper company compared to theirs: "For my peers in corporate chains, it's more about hitting that mark. If that means bodies go out the door, bodies go out the door. Any company needs to make profit, but at a family-owned paper there is that sense of family. It pains them to do layoffs. They also have this deep sense of community mission. They know that cutting staff is going to harm coverage. You do it as a last resort. They were willing to share in that financial loss to make sure the paper does not suffer." Smith started his newspaper career in 1987 at small newspapers in the suburbs of Hartford, Connecticut, before landing at the *Post and Courier*. He is not averse to the economic swings the newspaper industry has faced. In 2009 the Charleston-based newspaper did what Smith referred to as "select layoffs," and leadership enacted furloughs. At the end of that year, the owners told staff members that the revenue downturn was not as bad as anticipated. Management returned pay to newsroom staff.

Pay and basic morale offer one difference between hedge funds and family owners. Other differences come in coverage and impact. South Carolina's largest daily newspaper, the *Post and Courier*, punches well above its weight class, including through the work of its six-person projects team. It counts a 2015 Pulitzer Prize for public service among its accomplishments, and it has been a finalist six times since 2011, including most recently for local reporting in 2021.[70] Smith sees the impact of this work for audiences, noting that investigations drive both subscriptions and web traffic. "It's a no-brainer," Smith said. "This is unique content that you can't get anywhere else. It's what people want to read." Smith's team has bolstered partnerships with seventeen of the state's news organizations to look after South Carolina's hundreds of local governments and special purpose districts, creating a searchable database for public use.

Smith and I both grew up in Connecticut reading the *Hartford Courant*, a newspaper with colonial roots. We talked for a few minutes during our October 2021 interview about our hometown newspaper, remembering its award-winning 1992 series called "Streets of Despair," which focused on the capital city's competing crises of addiction, AIDS, and prostitution.[71] Tribune, in December 2020 by then with nearly one-third of its shares controlled by Alden, closed the newspaper's headquarters on Broad Street, where photojournalists, editors, and reporters had planned and executed that series and others credited with revamping Connecticut's legislation around addiction and treatment, a model copied by other places nationwide.[72] The closure came two months after the newspaper celebrated its 256th anniversary, a fact noted in Tribune's 2020 annual report. That same Form 10-K noted that the newspaper's 2020 staffing levels were down 30 percent from the prior year as a result of Tribune's "strategy to flatten its management organization."[73] Those cuts came despite Tribune's windfall selling of BestReviews to Nexstar for $160 million, another company Alden has invested in. On the phone, Smith noted the stark difference at the Connecticut daily between 1992 and today. "Now it's just," Smith paused. "It's looking pretty rough."

Nonprofit News

Another paper also influenced during this era by Alden escaped a similar fate. The *Salt Lake Tribune* is notable for being the first major newspaper to switch to 501(c)(3) nonprofit status. In January 2021 leadership provided readers an update on its transition, with its executive editor writing: "We are a 150-year-old startup." An editorial cartoon accompanying the piece read: "Radio Couldn't Kill Us. TV Couldn't Kill Us. The Internet Couldn't Kill Us. 2020 Couldn't Kill Us."[74] It could have added another: "Alden Global Capital Couldn't Kill Us," as it had spent several years in MediaNews Group's portfolio. At the time of its nonprofit move, the paper explained: "In the last 15 years, our country has lost almost 2,000 newspapers. And The Tribune was nearly one of them. We couldn't let that happen."[75] In November 2021 executive editor Lauren Gustus updated readers on developments, which included a 23 percent boost in the size of the paper's newsroom staff, the creation of the three-person Innovation Lab reporting team, the start of a 401(k) match, and paid parental leave. Gustus wrote: "The Tribune will welcome more journalists in 2022, because you've told us many times over that this is what you want and because if we are not holding those in public office to account, there are few others who will."[76]

The Institute for Nonprofit News lists more than four hundred newsrooms operating in October 2022. Nonprofit newsrooms, documented by Magda Konieczna in *Journalism without Profit*, consider their public service mission essential.[77] I talked to nonprofit newsroom founders and editors in Columbus, Ohio; Ft. Lauderdale, Florida; Ithaca, New York; Jacksonville, Florida; New Orleans; and San Jose, California, to hear about that mission today. After Hurricane Katrina, as New Orleans started to rebuild, Karen Gadbois saw an opportunity in the void there, watching as the local newspaper faced cuts and consolidation. She thought: "There may be a place for us."[78] Gadbois cofounded The Lens, which can boast some of the most-coveted prizes in journalism, including a Peabody Award and an Alfred I. duPont Award. The Society of Professional Journalists awarded Gadbois its Ethics in Journalism Award in 2012 for her reporting on police policy to release murder victims' criminal records. In California, Ramona Giwargis founded the *San Jose Spotlight*. She had worked at the *Mercury News* and at the *Las Vegas Review-Journal*, and both provided opportunities for her to see a for-profit system unable to address its community's needs. "What got cut was local," Giwargis told me in July 2020. "People were craving local journalism. 'What did the planning commission decide?' That's the kind of journalism they want. That's the type of journalism that suffered." At the time of our interview, Giwargis had marshaled those community concerns and needs into a growing nonprofit newsroom funded through donations, allowing her to hire three full-time reporters.

While work through nonprofits founded by Gadbois and Giwargis covers cities and local issues, other sites are finding their niche covering content areas. Nonprofit newsrooms are covering regional ecology, justice, and culture issues like *Southerly*; the intersection of poverty, power, and policy at the Memphis-based *MLK50: Justice Through Journalism*; and the environment at *Inside Climate News*. The industry today includes powerhouses like ProPublica and the Center for Public Integrity and small sites like Columbus, Ohio's *Matter News*, which in 2020 was operating with a mostly volunteer staff and a $30,000 annual budget out of cofounder Cassie Young's living room.[79] "Local news often lacks diversity or context. We're here to bring it," its website reads.[80] In October 2020 I spoke with Andrew Pantazi, who at the time was an award-winning investigative reporter at the Gannett-owned *Florida Times-Union*. Pantazi, who had tracked Gannett layoffs, told me: "I sympathize with readers who want to support journalism, but I have a hard time telling them subscribing is going to support journalism. The company doesn't care about reinvesting that money. I want to see the paper continue to exist, but I don't know if it's worth saving. This business model is not healthy for democracy." In late 2020 Pantazi left the newspaper and launched a nonprofit news outlet focused on "investigating racism, poverty and barriers to opportunity" in Jacksonville called *The Tributary*.[81] He publishes online in the city where he has worked for a decade that also is his hometown. He was weighing that move when we spoke, and his enthusiasm for the field differed sharply from his frustration with Gannett. "The point is to have the journalism," Pantazi said, "not for there to be a thing called the *Florida Times-Union*." *Matter News* and *The Tributary* are among hundreds of nonprofit newsrooms that are not just a phenomenon unto themselves but growing as a direct result of the loss of public accountability reporting in newspaper markets decimated by private investment funds.

Studying these innovations and talking to newsroom founders working in the void has left me hopeful for the state of the field itself, a broader view of digital journalism beyond just newspapers. The nonprofit and independent media system emerging in response to our crisis can provide accountability reporting and provide paths to more equitable news in the public interest. People will support high-quality news if they are offered something worth paying for. But we are entering a period of extreme fragmentation, and what works in Salt Lake City may not work in Schenectady, New York. Audiences must be reengaged with a system that is providing them local and subject-matter news content that can inform their civic lives as an entire generation has grown up seeing it disintegrate. And $1 billion redirected from legislation that benefits for-profit newspapers to the Institute for Nonprofit News could mean better local journalism and engagement across the country.

Independent For-Profit News

Nonprofit news outlets are not the only reputable, reliable, or dependable outlets working today, and the void left by corporate chains and private investment funds has spun off other sites with innovative business models. Among them is S. Mitra Kalita's work in Queens, New York, an effort described as decentralizing the news.[82] She wrote: "Our Epicenter-NYC community rests on the simple but revolutionary idea that we journalists often do not have the answers. You do. Our role is one of disseminating, facilitating, connecting, enabling, spotlighting."[83] Epicenter is under the umbrella of URL Media, which Kalita cofounded as a network, building on the work of organizations like the *Haitian Times* and focused on "journalism in service of community." That for-profit list operating in the public interest also includes sports and culture site *Defector*, which was launched by a group of journalists who fled *Deadspin* after it was gutted by Great Hill Partners, its private equity owner.[84] After its first year, *Defector* had thirty-six thousand active subscribers, who were responsible for 95 percent of its $3.2 million in revenue. More than half of that funds employee compensation and benefits.[85]

Facing the Future

Private investment funds are a barrier to high-quality reporting, but incredible public-interest work still gets done at these chains I have critiqued. The Gannett-owned *Indianapolis Star* in 2016 published work implicating USA Gymnastics and its role in team doctor Larry Nassar's years of sexual abuse.[86] After its reporting, 150 women stepped forward to accuse the disgraced doctor, who is serving a 175-year prison sentence. In December 2019 at the *Miami Herald*, part of the McClatchy chain before and since Chatham took control, investigative reporter Julie K. Brown broke the story of politically connected multimillionaire Jeffrey Epstein's years of sex trafficking. Brown's reporting also showed that Epstein received leniency from a prosecutor who went on to serve as Donald Trump's labor secretary.[87] This is headline-making work, and it is crucial. But imagine how much more those journalists still at hedge fund newsrooms and other corporate chains could do if they were not constrained by the financial world's locusts. What's overwhelmingly lost in this investment and ownership structure is the day-to-day accountability checks in small towns and cities after people like Kristen Doerschner are laid off. That has consequences for communities nationwide.

I cannot help but worry how stronger private investment fund ownership will limit future investigative and community beat work as newspapers move ahead under a more efficient and empowered oligarchy and trust further disintegrates. Leon Black, Apollo's billionaire cofounder, had financial ties to Epstein.[88] Consider a newspaper company beholden to Black and a firm's investment allowing reporting like Brown's to move through. Then consider that Apollo, after financing a megamerger in 2019, gained a voice over operations at Gannett.[89] Local newspaper coverage can keep corporate management in check, and its disappearance may be good news for misconduct, according to work from researchers, including Jonas Heese, Gerardo Pérez-Cavazos, and Caspar David Peter at Harvard Business School.[90] Outside of corruption and criminal activity is the threat of news that ignores issues such as corporate corruption and climate change because it doesn't have the staff or fears market swings. In a September 2019 piece for the *New Yorker*, Bill McKibben said that BlackRock's ties to the fossil fuel industry mean that "no one else is trying as diligently to make money off the destruction of the planet."[91] Imagine reliable climate coverage from a news company beholden to a firm like that, and then consider that BlackRock has owned shares of both Gannett and Lee Enterprises.

While I lament the loss of strong local newspapers, I understand that hidden among the righteousness and the memories of wrongs righted by newspapers exists a darker side. Even before private investment fund control, as newspapers made stratospheric revenue for family and chain owners, low-income citizens and people of color were left out of many editors' day-to-day decision-making. Robert Spencer Knotts, sixty-eight, a former *Sun-Sentinel* investigative reporter, remembered this of Tribune executives: "They were very happy pandering to the white readers that were the bulk of their circulation because that's who advertisers wanted. The system, on some levels, was very rotten."[92] I hope there is opportunity on the flip side to our local newspaper crisis, scaffolding the parts that worked and fixing those that didn't. I also hope it's not too late. Writing about climate threats and rising authoritarianism, Perry Parks expressed a need for "a jolt in journalism theory commensurate with the urgent state of planetary affairs that journalism's weaknesses have helped to precipitate and that its strengths might help to contain."[93] Assessing the newspaper industry and its decline means facing hard truths about what worked throughout its history and admitting what failed as citizens face this future. The alternative is even more troubling.

The rise of hedge fund ownership comes against the backdrop of a great partisan divide across America, a divide that researchers have found is exacerbated by a loss of local newspapers and growing due to hyperpartisan sites funded by dark money designed to look like local news.[94] While nonprofit news and independent sites are helping to fill the void, what's worse is that corporations, too, are using information channels to create content, and these hyperpartisan outlets are shaping our understanding of politics, social justice, and inequality itself absent a strong local news ecosystem. Multinational energy company Chevron launched a website designed to look like local news.[95] There also is a growing stable of "pink slime" outlets, which Priyanjana Bengani has shown look like digital local news that "further partisan talking points and collect user data."[96] Democratic society is feeling these effects. In October 2022 more than 370 candidates running for office were campaigning on the lie that a democratically viable election was rigged.[97] Perhaps there has never been a greater need for independent newspapers and the connection and authority their coverage has provided communities historically, especially considering that nationally produced social media, cable, and talk radio content driving local conversations everywhere has partisanship as a feature, not a bug. We are in a battle for facts, truth, and democracy itself. And we have a market, legislative, and regulatory system that has failed at nearly every turn.

The product of that failure is a newspaper system, a local television network, and an online echo chamber run and influenced by elites with ties to multinational businesses and political party machines increasingly leaving average citizens out of the most essential debates that impact them but inflaming others. Maybe that is the point. Alongside the erosion of public interest newspaper journalism is a domination of political deal-making and a growing wealth gap. US Census figures show that in 2021 nearly 12 percent of Americans lived in poverty, while the number of billionaires and their influence over the economy grows.[98] Private investment funds impact sectors that help that poverty fester: everything from high-interest loans to housing and pharmaceuticals to insurance is touched by their greed. It is the very inequality that news organizations should address, but that coverage will disappear as private investment funds continue to thrive in an increasingly deregulated marketplace. News organizations increasingly have been stripped of power to investigate issues, and we are left as a society with few institutions that will.

The press and its relationship to society is certainly due for both a reckoning and a radical rethink for reasons articulated in my concept of the private investment era and for those beyond its scope. I also know that we cannot keep blaming the internet alone for a structural crisis perpetuated by some of the world's wealthiest funds. So, I hope this work further helps shift part of the blame for our local newspaper crisis away from the internet to where it belongs: onto the private investment funds that for years have gutted local newspapers and grown wealthier off the backs of what is left of them. My hope is that this work, by providing a map of the last twenty years, follows other structural critiques and watchdog work concerned not just about the existence of this control but also about how the hunt for it extracts agency and power from average citizens. Understanding the core issues means better solutions, and we can and should demand a media system that benefits democracy. Considering all of these important issues, what is clearer to me now than it was five years ago when I sat for that NBC News *THINK* interview is that whatever potential exists for newspapers to investigate and to address a myriad of issues on behalf of society cannot exist under private investment fund control. All eras must end.

Notes

Introduction: What Crisis?

1. "Margot Susca: Local News Doesn't Have a Profit Problem, Corporations Do," NBCNews.com, NBCUniversal News Group, January 22, 2018, https://www.nbcnews.com/think/video/margot-susca-local-news-doesn-t-have-a-profit-problem-corporations-do-1142609987867.

2. "FCC Modernizes Broadcast Ownership Rules," Federal Communications Commission, November 16, 2017, https://www.fcc.gov/document/fcc-modernizes-broadcast-ownership-rules.

3. Nexstar Media Group, Inc., Form 10-K, annual report for the fiscal year ended December 31, 2017 (February 28, 2018), https://sec.report/Document/0001564590-18-003921/; "FCC Fact Sheet: Review of the Commission's Broadcast Ownership Rules, Joint Sales Agreements, and Shared Services Agreements, and Comment Sought on an Incubator Program," n.d., https://docs.fcc.gov/public/attachments/DOC-347796A2.pdf.

4. "Rosenworcel Statement, FCC Modernizes Broadcast Ownership Rules," Federal Communications Commission, November 16, 2017, https://www.fcc.gov/document/fcc-modernizes-broadcast-ownership-rules/rosenworcel-statement.

5. "Prometheus v FCC Is Going to the Supreme Court," Prometheus Radio Project, https://www.prometheusradio.org/prometheus-v-fcc-going-supreme-court.

6. Opinion of the court, Prometheus Radio Project et al., v. Federal Communications Commission et al., nos. 17–1107, 17–1109, 17–1110, 17–1111, https://www2.ca3.uscourts.gov/opinarch/171107p.pdf.

7. Brief for Gray Television, Inc., as Amicus Curiae, Federal Communications Commission et al., v. Prometheus Radio Project et al., nos. 19–1231 and 19–1241 (2020), *SCOTUSblog*,

https://www.supremecourt.gov/DocketPDF/19/19-1231/143930/20200520153611355
_39832%20Anderson%20Brief.pdf; Amy Howe, "Federal Communications Commission v. Prometheus Radio Project," *SCOTUSblog*, January 19, 2021, https://www.scotusblog.com/case-files/cases/federal-communications-commission-v-prometheus-radio-project/.

8. "FCC v. Prometheus Radio Project," Oyez, accessed January 24, 2021, https://www.oyez.org/cases/2020/19-1231.

9. Alden Global Capital LLC, Form 13F-HR, quarterly report filed by institutional managers, holdings, filed by Broadridge Financial Solutions, Inc., with the US Securities and Exchange Commission, May 15, 2020, from US Securities and Exchange Commission website, https://sec.report/Document/0001567619-20-010364/.

10. Edmund Lee and Tiffany Hsu, "Hedge Fund Called 'Destroyer of Newspapers' Bids for USA Today Owner Gannett," *New York Times*, January 14, 2019, https://www.nytimes.com/2019/01/14/business/dealbook/gannett-takeover-offer-mng.html.

11. Alden Global Capital LLC, form 13-F, report for the quarter ending June 30, 2020, from the US Securities and Exchange Commission website, https://sec.report/Document/0001567619-20-015309/.

12. Palash Ghosh, "No End in Sight to BlackRock's Growth as It Approaches $10T," *Pensions & Investments*, November 29, 2021, 1.

13. Penny Abernathy, "The State of Local News," Local News Initiative, Northwestern University, June 29, 2022, https://localnewsinitiative.northwestern.edu/research/state-of-local-news/report/.

14. Carl O'Donnell and Liana B. Baker, "Apollo to Buy Cox TV Stations in Broadcast Push," *Reuters*, February 15, 2019, https://www.reuters.com/article/us-cox-media-m-a-apollo-glo-mgmt/apollo-to-buy-cox-tv-stations-in-broadcast-push-idUSKCN1Q42IS; "TEGNA to Be Acquired by Standard General for $24.00 per Share," Tegna Inc., February 22, 2022, https://www.tegna.com/tegna-to-be-acquired-by-standard-general-for-24-00-per-share/.

15. Hsiang Iris Chyi, Seth C. Lewis, and Nan Zheng, "A Matter of Life and Death? Examining How Newspapers Covered the Newspaper 'Crisis,'" *Journalism Studies* 13, no. 3 (2012): 305–24, https://doi.org/10.1080/1461670x.2011.629090.

16. Elizabeth Grieco, "U.S. Newspapers Have Shed Half of Their Newsroom Employees Since 2008," Pew Research Center, April 20, 2020, https://www.pewresearch.org/fact-tank/2020/04/20/u-s-newsroom-employment-has-dropped-by-a-quarter-since-2008/.

17. Michelle M. Harner, "Activist Distressed Debtholders: The New Barbarians at the Gate," *Washington University Law Review* 89, no. 1 (2011): 155–206.

18. McKay Coppins, "A Secretive Hedge Fund Is Gutting Newsrooms: Inside Alden Global Capital," *The Atlantic*, October 14, 2021, https://www.theatlantic.com/magazine/archive/2021/11/alden-global-capital-killing-americas-newspapers/620171/.

19. Jason Kelly, *The New Tycoons: Inside the Trillion Dollar Private Equity Industry That Owns Everything* (Hoboken, NJ: Wiley, 2012), xix.

20. Penelope Muse Abernathy, *The Rise of the New Media Baron and the Emerging Threats of News Deserts*, University of North Carolina at Chapel Hill, Center for Innovation and Sus-

tainability in Local Media, 2016, http://newspaperownership.com/newspaper-ownership
-report/.

21. Robert G. Picard, "Institutional Ownership of Publicly Traded US Newspaper
Companies," *Journal of Media Economics* 7, no. 4 (1994): 49–64, https://doi.org/10.1207/
s15327736me0704_4.

22. Robert G. Picard and Tony Rimmer, "Weathering a Recession: Effects of Size and
Diversification on Newspaper Companies," *Journal of Media Economics* 12, no. 1 (1999):
1–18, https://doi.org/10.1207/s15327736me1201_1; Robert G. Picard and Aldo Van
Weezel, "Capital and Control: Consequences of Different Forms of Newspaper Ownership," *International Journal on Media Management* 10, no. 1 (2008): 22–31, https://doi.org/
10.1080/14241270701820473.

23. Robert G. Picard, *The Economics and Financing of Media Companies* (New York:
Fordham University Press, 2011), viii.

24. In conversation with the author, October 2020.

25. John Nerone and Kevin G. Barnhurst, "US Newspaper Types, the Newsroom, and
the Division of Labor, 1750–2000," *Journalism Studies* 4, no. 4 (2003): 435–49, https://
doi.org/10.1080/1461670032000136541.

26. Robert G. Picard, *The Press and the Decline of Democracy: The Democratic Socialist
Response in Public Policy* (Westport, CT: Greenwood Press, 1985), 6.

27. John Stuart Mill, *Considerations on Representative Government* (Buffalo, NY: Prometheus Books, 1861).

28. Ida B. Wells, *Southern Horrors: Lynch Law in All Its Phases* (1892), https://www
.encyclopediavirginia.org/Southern_Horrors_Lynch_Law_in_All_Its_Phases_by_Ida
_B_Wells_1892.

29. C. Edwin Baker, *Human Liberty and Freedom of Speech* (New York: Oxford University Press, 1989), 263.

30. Leonard Downie Jr. and Michael Schudson, *The Reconstruction of American Journalism*, October 20, 2009, https://revsonfoundation.org/wp-content/uploads/publications/
The-Reconstruction-of-American-Journalism.pdf.

31. *Losing the News: The Decimation of Local Journalism and the Search for Solutions*, PEN
America, November 20, 2019, https://pen.org/wp-content/uploads/2019/11/Losing
-the-News-The-Decimation-of-Local-Journalism-and-the-Search-for-Solutions-Report
.pdf, quote appears on p. 4.

32. Robert W. McChesney, *Rich Media, Poor Democracy: Communication Politics in
Dubious Times* (New York: New Press, 2000), xv.

33. C. Edwin Baker, *Media, Markets, and Democracy* (Cambridge: Cambridge University
Press, 2002), 56.

34. Thomas F. Corrigan, "Making Implicit Methods Explicit: Trade Press Analysis in
the Political Economy of Communication," *International Journal of Communication* 12
(2018): 2751, https://ijoc.org/index.php/ijoc/article/view/6496.

35. On these debates, see Brian McNair, "Journalism and Democracy," in *The Handbook of Journalism Studies*, ed. Karin Wahl-Jorgensen and Thomas Hanitzsch (New York:

Routledge, 2009), 237–49, https://cpb-us-e1.wpmucdn.com/sites.psu.edu/dist/0/9235/files/2014/01/Handbook-Journalism-and-Democracy.pdf; Eli M. Noam, *Media Ownership and Concentration in America* (New York: Oxford University Press, 2009).

36. Clifford G. Christians, Theodore Glasser, Denis McQuail, Kaarle Nordenstreng, and Robert A. White, *Normative Theories of the Media: Journalism in Democratic Societies* (Urbana: University of Illinois Press, 2010); Daniel C. Hallin and Paolo Mancini, *Comparing Media Systems: Three Models of Media and Politics* (Cambridge: Cambridge University Press, 2004).

37. Ronald V. Bettig, "Private Equity, Private Media," *Democratic Communiqué* 23, no. 1 (2009), https://scholarworks.umass.edu/democratic-communique/vol23/iss1/2.

38. Rodney Benson, "Maybe Things Aren't So Bad, or Are They? Michael Schudson's Ambivalent Critique of Commercialism," *Journalism Studies* 18, no. 10 (2017): 1210–23, DOI: 10.1080/1461670X.2017.1335608, quote appears on p. 1219.

39. Robert W. McChesney and John Nichols, *The Death and Life of American Journalism: The Media Revolution That Will Begin the World Again* (New York: Nation Books, 2011), 11.

40. Victor Pickard, *Democracy without Journalism? Confronting the Misinformation Society* (New York: Oxford University Press, 2019), 89.

41. Ignacio Siles and Pablo J. Boczkowski, "Making Sense of the Newspaper Crisis: A Critical Assessment of Existing Research and an Agenda for Future Work," *New Media & Society* 14, no. 8 (2012): 1375–94, https://doi.org/10.1177/1461444812455148.

42. Margaret Sullivan, *Ghosting the News: Local Journalism and the Crisis of American Democracy* (New York: Columbia Global Reports, 2020), 95.

43. Alex S. Jones, *Losing the News: The Future of the News That Feeds Democracy* (New York: Oxford University Press, 2010), 151; Christopher William Anderson, *Rebuilding the News: Metropolitan Journalism in the Digital Age* (Philadelphia, PA: Temple University Press, 2013), 1.

44. Dean Starkman, *The Watchdog That Didn't Bark: The Financial Crisis and the Disappearance of Investigative Journalism* (New York: Columbia University Press, 2014).

45. Richard Tofel, *Why American Newspapers Gave Away the Future* (Now and Then Reader LLC, 2012); Kristen Hare, "The Coronavirus Has Closed More Than 60 Local Newsrooms across America. And Counting," *Poynter*, January 7, 2021, https://www.poynter.org/locally/2021/the-coronavirus-has-closed-more-than-60-local-newsrooms-across-america-and-counting/.

46. Marc Edge, "Newspapers' Annual Reports Show Chains Profitable," *Newspaper Research Journal* 35, no. 4 (September 2014): 66–82, https://doi.org/10.1177/07395329 1403500406; Lee Enterprises, Inc., Schedule 14A, Definitive Proxy Statement, January 15, 2021, from Lee Enterprises website, https://lee.gcs-web.com/static-files/e9d291d8-523a -4d4f-933b-1bbcca71710b.

47. IBISWorld, "US Industry Reports (NAICS)," n.d., Newspaper Publishing in the US, Report 51111, IBISWorld.

48. Ken Doctor, "Newsonomics: Alden Global Capital Is Making So Much Money Wrecking Local Journalism It Might Not Want to Stop Anytime Soon," *Nieman Lab*, May 1, 2018,

https://www.niemanlab.org/2018/05/newsonomics-alden-global-capital-is-making-so-much-money-wrecking-local-journalism-it-might-not-want-to-stop-anytime-soon/.

49. Derek Thompson, "The Collapse of Print Advertising in 1 Graph," *The Atlantic*, February 28, 2012, https://www.theatlantic.com/business/archive/2012/02/the-collapse-of-print-advertising-in-1-graph/253736/.

50. Nikki Usher, "Newsroom Moves and the Newspaper Crisis Evaluated: Space, Place, and Cultural Meaning," *Media, Culture & Society* 37, no. 7 (October 2015): 1005–21, https://doi.org/10.1177/0163443715591668.

51. Dan Kennedy, *The Return of the Moguls: How Jeff Bezos and John Henry Are Remaking Newspapers for the Twenty-First Century* (Lebanon, NH: ForeEdge, an imprint of the University Press of New England, 2018).

52. James Rufus Koren, "What's Next for Orange County Register Buyer Digital First?," *Los Angeles Times*, April 14, 2016, https://www.latimes.com/business/la-fi-digital-first-oc-20160414-story.html; Rick Edmonds, "Stewart Bainum Jr. Is Advertising for Help to Launch a 'High Profile, Well-Funded' News Startup in Baltimore," Poynter Institute for Media Studies, August 10, 2021, https://www.poynter.org/business-work/2021/stewart-bainum-jr-is-advertising-for-help-to-launch-a-high-profile-well-funded-news-startup-in-baltimore/.

53. Britt Robson, "New Owner Glen Taylor: Less Liberal Star Tribune Ahead," *Minn Post*, April 17, 2014, https://www.minnpost.com/business/2014/04/new-owner-glen-taylor-less-liberal-star-tribune-ahead/.

54. "SEC Forms List," US Securities and Exchange Commission, accessed January 12, 2021, https://www.sec.gov/forms.

55. Gannett Co. Inc., Form 10-K, annual report for the fiscal year ended December 31, 2020 (February 26, 2021), https://d18rnop25nwr6d.cloudfront.net/CIK-0001579684/738c2ddb-7f33-48c7-80f9-0c2a79094433.pdf.

56. Gannett Co. Inc., Form 10-K, annual report for the fiscal year ended December 31, 2019 (March 2, 2020), https://d18rnop25nwr6d.cloudfront.net/CIK-0001579684/b1282d40-f154-4de6-9629-a7a96f8bdfb0.pdf.

57. Adam Levy, "Can You Buy a Stock and Sell It in the Same Day?," Motley Fool, September 2, 2021, https://www.fool.com/investing/stock-market/basics/buy-and-sell-stock-same-day/.

58. David Inge, Clifford Christians, and Steve Jones, "The Career of Dean James Carey, Former Dean of the College of Communications at UIUC," Will Livestreams, University of Illinois, Illinois Public Media, October 26, 2006, https://will.illinois.edu/focus/program/focus061026a.

59. James W. Carey, "The Discovery of Objectivity," *American Journal of Sociology* 87, no. 5 (1982): 1182–88.

60. Jacob Bogage, "Gannett Will Furlough Workers at More Than 100 Newspapers over the Next Three Months," *Washington Post*, March 30, 2020, https://www.washingtonpost.com/business/2020/03/30/gannett-newspapers-furloughs/.

61. John Gittelsohn, "Controlled Choice," *Sun-Sentinel*, October 3, 2018, https://www.sun-sentinel.com/news/fl-xpm-1994-10-16-9410150348-story.html.

62. Herbert J. Gans, "What Can Journalists Actually Do for American Democracy?," *Harvard International Journal of Press/Politics* 3, no. 4 (1998): 6–12.

Chapter 1. The Private Investment Era

1. Jennifer Saba and Ben Berkowitz, "Warren Buffett to Buy Media General Newspapers," Reuters, May 17, 2012, https://www.reuters.com/article/us-mediageneral/warren
-buffett-to-buy-media-general-newspapers-idUSBRE84G0M920120517.

2. "Berkshire Hathaway Inc. 2012 Annual Report," Berkshire Hathaway Inc., https://
www.berkshirehathaway.com/2012ar/2012ar.pdf.

3. Jia Lynn Yang and Steven Mufson, "Warren Buffett in Negotiations to Relinquish
$1.1 Billion Stake in Graham Holdings," *Washington Post*, February 13, 2014, https://www
.washingtonpost.com/business/economy/warren-buffett-in-negotiations-to-relinquish
-11billion-stake-in-graham-holdings/2014/02/13/bf6d0a92-94f8-11e3-83b9-1f024193bb84
_story.html; "Lee Enterprises to Buy Berkshire Hathaway Newspaper Operations;
Berkshire Hathaway to Finance All Debt," NASDAQ OMX's News Release Distribution Channel, January 29, 2020, https://www.globenewswire.com/news-release/2020/
01/29/1976653/0/en/Lee-Enterprises-to-Buy-Berkshire-Hathaway-Newspaper-Operations
-Berkshire-Hathaway-to-Finance-All-Debt.html.

4. Peter Wells and E. Platt, "Buffett Shifts Newspaper Investment Strategy," *Financial Times*,
January 29, 2020, https://www.ft.com/content/59cb4100-4293-11ea-abea-0c7a29cd66fe.

5. Nicole Friedman, "Warren Buffett Is Giving Up on Newspapers; Lee Enterprises Is
Acquiring Berkshire Hathaway Media Group's Publications for $140 Million," *Wall Street
Journal*, January 29, 2020, https://www.wsj.com/articles/warren-buffett-is-giving-up-on
-newspapers-11580301637.

6. "Goldman's Path to Becoming More Like JPMorgan," FT.com, January 30, 2020, https://
www.proquest.com/trade-journals/goldman-s-path-becoming-more-like-jpmorgan/doc
view/2348541456/se-2.

7. Lee Enterprises, Inc., Form 10-K, annual report for the fiscal year ended September 27,
2020 (December 11, 2020), https://investors.lee.net/static-files/e1cbdb61-c7c1-40f2-b0fb
-08064d65294d.

8. Berkshire Hathaway, Inc., Form 10-Q, quarterly report for the quarterly period ended
March 31, 2022 (May 2, 2022), https://sec.report/Document/0001564590-22-016907/.

9. Joshua Benton and Ken Doctor, "Turns Out Warren Buffett Won't Be the Billionaire
Who Saves Newspapers Either," NiemanLab, January 29, 2020, https://www.niemanlab
.org/2020/01/turns-out-warren-buffett-wont-be-the-billionaire-who-saves-newspapers
-either.

10. Kerry Dolan, Jennifer Wang, and Chase Peterson-Withorn, eds., "Forbes Billionaires 2021: The Richest People in the World," Forbes, n.d., https://www.forbes.com/
billionaires/.

11. Rodney Benson, "The New American Media Landscape," in *The Death of Public
Knowledge? How Free Markets Destroy the General Intellect*, ed. Aeron Davis (London:
Goldsmiths' Press, 2017), 69–85.

12. Nicole Bullock, "Profit Margin Question Hanging Over US Stocks," FT.com, May 18, 2018, https://www-proquest-com.proxyau.wrlc.org/trade-journals/profit-margin -question-hanging-over-us-stocks/docview/2072460682/se-2?accountid=8285.

13. Robert Channick, "Hedge Fund Alden Closes $633 Million Tribune Publishing Acquisition; Newspaper Chain Is Delisted from Stock Market," *TCA Regional News*, May 24, 2021.

14. Bill Grueskin, Ava Seave, and Lucas Graves, "Chapter Seven: Dollars and Dimes," *Columbia Journalism Review*, May 10, 2011, https://archives.cjr.org/the_business_of_digital _journalism/chapter_seven_dollars_and_dimes.php.

15. New Media Investment Group, Inc., Form 10-K, annual report for the fiscal year ending December 29, 2013 (March 19, 2014), from the US Securities and Exchange Commission website, https://www.sec.gov/Archives/edgar/data/1579684/000119312514106565/ d694452d10k.htm; New Media Investment Group, Inc., Form 10-K, annual report for the fiscal year ending December 30, 2018 (February 27, 2019), from the Gannett website, https://investors.gannett.com/financials/sec-filings/sec-filings-details/default.aspx ?FilingId=13260522.

16. Sara Fischer, "Alden Global Capital Sues Lee Enterprises after Rejected Takeover Bid," *Axios*, December 15, 2021, https://www.axios.com/alden-global-lee-enterprises -suit-91e30f51-7ea7-4b1a-a3da-3098eafaa97b.html.

17. "Lee," Nasdaq, accessed October 14, 2022, https://www.nasdaq.com/market-activity/ stocks/lee/institutional-holdings.

18. Lou Ureneck, "Newspapers Arrive at Economic Crossroads," Nieman Reports, Nieman Foundation for Journalism at Harvard, February 17, 2021, https://niemanreports.org/ articles/newspapers-arrive-at-economic-crossroads/.

19. In conversation with the author, October 2021.

20. Bill Pate to Sam Zell, August 9, 2007, Equity Group Investments, LLC, memorandum, EGI-LAW 00178270, https://admin.epiq11.com/onlinedocuments/trb/examinerreports/ EX%200786.pdf.

21. Gerald A. Epstein, ed., *Financialization and the World Economy* (Cheltenham: Edward Elgar Publishing, 2005).

22. Núria Almiron, *Journalism in Crisis: Corporate Media and Financialization* (New York: Hampton Press, 2010).

23. Dwayne Winseck, "Financialization and the 'Crisis of the Media': The Rise and Fall of (Some) Media Conglomerates in Canada," *Canadian Journal of Communication* 35, no. 3 (2010): 365–94, doi: 10.22230/cjc.2010v35n3a2392.

24. "Defined Benefit Pension Plans: Plans Face Valuation and Other Challenges When Investing in Hedge Funds and Private Equity," US Government Accountability Office (GAO), July 20, 2010, https://www.gao.gov/products/GAO-10-915T.

25. William Fung and David A. Hsieh, "A Primer on Hedge Funds," *Journal of Empirical Finance* 6, no. 3 (1999): 309–31.

26. Jeffrey C. Hooke, *The Myth of Private Equity: An Inside Look at Wall Street's Transformative Investments* (New York: Columbia University Press, 2021), 17.

27. Edward I. Altman, "The Role of Distressed Debt Markets, Hedge Funds, and Recent Trends in Bankruptcy on the Outcomes of Chapter 11 Reorganizations," *American Bankruptcy Institute Law Review* 22, no. 1 (2014): 75.

28. Steven Drobny, *The Invisible Hands: Top Hedge Fund Traders on Bubbles, Crashes, and Real Money* (Hoboken, NJ: John Wiley & Sons, Inc., 2011), 3.

29. Gerald Epstein, *The Asset Management Industry in the United States*, no. 271, Naciones Unidas Comisión Económica para América Latina y el Caribe (CEPAL), 2019, https://repositorio.cepal.org/bitstream/handle/11362/45045/1/S1900994_en.pdf.

30. George Schultze, *The Art of Vulture Investing: Adventures in Distressed Securities Management* (New York: John Wiley & Sons, 2012).

31. A. Scott Carson, "Vulture Investors, Predators of the 90s: An Ethical Examination," *Journal of Business Ethics* 17, no. 5 (1998): 543–55, https://doi.org/10.1023/A:1005718715162.

32. Wulf Kaal and Dale Oesterle, "The History of Hedge Fund Regulation in the United States," *CLS Blue Sky Blog*, Trustees of Columbia University in the City of New York, February 29, 2016, https://clsbluesky.law.columbia.edu/2016/02/29/the-history-of-hedge-fund-regulation-in-the-united-states/.

33. Aaron Glantz, *Homewreckers: How a Gang of Wall Street Kingpins, Hedge Fund Magnates, Crooked Banks, and Vulture Capitalists Suckered Millions out of Their Homes and Demolished the American Dream* (New York: Custom House, 2019).

34. Ann-Kristin Achleitner and Christoph Kaserer, "Private Equity Funds and Hedge Funds: A Primer," Working Paper no. 2005–03, Technische Universität München, Center for Entrepreneurial and Financial Studies (CEFS), https://www.econstor.eu/handle/10419/48439.

35. Peter Temple, *Hedge Funds: Courtesans of Capitalism* (Chichester: J. Wiley, 2001), 1.

36. Jennifer Ralph Oppold, "The Changing Landscape of Hedge Fund Regulation: Current Concerns and a Principle-Based Approach," *University of Pennsylvania Journal of Business & Employment Law* 10, no. 4 (2007–8): 833.

37. Temple, *Hedge Funds*.

38. Temple, *Hedge Funds*, 8.

39. The article, originally published in April 1966, is Carol J. Loomis, "The Jones Nobody Keeps Up With (Fortune, 1966)," *Fortune*, December 29, 2015, https://fortune.com/2015/12/29/hedge-funds-fortune-1966/.

40. Christine Haughney, "Carol Loomis, Editor for Warren Buffett, Leaves Job after 60 Years," *New York Times*, July 3, 2014, https://www.nytimes.com/2014/07/04/business/media/carol-loomis-editor-for-warren-buffett-leaves-job-after-60-years.html.

41. Stephen Taub, "The Bucks Stop Here," *Institutional Investor* 29, no. 8 (2004): 1–56.

42. René M. Stulz, "Hedge Funds: Past, Present, and Future," *Journal of Economic Perspectives* 21, no. 2 (2007): 175–94.

43. Ronen Palan, Richard Murphy, and Christian Chavagneux, *Tax Havens* (Ithaca, NY: Cornell University Press, 2013); Daniel Barth, Juha Joenväärä, Mikko Kauppila, and Russ Wermers, "The Hedge Fund Industry Is Bigger (and Has Performed Better)

Than You Think," Office of Financial Research Working Paper, version updated March 8, 2021, https://www.financialresearch.gov/working-papers/files/OFRwp-20-01_the-hedge
-fund-industry-is-bigger-and-has-performed-better-than-you-think-revised.pdf.

44. Stefano Lavinio, *The Hedge Fund Handbook: A Definitive Guide for Analyzing and Evaluating Alternative Investments* (New York: McGraw-Hill, 2000).

45. Joseph G. Nicholas, *Investing in Hedge Funds* (New York: John Wiley and Sons, 2010); Joseph A. Franco, "Bending the Investment Advisers Act's Regulatory Arc," *Fordham Journal of Corporate & Financial Law* 26, no. 1 (2021): 1–104; H. Norman Knickle, "The Investment Company Act of 1940: SEC Enforcement and Private Actions," *Annual Review of Banking and Financial Law* 23 (2004): 777.

46. "Investor Bulletin Hedge Funds," US Securities and Exchange Commission, n.d., https://www.sec.gov/files/ib_hedgefunds.pdf.

47. Steven N. Kaplan and Per Strömberg, "Leveraged Buyouts and Private Equity," *Journal of Economic Perspectives* 23, no. 1 (2009): 121–46, doi: 10.1257/jep.23.1.121.

48. "Private Equity Passes the Baton," *Daily Upside*, February 7, 2021, https://www
.thedailyupside.com/private-equity-passes-the-baton/.

49. Eileen Appelbaum and Rosemary Batt, *Private Equity at Work: When Wall Street Manages Main Street* (New York: Russell Sage Foundation, 2014), 53.

50. Itzhak Ben-David, Francesco Franzoni, Rabih Moussawi, and John Sedunov, "The Granular Nature of Large Institutional Investors," *Management Science* 67, no. 11 (2021): 6629–59, https://doi.org/10.1287/mnsc.2020.3808.

51. William Bratton and Joseph A. McCahery, eds., *Institutional Investor Activism: Hedge Funds and Private Equity, Economics and Regulation* (Oxford: Oxford University Press, 2015).

52. Henry Ordower, "The Regulation of Private Equity, Hedge Funds, and State Funds," *American Journal of Comparative Law* 58, no. 1, supplement (2010): 295–322, https://doi.org/
10.5131/ajcl.2009.0035.

53. Tamar Frankel, "Private Investment Funds: Hedge Funds' Regulation by Size," *Rutgers Law Journal* 39, no. 3 (2007): 657.

54. Bratton and McCahery, *Institutional Investor Activism*.

55. Luis A. Aguilar, "Institutional Investors: Power and Responsibility," speech presented to J. Mack Robinson College of Business, Center for the Economic Analysis of Risk (CEAR), Department of Finance, CEAR Workshop, Georgia State University, April 19, 2013.

56. Colleen Honigsberg, "Hedge Fund Regulation and Fund Governance: Evidence on the Effects of Mandatory Disclosure Rules," *Journal of Accounting Research* 57, no. 4 (2019), https://ssrn.com/abstract=3463936.

57. "Alden Global Opportunities Fund (Cayman), L.P.," Securities and Exchange Commission, January 14, 2014, https://sec.report/CIK/0001453506; Epstein, *The Asset Management Industry*, 20.

58. Kevin Phillips, *Bad Money: Reckless Finance, Failed Politics, and the Global Crisis of American Capitalism* (New York: Penguin, 2009).

59. Mark R. Desjardine, Emilio Marti, and Rodolphe Durand, "Why Activist Hedge Funds Target Socially Responsible Firms: The Reaction Costs of Signaling Corporate Social Responsibility," *Academy of Management Journal* 64, no. 3 (2021): 851–72, doi:10.5465/amj.2019.0238.

60. Penelope Muse Abernathy, *The Rise of a New Media Baron and the Emerging Threat of News Deserts*, University of North Carolina at Chapel Hill, Center for Innovation and Sustainability in Local Media, 2016, http://newspaperownership.com/newspaper-ownership-report/.

61. "Freedom Communications, Inc.: Company Profile, Information, Business Description, History, Background Information on Freedom Communications, Inc.," Reference for Business, accessed January 5, 2021, https://www.referenceforbusiness.com/history2/70/Freedom-Communications-Inc.html.

62. R. Reiff, "Freedom Fighter: Register Heir Seeks Sale," *Orange County Business Journal*, August 5, 2002, http://www.rickreiff.com/stories/20805.html.

63. E. Scott Reckard, "Freedom Communications Deal Would Boost Debt to $1 Billion," *Los Angeles Times*, November 20, 2003, https://www.latimes.com/archives/la-xpm-2003-nov-20-fi-freedom20-story.html.

64. John Ward and Carol Adler Zsolnay, "Freedom Communications, Inc.: Family Enterprise or Liquidity?," 5–307–504, 2007, Kellogg School of Management at Northwestern University, Evanston, IL, https://doi.org/10.1108/case.kellogg.2016.000127.

65. Mark Hampton, "The Fourth Estate Ideal in Journalism History," in *The Routledge Companion to News and Journalism* (New York: Routledge, 2010), 3–12.

66. Steve Williams, "After 35 Years, It's Time to Go," *Daily Press*, October 10, 2015, https://www.vvdailypress.com/article/20151010/NEWS/151019990?fbclid=IwAR2v_3_h35GMpQoaqOaSFtton_qviIue1fCyipt2GYtBVonKUsyx9l_QWRA.

67. Williams, "After 35 Years."

68. In conversation with the author, January 2021.

69. Ward and Zsolnay, "Freedom Communications," 10.

70. Xiang Ji, "Freedom Bankruptcy Hits Blackstone," *Institutional Investor*, October 6, 2009, https://www.institutionalinvestor.com/article/b150qbohbo6b9j/freedom-bankruptcy-hits-blackstone.

71. "Freedom Recapitalization Completed," Blackstone Group, May 18, 2004, https://www.blackstone.com/press-releases/article/freedom-recapitalization-completed/; "The Blackstone Group and Providence Equity Partners Acquires Freedom Communications," Mergr, M&A Deal Summary, October 14, 2003, https://mergr.com/the-blackstone-group-acquires-freedom-communications.

72. "Freedom Communications, Blackstone Communications Partners and Providence Equity Partners Sign Definitive Capitalization Agreement," Blackstone Group, October 14, 2003, https://www.blackstone.com/press-releases/article/freedom-communications-blackstone-communications-partners-and-providence-equity-partners-sign-definitive-capitalization-agreement/.

73. Ji, "Freedom Bankruptcy"; Reckard, "Freedom Communications Deal."

74. In early 2021 I contacted by email three other members of the extended Hoiles family. Two responded that they had no interest in talking with me. A third did not respond.

75. Michael J. de la Merced, "Freedom Communications Files for Bankruptcy Protection," *New York Times*, September 1, 2009, https://www.nytimes.com/2009/09/02/business/media/02freedom.html?_r=1&ref=business.

76. "Freedom Communications, Blackstone."

77. Richard Morgan, "Let Freedom Ring," *The Deal*, July 25, 2005.

78. Kimi Yoshino, "O.C. Register to Cut Workforce," *Los Angeles Times*, September 30, 2006, https://www.latimes.com/archives/la-xpm-2006-sep-30-fi-ocregister30-story.html.

79. Bratton and McCahery, *Institutional Investor Activism*.

80. James Skorheim v. Scott N. Flanders et al., U.S. District Court Central District of California Case No. SACV10–789 AG (2011).

81. The court records used the parentheses included here.

82. "Register Owner Puts Off Buyout of 2 Partners," *Los Angeles Times*, January 28, 2007, Business, C3.

83. "Freedom Recapitalization Completed," paragraph 19.

84. "Freedom Recapitalization Completed," paragraph 20.

85. David Carey and John D. Morris, *King of Capital: The Remarkable Rise, Fall, and Rise Again of Steve Schwarzman and Blackstone* (New York: Crown, 2012).

86. Glantz, *Homewreckers*.

87. Georg Szalai, "Univision Deal Closes: Investor Group Takes Majority Stake, Wade Davis Becomes CEO," *Hollywood Reporter*, December 29, 2020, https://www.hollywoodreporter.com/business/business-news/univision-deal-closes-investor-group-takes-majority-stake-wade-davis-becomes-ceo-4096228/.

88. "Covington Advises Providence Equity Partners on $1.2 Billion Acquisition of Clear Channel," *Covington*, April 20, 2007, https://www.cov.com/en/news-and-insights/news/2007/04/covington-advises-providence-equity-partners-on-$1–2-billion-acquisition-of-clear-channel.

89. Ji, "Freedom Bankruptcy."

90. "VNU Agrees to Public Offer from Private Equity Group That Values Company at EUR 28.75 per Common Share, or Approximately EUR 7.5 Billion in Cash," Blackstone Group, press release, March 8, 2006, https://www.blackstone.com/press-releases/article/vnu-agrees-to-public-offer-from-private-equity-group-that-values-company-at-eur-28-75-per-common-share-or-approximately-eur-7–5-billion-in-cash/.

91. Michael Flaherty, "Nielsen Cuts 1,250 Service Jobs Worldwide," Reuters, October 1, 2007, https://www.reuters.com/article/uk-nielsen-jobs/nielsen-cuts-1250-service-jobs-worldwide-idUKN3019663220071001.

92. "Freedom Communications Announces Sale of Four Midwest Newspapers," *Business Wire*, May 17, 2012, https://www.businesswire.com/news/home/20120517005312/en/freedom-communications-announces-sale-of-four-midwest-newspapers.

93. Blackstone Group, accessed March 4, 2021, https://www.blackstone.com/the-firm/.

94. Blackstone Group, Form 10-K, annual report filed by the Blackstone Group LP with the US Securities and Exchange Commission for the year ending December 31, 2017 (March 1, 2018), US Securities and Exchange Commission, https://www.sec.gov/Archives/edgar/data/1393818/000119312518067079/d522506d10k.htm#tx522506_16.

95. Dennis K. Berman, "Journal Register Cements Deal for 21st Century Newspapers," *Wall Street Journal*, July 6, 2004, Eastern edition.

96. "The Blackstone Group and Providence Equity Partners Acquires."

97. "Freedom Emerges from Bankruptcy," *McClatchy-Tribune Business News*, May 1, 2010.

98. Russell Adams, "Freedom Communications Explores Sale of More Newspapers," *Wall Street Journal*, March 14, 2012, https://www.wsj.com/articles/SB10001424052702304692804577281672579297542.

99. Michelle M. Harner, "Activist Distressed Debtholders: The New Barbarians at the Gate," *Washington University Law Review* 89, no. 1 (2011): 155–206.

100. Beau Yarbrough, "Media: Digital First Closes Deal to Buy the Press-Enterprise," *Press-Enterprise*, March 31, 2016, https://www.pe.com/2016/03/31/media-digital-first-closes-deal-to-buy-the-press-enterprise/; Yarbrough, "Attorney: Freedom Communications to Sell to Digital First Media," *Daily News*, March 19, 2016, https://www.dailynews.com/2016/03/19/attorney-freedom-communications-to-sell-to-digital-first-media/.

Chapter 2. Democracy for Sum

1. Nina Kvalheim and Jens Barland, "Commercialization of Journalism," in *Oxford Research Encyclopedia of Communication*, 2019, oxfordre.com/communication/search?siteToSearch=communication&q="Commercialization+of+journalism."&searchBtn=Search&isQuickSearch=true.

2. C. Edwin Baker, *Media Concentration and Democracy: Why Ownership Matters* (Cambridge: Cambridge University Press, 2006).

3. Edwin H. Ford and Edwin Emery, eds., *Highlights in the History of the American Press: A Book of Readings* (Minneapolis: University of Minnesota Press, 1954).

4. Edwin H. Ford, "Colonial Pamphleteers," in Ford and Emery, *Highlights in the History*, 64–74.

5. Jordan E. Taylor, "Enquire of the Printer: Newspaper Advertising and the Moral Economy of the North American Slave Trade, 1704–1807," *Early American Studies: An Interdisciplinary Journal* 18, no. 3 (2020): 287–323, doi:10.1353/eam.2020.0008.

6. Arthur M. Schlesinger, "The Colonial Newspapers and the Stamp Act," *New England Quarterly* 8, no. 1 (1935): 63–83, doi:10.2307/359430.

7. Edwin Emery, *The Press and America: An Interpretative History of the Mass Media* (New York: Prentice-Hall, 1972).

8. Albert Henry Smyth, "Franklin as a Printer," in Ford and Emery, *Highlights in the History*, 75–82.

9. Emery, *The Press and America*, 43.

10. Sidney Kobre, *The Development of the Colonial Newspaper* (Pittsburgh, PA: Colonial Press, 1944), 153.

11. Eric W. Nye, "Pounds Sterling to Dollars: Historical Conversion of Currency," August 16, 2021, https://www.uwyo.edu/numimage/currency.htm.

12. Jeffrey L. Pasley, *The Tyranny of Printers: Newspaper Politics in the Early American Republic* (Charlottesville: University of Virginia Press, 2002).

13. Robert W. McChesney, *The Political Economy of Media: Enduring Issues, Emerging Dilemmas* (New York: Monthly Review Press, 2008), 495.

14. Victor Pickard, *Democracy without Journalism? Confronting the Misinformation Society* (Oxford: Oxford University Press, 2019).

15. Mark Feldstein, "A Muckraking Model: Investigative Reporting Cycles in American History," *Harvard International Journal of Press/Politics* 11, no. 2 (April 2006): 105–20, https://doi.org/10.1177/1081180X06286780.

16. Simon Newton Dexter North, *History and Present Condition of the Newspaper and Periodical Press of the United States: With a Catalogue of the Publications of the Census Year* (Washington, DC: Government Printing Office, 1884), https://upload.wikimedia.org/wikipedia/commons/2/27/History_and_present_condition_of_the_newspaper_and_periodical_press_of_the_United_States%2C_with_a_catalogue_of_the_publications_of_the_census_year_%28IA_cu31924083814453%29.pdf.

17. Daxton R. "Chip" Stewart, "Freedom's Vanguard: Horace Greeley on Threats to Press Freedom in the Early Years of the Penny Press," *American Journalism* 29, no. 1 (2012): 60–83.

18. David L. Jamison, "Newspapers and the Press," Nineteenth Century US Newspapers, Cengage Learning, 2008, https://www.gale.com/binaries/content/assets/gale-us-en/primary-sources/intl-gps/intl-gps-essays/full-ghn-contextual-essays/ghn_essay_19usn_jamison1_website.pdf.

19. Pasley, *The Tyranny of Printers*, 9.

20. Pasley, *The Tyranny of Printers*.

21. Jeffrey L. Pasley, "The Two National 'Gazettes': Newspapers and the Embodiment of American Political Parties," *Early American Literature* 35, no. 1 (2000): 51–86, quote on 52.

22. Part 4 introduction, in Ford and Emery, *Highlights in the History*, 135–37.

23. Pasley, "The Two National 'Gazettes.'"

24. George H. Douglas, *The Golden Age of the Newspaper* (Westport, CT: Greenwood Publishing Group, 1999).

25. Douglas, *The Golden Age of the Newspaper*, 45.

26. J. Nerone, "Penny Press," in *The International Encyclopedia of Communication*, ed. W. Donsbach, 2008, https://doi-org.proxyau.wrlc.org/10.1002/9781405186407.wbiecp018.

27. Sharon McQueen, "From Yellow Journalism to Tabloids to Clickbait: The Origins of Fake News in the United States," in *Information Literacies and Libraries in the Age of Fake News* (Santa Barbara, CA: Libraries Unlimited, 2018), 12–35.

28. James Lundberg, "How Horace Greeley Turned Newspapers Legitimate and Saved the Media from Itself," *Smithsonian Magazine*, March 6, 2020, https://www.smithsonianmag.com/history/how-horace-greeley-invented-persona-crusading-journalist-180974348/.

29. Stewart, "Freedom's Vanguard."

30. John Nerone, "Penny Press," in *The International Encyclopedia of Communication*, ed. Wolfgang Donsbach (Malden, MA: Blackwell, 2008), 3539.

31. Andie Tucher, "PrinceOfDarkness@ NYHerald. com: How the Penny Press Caused the Decline of the West," *American Journalism* 17, no. 4 (2000): 121–27.

32. Frank W. Scott, "Newspapers, 1775–1860," in *A History of American Literature*, ed. William Trent, John Erskine, Stuart Sherman, and Car van Doren (Cambridge: Cambridge University Press, 1919), 176–95, 190.

33. Adam Tuchinsky, *Horace Greeley's "New-York Tribune": Civil War–Era Socialism and the Crisis of Free Labor* (Ithaca, NY: Cornell University Press, 2011), 9.

34. John D. Stevens, *Sensationalism and the New York Press* (New York: Columbia University Press, 1991), 19.

35. Mark Bernhardt, "Taking Sides in the 'Bloodless Croton War': The Coverage of the Croton Aqueduct Strike and Labor's Relationship with the Penny Press," *New York History* 97, no. 1 (2016): 9–33; quote from Martin Oppenheimer, "The Rise and Fall of the Muckrakers," *New Politics* 16, no. 2 (Winter 2017): 87–96.

36. Gamaliel Bradford, "Horace Greeley," in Ford and Emery, *Highlights in the History*, 160–74, 170.

37. Lundberg, "How Horace Greeley Turned."

38. Lundberg, "How Horace Greeley Turned," paragraph 21.

39. David O. Dowling, "Emerson's Newspaperman: Horace Greeley and Radical Intellectual Culture, 1836–1872," *Journalism & Communication Monographs* 19, no. 1 (2017): 7–74.

40. Maria Petrova, "Newspapers and Parties: How Advertising Revenues Created an Independent Press," *American Political Science Review* 105, no. 4 (2011): 790–808, https://doi.org/10.1017/S0003055411000360.

41. Stevens, *Sensationalism*, 39.

42. Petrova, "Newspapers and Parties."

43. Stevens, *Sensationalism*, 39.

44. Erin K. Coyle, "E. L. Godkin's Criticism of the Penny Press: Antecedents to a Legal Right to Privacy," *American Journalism* 31, no. 2 (2014): 262–82, https://doi-org.proxyau.wrlc.org/10.1080/08821127.2014.905362.

45. Douglas, *The Golden Age*.

46. Gregory A. Borchard, *A Narrative History of the American Press* (New York: Routledge, 2018).

47. Michael Schudson, *Discovering the News: A Social History of American Newspapers* (New York: Basic Books, 1981), 16.

48. Schudson, *Discovering the News*, 132.

49. John William Tebbel, *The Compact History of the American Newspaper* (New York: Hawthorn Books, 1963).

50. Douglas, *The Golden Age*.

51. W. Joseph Campbell, *The Year That Defined American Journalism: 1897 and the Clash of Paradigms* (New York: Routledge, 2013), 9.

52. Gerald J. Baldasty, *The Commercialization of News in the Nineteenth Century* (Madison: University of Wisconsin Press, 1992).

53. Kenneth Whyte, *The Uncrowned King: The Sensational Rise of William Randolph Hearst* (Toronto: Vintage Canada, 2009).

54. Aurora Wallace, *Media Capital: Architecture and Communications in New York City* (Urbana: University of Illinois Press, 2012), 7.

55. David Halberstam, *The Powers That Be* (Urbana: University of Illinois Press, 2000).

56. Schudson, *Discovering the News*.

57. Joyce Milton, *The Yellow Kids: Foreign Correspondents in the Heyday of Yellow Journalism* (New York: Open Road Media, 2014).

58. Emery, *The Press and America*, 292.

59. Halberstam, *The Powers That Be*.

60. Daniel W. Pfaff, *No Ordinary Joe: A Life of Joseph Pulitzer III* (Columbia: University of Missouri Press, 2005), ProQuest Ebook Central.

61. Emery, *The Press and America*.

62. James Boylan, *Pulitzer's School: Columbia University's School of Journalism, 1903–2003* (New York: Columbia University Press, 2003), 3.

63. Edwin Emery, Michael C. Emery, and Nancy L. Roberts, *The Press and America: An Interpretive History of the Mass Media* (Boston: Allyn and Bacon, 1996), 171.

64. William Andrew Swanberg, *Citizen Hearst: A Biography of William Randolph Hearst* (New York: Collier Books, 1961).

65. Douglas, *The Golden Age*, 273.

66. Emery, *The Press and America*, 381.

67. David Croteau and William D. Hoynes, *The Business of Media: Corporate Media and the Public Interest* (Newbury Park, CA: Pine Forge Press, 2006), 25.

68. Douglas, *The Golden Age*, 191.

69. Steve Weinberg, *Taking on the Trust: How Ida Tarbell Brought Down John D. Rockefeller and Standard Oil* (New York: W. W. Norton, 2008), ix.

70. Oppenheimer, "The Rise and Fall."

71. Linda McMurry Edwards, *To Keep the Waters Troubled: The Life of Ida B. Wells* (Oxford: Oxford University Press, 2000).

72. John Hersey, "Hiroshima," *New Yorker*, August 23, 1946, https://www.newyorker.com/magazine/1946/08/31/hiroshima; M. Yavenditti, "John Hersey and the American Conscience: The Reception of 'Hiroshima,'" *Pacific Historical Review* 43, no. 1 (1974): 24–49, doi:10.2307/3637589.

73. James Hamilton, *Democracy's Detectives: The Economics of Investigative Journalism* (Cambridge, MA: Harvard University Press, 2016).

74. Lucia Moses, "Profiting from Experience," *Editor & Publisher* 136, no. 5 (February 2003): 11–12.

75. Edward S. Herman, *Corporate Control, Corporate Power* (New York: Cambridge University Press, 1981), 12.

76. Robert G. Picard, "A Business Perspective on Challenges Facing Journalism," in *The Changing Business of Journalism and Its Implications for Democracy*, ed. David A. L. Levy and Rasmus Kleis Nielsen (Oxford: Reuters Institute for the Study of Journalism, 2010), 17–24, 22.

77. C. Edwin Baker, *Advertising and a Democratic Press* (Princeton, NJ: Princeton University Press, 1994).

78. Edward S. Herman and Noam Chomsky, *Manufacturing Consent: The Political Economy of Mass Media* (New York: Vintage, 1988).

79. Pickard, *Democracy without Journalism*, 29.

80. Fred Dews and Thomas Young, "Ten Noteworthy Moments in U.S. Investigative Journalism," Brookings Institution, October 20, 2014, https://www.brookings.edu/blog/brookings-now/2014/10/20/ten-noteworthy-moments-in-u-s-investigative-journalism/.

81. Edward Jay Epstein, "Did the Press Uncover Watergate?," July 1974, https://www.edwardjayepstein.com/archived/watergate.htm.

82. Michael S. Rosenwald, "Katharine Graham Was Burned in Effigy, but Refused to Give In during a Violent Strike," *Washington Post*, June 16, 2017, https://www.washingtonpost.com/news/retropolis/wp/2017/06/15/she-stood-up-katharine-grahams-fierce-fight-against-a-violent-pressmens-strike/.

83. Matt Schudel, "Ben H. Bagdikian, Journalist with Key Role in Pentagon Papers Case, Dies at 96," *Washington Post*, March 11, 2016, https://www.washingtonpost.com/local/obituaries/ben-h-bagdikian-media-critic-and-journalist-with-key-role-in-pentagon-papers-case-dies-at-96/2016/03/11/9515bb8c-e7bb-11e5-bc08-3e03a5b41910_story.html.

84. McChesney, *The Political Economy*, 19.

85. Pickard, *Democracy without Journalism?*

86. Robert W. McChesney, "September 11 and the Structural Limitations of US Journalism," in *Journalism after September 11*, ed. Barbie Zelizer and Stuart Allan (New York: Routledge, 2003), 109–18.

87. Lucia Moses, "Heard on the Street: Newspapers Still a Good Place to Be," *Editor & Publisher* 133, no. 1 (January 2000): 15, ABI/INFORM.

88. Charles Layton, "White Knights: Knight Ridder's Washington Bureau Has Distinguished Itself with Cutting-Edge Reporting on Everything from Saddam's Weapons of Mass Destruction to Coal Mine Safety," *American Journalism Review* 28, no. 2 (2006): 38–46.

89. Moses Ofome Asak and Tshepang Bright Molale, "Deconstructing De-legitimisation of Mainstream Media as Sources of Authentic News in the Post-truth Era," *Communicatio: South African Journal of Communication Theory and Research* 46, no. 4 (2020): 50–74, https://doi.org/10.1080/02500167.2020.1723664.

90. Philip Meyer and Stanley T. Wearden, "The Effects of Public Ownership on Newspaper Companies: A Preliminary Inquiry," *Public Opinion Quarterly* 48, no. 3 (1984): 564–77, 575.

91. John Soloski and Robert G. Picard, "The New Media Lords: Why Institutional Investors Call the Shots," *Columbia Journalism Review* 35, no. 3 (1996), https://go.gale.com/ps/i.do?p=AONE&u=googlescholar&id=GALE|A18714041&v=2.1&it=r&sid=AONE&asid=af33f06d.

92. Steven Drobny, *The Invisible Hands: Hedge Funds Off the Record—Rethinking Real Money* (New York: Wiley, 2010), 4.

93. Joseph A. McCahery, Zacharias Sautner, and Laura T. Starks, "Behind the Scenes: The Corporate Governance Preferences of Institutional Investors," *Journal of Finance* 71, no. 6 (2016): 2905–32, http://www.jstor.org/stable/44155408.

94. Robert G. Picard, "Institutional Ownership of Publicly Traded US Newspaper Companies," *Journal of Media Economics* 7, no. 4 (1994): 49–64, 51.

95. Picard, "Institutional Ownership," 54.

96. Ben H. Bagdikian, *The New Media Monopoly* (Boston: Beacon Press, 2004).

97. Herman and Chomsky, *Manufacturing Consent*, 2.

98. Stephen Lacy and Alan Blanchard, "The Impact of Public Ownership, Profits, and Competition on Number of Newsroom Employees and Starting Salaries in Mid-Sized Daily Newspapers," *Journalism and Mass Communication Quarterly* 80, no. 4 (Winter 2003): 949–68, 963.

99. Dean Starkman, *The Watchdog That Didn't Bark: The Financial Crisis and the Disappearance of Investigative Reporting* (New York: Columbia University Press, 2014), 4.

100. Aeron Davis, "Mediation, Financialization and the Global Financial Crisis: An Inverted Political Economy Perspective," in *The Political Economies of Media: The Transformation of the Global Media Industries*, ed. John Banks, Dal Yong Jin, and Dwayne Winseck (London: Bloomsbury, 2012).

101. On venture capital, see "Noted," *Wall Street Journal*, December 15, 2000, eastern edition, http://proxyau.wrlc.org/login?url=https://www-proquest-com.proxyau.wrlc.org/newspapers/noted/docview/398785109/se-2?accountid=8285.

102. Marc Edge, Hsiang Iris Chyi, Kelly Kaufhold, Mitch McKenney, and Dane S. Claussen, "Marking 40 Years of *Newspaper Research Journal*," *Newspaper Research Journal* 41, no. 1 (2020): 8–36, quote on 8.

103. Douglas, *The Golden Age*, 117.

104. Núria Almiron, *Journalism in Crisis: Corporate Media and Financialization* (Cresskill, NJ: Hampton Press, 2010).

105. Matthew Crain, "The Rise of Private Equity Media Ownership in the United States: A Public Interest Perspective," *International Journal of Communication* 3 (January 2009), https://ijoc.org/index.php/ijoc/article/view/381/307.

106. Bryan Burrough and John Helyar, *Barbarians at the Gate: The Fall of RJR Nabisco* (New York: Harper and Row, 1990).

107. Steve Gelsi, "Axel Springer Buys Politico and Forbes to Go Public by Merging with a SPAC in Busy Media Deal Day," MarketWatch, August 26, 2021, https://www.marketwatch.com/story/axel-springer-buys-politico-and-forbes-to-go-public-by-merging-with-a-spac-in-busy-media-deal-day-11629990968.

Chapter 3. Overharvesting

1. Philip Meyer, "Saving Journalism," *Columbia Journalism Review*, November–December 2004, 55–57, https://go.gale.com/ps/i.do?id=GALE%7CA124942968&sid=google

Scholar&v=2.1&it=r&linkaccess=abs&issn=0010194X&p=AONE&sw=w&userGroup
Name=anon%7Ec338e0a3.

2. Joe Pompeo, "The Hedge Fund Vampire That Bleeds Newspapers Dry Now Has the Chicago Tribune by the Throat," *Vanity Fair*, February 5, 2020, https://www.vanityfair.com/news/2020/02/hedge-fund-vampire-alden-global-capital-that-bleeds-newspapers-dry-has-chicago-tribune-by-the-throat.

3. "US Industry Reports (NAICS)," January 2022, Newspaper Publishing in the US, Report 51111, IBISWorld.

4. Michael Barthel and Kirsten Worden, "Newspaper Fact Sheet," Pew Research Center, June 29, 2021, https://www.pewresearch.org/journalism/fact-sheet/newspapers/.

5. "US Industry Reports (NAICS)," July 2021, Private Equity, Hedge Funds & Investment Vehicles in the US, Report 52599, IBISWorld.

6. Christine Haughney, "For the Hartford Courant, 250 Years in Print," *New York Times*, October 26, 2014, https://www.nytimes.com/2014/10/27/business/media/for-the-hartford-courant-250-years-in-print.html.

7. Mark Fitzgerald and Jennifer Saba, "Owners Up to It?," *Editor & Publisher* 142, no. 12 (December 2009): 24–26.

8. In conversation with the author, November 2021.

9. Scott Sherman, "The Evolution of Dean Singleton," *Columbia Journalism Review*, March 2003, 32–41, ABI/INFORM.

10. "Honoring Dean Singleton with 2021 Journalism in the Public Interest Award," University of Denver, September 27, 2021, https://liberalarts.du.edu/news-events/all-articles/honoring-dean-singleton-2021-journalism-public-interest-award.

11. Randy Holhut, email message to author, October 12, 2022.

12. In conversation with the author, November 2021.

13. "Welcome to *The Commons*—News and Views for Windham County, Vermont," accessed October 14, 2022, http://www.commonsnews.org/site/sitenext/index.php#.

14. Robert Neuwirth, "Lean Dean," *Editor & Publisher* 132, no. 38 (September 1999): 26–32, ABI/INFORM, quote appears in paragraph 7.

15. John Moore, "William Dean Singleton on Legacy, Promises and a Theatre Named in His Honor," Denver Center for the Performing Arts, September 22, 2021, https://www.denvercenter.org/news-center/william-dean-singleton-on-legacy-promises-and-a-theatre-named-in-his-honor/.

16. "2nd WSJ Update: MediaNews Holding Co Will File for Bankruptcy," *Dow Jones Institutional News*, January 15, 2010, https://www.proquest.com/wire-feeds/2nd-wsj-update-medianews-holding-co-will-file/docview/2174836618/se-2.

17. Mark Fitzgerald and Jennifer Saba, "'Til Debt Do Us Part," *Editor & Publisher* 141, no. 6 (June 2008): 24–26, 28–29, ABI/INFORM.

18. In re Affiliated Media, Inc., 2010 Bankr. LEXIS 5732 (United States Bankruptcy Court for the District of Delaware March 4, 2010, Decided).

19. "WSJ: Alden Global Considers Consolidating Newspaper Holdings," *Dow Jones Institutional News*, January 18, 2011, ABI/INFORM.

20. Aldo Svaldi and Steve Raabe, "MediaNews Makes Changes," *Denver Post,* January 18, 2011, https://www.denverpost.com/2011/01/18/medianews-makes-changes/.

21. Moore, "William Dean Singleton"; Michael Roberts, "Dean Singleton on Resigning from the Post: 'They've Killed a Great Newspaper,'" *Westword,* May 7, 2018, https://www.westword.com/news/dean-singleton-on-resigning-from-the-denver-post-theyve-killed-a-great-newspaper-10287146.

22. Jennifer Bjorhus, "'Lean Dean' to Critics, Shrewd CEO to Fans," *Knight Ridder Tribune Business News,* April 27, 2006, 1, ABI/INFORM.

23. "3 Top Figures at Denver Post, Including Former Owner, Quit," *AP News,* May 5, 2018, https://apnews.com/cae12ecbd3cf4a3185edad7171d600ce.

24. David Sirota, "Newspaper Mogul Dean Singleton: Bias Charges 'Totally Baloney,'" *Salon,* October 9, 2012, https://www.salon.com/2012/10/08/interview_with_newspaper_mogul_dean_singleton_a_modern_day_citizen_kane/.

25. Steve Raabe, "Singleton to Retire from Denver Post Owner MediaNews Group," *Denver Post,* June 13, 2016, https://www.denverpost.com/2013/11/04/singleton-to-retire-from-denver-post-owner-medianews-group/.

26. Martin Langeveld, "The Shakeup at MediaNews: Why It Could Be the Leadup to a Massive Newspaper Consolidation," Nieman Lab, President and Fellows of Harvard College, January 20, 2011, https://www.niemanlab.org/2011/01/the-shakeup-at-medianews-why-it-could-be-the-leadup-to-a-massive-newspaper-consolidation/.

27. "SoftBank Group Completes Acquisition of Fortress Investment Group," Fortress Investment Group, December 27, 2017, https://www.fortress.com/shareholders/news/2017-12-27-softbank-group-completes-acquisition-of-fortress-investment-group.

28. Michelle Celarier, "The Fall of Fortress," *Institutional Investor,* October 2, 2017, https://www.institutionalinvestor.com/article/b1505p66vqo6cy/the-fall-of-fortress.

29. Alan Ohnsman and Antoine Gara, "Inside a Wall Street Tycoon's Plan to Get Americans off the Highway—and on His Trains," *Forbes,* June 11, 2020, https://www.forbes.com/sites/alanohnsman/2020/06/11/inside-a-wall-street-tycoons-plan-to-get-americans-off-the-highway-and-on-his-trains/?sh=7e7c14d7a04f.

30. Ohnsman and Gara, "Inside a Wall Street Tycoon's Plan."

31. Fortress Investment Group LLC, Form 10-K/A, annual report filed by Donnelley Financial Solutions for the fiscal year ended December 31, 2016 (April 28, 2017), from the US Securities and Exchange Commission website, https://sec.report/Document/0001193125-17-148688/.

32. Fortress Investment Group LLC, Form 10-K, annual report for the fiscal year ended December 31, 2016 (February 28, 2017), from the Fortress Investment Group website, https://www.fortress.com/shareholders/financial-reports-and-filings/2016/Q4/fourth-quarter-2016-10K.pdf.

33. Jeff Vasishta, "Milwaukee Bucks Owner Wes Edens Lands $20 Million Manhattan Penthouse," *Dirt,* October 13, 2020, https://www.dirt.com/moguls/finance/wes-eden-house-manhattan-1203344898/.

34. Celarier, "The Fall of Fortress."

35. GateHouse Media, Inc., Form 10-K, annual report for the fiscal year ending December 31, 2007 (March 17, 2008), from the US Securities and Exchange Commission website, https://www.sec.gov/Archives/edgar/data/1368900/000114420408015835/v096277_10k.htm; Dennis K. Berman, "Fortress Capital Will Buy Publisher Liberty Group," *Wall Street Journal*, May 11, 2005, https://www.wsj.com/articles/SB111577592873230054.

36. "Liberty Group Publishing to Be Acquired by Fortress Investment Group LLC," Dirks, Van Essen & April, May 11, 2005, https://www.dirksvanessen.com/press_releases/print_view/112/liberty-group-publishing-to-be/, quote appears in paragraph 3.

37. Berman, "Fortress Capital Will Buy."

38. "Selling Your Publication: Shoppers and Pennysavers," McInnis and Associates, 2013, http://www.ads-on-line.com/newbasiccourse/products/chaptereight6.html.

39. Leon Lazaroff, "Liberty Newspaper Chain Put on the Block," *Chicago Tribune*, August 5, 2004, https://www.chicagotribune.com/news/ct-xpm-2004-08-05-0408050296-story.html.

40. GateHouse Media, Inc., Form 10-K, annual report filed by Donnelley Financial Solutions for the fiscal year ended December 30, 2012 (March 7, 2013), from the US Securities and Exchange Commission website, https://sec.report/Document/0001193125-13-096322/.

41. Mark Fitzgerald, "The Gatekeeper," *Editor & Publisher* 140, no. 2 (February 2007): 52–56; Jim Waterson, "Trump Pardons Fraudster Conrad Black after Glowing Biography," *Guardian*, May 16, 2019, https://www.theguardian.com/business/2019/may/15/conrad-black-trump-pardons-ex-media-mogul.

42. Gene Roberts, *Leaving Readers Behind: The Age of Corporate Newspapering* (Fayetteville: University of Arkansas Press, 2004).

43. GateHouse Media, Inc., Form 10-K, annual report for the fiscal year ending December 31, 2007 (March 17, 2008), from the US Securities and Exchange Commission website, https://www.sec.gov/Archives/edgar/data/1368900/000114420408015835/v096277_10k.htm; Lynn Cowan, "GateHouse Media Rises 18% in IPO; Two Others Mixed," *Wall Street Journal*, October 26, 2006, eastern edition, https://www.wsj.com/articles/SB116181541143803910.

44. GateHouse Media, Inc., final prospectus: initial public offering, 13,800,000 shares, October 24, 2006, Mergent Archives Database, https://www-mergentarchives-com.proxyau.wrlc.org/viewReport.php?rtype=annualReports&documentID=485088&companyName=Gatehouse%20Media%20Inc&reportType=1&country=United%20States; Steven Syre, "The Boston Globe Boston Capital Column," *McClatchy-Tribune Business News*, October 24, 2006.

45. "Constantine Dakolias: TRD Research," *Real Deal*, accessed March 2, 2021, https://therealdeal.com/new-research/topics/people/constantine-dakolias/.

46. Christopher Rowland, "Despite Debt, Chain Seeks More Papers," *McClatchy-Tribune Business News*, August 1, 2006.

47. "Fortress Investment Group LLC Corporate Investment Arm Profile," S&P Capital IQ, Color Notes, https://www.capitaliq.com/CIQDotNet/company.aspx?companyId=666715.

48. Rowland, "Despite Debt."

49. GateHouse Media, Inc., Form 10-K, annual report for the fiscal year ending December 31, 2007 (March 17, 2008), from the US Securities and Exchange Commission website, https://www.sec.gov/Archives/edgar/data/1368900/000114420408015835/v096277_10k.htm.

50. Jennifer Saba, "After Job Cuts in '07, What's Ahead?," *Editor & Publisher* 141, no. 1 (January 2008): 14; "GateHouse Media Announces Second Quarter Dividend of $0.40, an Increase of 25% Since IPO," US Securities and Exchange Commission, June 18, 2007, https://www.sec.gov/Archives/edgar/data/1368900/000119312507138084/dex991.htm.

51. GateHouse Media, Inc., Form 10-K, annual report for the fiscal year ending December 31, 2012 (March 7, 2013), quote appears on p. 39, from the US Securities and Exchange Commission website, https://www.sec.gov/Archives/edgar/data/1368900/000119312513096322/d475356d10k.htm.

52. New Media Investment Group, Inc., Form 10-K, annual report for the fiscal year ending December 29, 2013 (March 19, 2014), https://www.sec.gov/Archives/edgar/data/1579684/000119312514106565/d694452d10k.htm, 50–51.

53. New Media Investment Group, December 29, 2013, 166.

54. "New Media Announces First Quarter 2014 Results," New Media Investment Group, Inc., May 1, 2014, https://s1.q4cdn.com/307481213/files/doc_news/2014/05/1/New-Media-Announces-First-Quarter-2014-Results.pdf.

55. David L. Harris, "GateHouse Media Executive Pay Jumps as Acquisition Spree Continues," *Boston Business Journal*, April 21, 2016.

56. New Media Investment Group, Inc., Form 10-K, annual report for the fiscal year ending December 25, 2016 (February 21, 2017), from the US Securities and Exchange Commission website, https://www.sec.gov/Archives/edgar/data/1579684/000157968417000005/newm-20161225x10k.htm, 69.

57. Gannett Co., Inc., Form 10-K, annual report for the fiscal year ended December 31, 2019 (March 2, 2020), https://d18rnop25nwr6d.cloudfront.net/CIK-0001579684/b1282d40-f154-4de6-9629-a7a96f8bdfb0.pdf.

58. James Fontanella-Khan, Eric Platt, and Anna Nicolaou, "MNG Enterprises Unveils $1.4bn Bid for USA Today Owner Gannett," FT.com, January 14, 2019, ABI/INFORM.

59. Gannett Co., Inc., Form 10-K, annual report for the fiscal year ending December 31, 2020 (February 26, 2021), https://d18rnop25nwr6d.cloudfront.net/CIK-0001579684/738c2ddb-7f33-48c7-80f9-0c2a79094433.pdf.

60. Gannett Co., Inc., Schedule 14-A (April 28, 2021), https://d18rnop25nwr6d.cloudfront.net/CIK-0001579684/6ee6b199-e99e-4288-8998-b1bb54adfdd8.pdf.

61. "About Fortress," Fortress Investment Group, n.d., https://www.fortress.com/about; Christopher Rowland, "Can Suburban Newspapers Deliver? Investors See Promise," *Knight Ridder Tribune Business News*, May 16, 2006.

62. Sara Fischer and Kerry Flynn, "Gannett Shed Nearly Half Its Workforce Since Gatehouse Merger," March 7, 2023, *Axios*, https://www.axios.com/2023/03/07/gannett-changes-leadership-workers.

63. Savannah Jacobson, "The Most Feared Owner in American Journalism Looks Set to Take Some of Its Greatest Assets," *Columbia Journalism Review*, June 29, 2020, https://www.cjr.org/special_report/alden-global-capital-medianews-tribune-company.php.

64. Form 13F-SEC, US Securities and Exchange Commission, n.d., https://www.sec.gov/pdf/form13f.pdf.

65. Alden Global Capital, Form 13-F, annual report for the calendar year or quarter ending December 31, 2010 (February 14, 2011), from the US Securities and Exchange Commission website, https://www.sec.gov/Archives/edgar/data/0001492343/000090266411000446/p11-0476form13fhr.txt.

66. Alden Global Capital, Form 13-F, annual report for the calendar year or quarter ending December 31, 2009 (February 6, 2010), https://www.sec.gov/Archives/edgar/data/0001469694/000090266410000699/p10-0293form13fhr.txt.

67. Joe Nocera, "Imagine If Gordon Gekko Bought News Empires," *Bloomberg*, March 26, 2018, https://www.bloomberg.com/opinion/articles/2018-03-26/alden-global-capital-s-business-model-destroys-newspapers-for-little-gain.

68. Alden Global Capital LLC, Form ADV, Uniform Application for Investment Adviser Registration and Report by Exempt Reporting Advisers (March 30, 2020), from the US Securities and Exchange Commission website, https://reports.adviserinfo.sec.gov/reports/ADV/161333/PDF/161333.pdf.

69. Tribune Publishing Company, Schedule 13D, filed by Alden Global Capital (December 14, 2020), from the US Securities and Exchange Commission website, https://www.sec.gov/Archives/edgar/data/1593195/000119312520330238/d80296dsc13da.htm.

70. Anna Nicolaou and James Fontanella-Khan, "The Fight for the Future of America's Local Newspapers," *Financial Times*, January 21, 2021, https://www.ft.com/content/5c22075c-f1af-431d-bf39-becf9c54758b.

71. Rick Edmonds, "As Print and Digital Newsrooms Struggle, Local Broadcast Stations Are Making Money 'Hand over Fist,'" Poynter, December 11, 2019, https://www.poynter.org/business-work/2019/the-rich-get-richer-local-broadcast-readies-for-a-3-2-billion-political-ad-bonanza-in-2020/.

72. Mary Ann Milbourn, "Register Owner Bought by Private Firm," *McClatchy-Tribune Business News*, June 11, 2012.

73. "Press Release: MediaNews Group to Solicit," *Dow Jones Institutional News*, September 30, 2016.

74. "Newsonomics: Do Newspaper Companies Have a Strategy beyond Milking Papers for Profit?," Nieman Lab, accessed October 14, 2022, https://www.niemanlab.org/2015/07/newsonomics-do-newspaper-companies-have-a-strategy-beyond-milking-papers-for-profit/.

75. Tribune Publishing Company, Form 10-K, annual report for the period ending December 29, 2019 (March 11, 2020), from the US Securities and Exchange Commission website, https://www.sec.gov/Archives/edgar/data/1593195/000159319520000024/tpco-20191229.htm.

76. "Tribune Publishing Company Announces Sale of BestReviews LLC to Nexstar Inc. for $160 Million," Tribune Publishing, December 16, 2020, https://investor.tribpub .com/news-releases/news-release-details/tribune-publishing-company-announces-sale -bestreviews-llc.

77. Katie Robertson, "The Hartford Courant's Newsroom Is Closing Down," *New York Times*, December 4, 2020, https://www.nytimes.com/2020/12/04/business/media/the -hartford-courants-newsroom-is-closing-down.html.

78. Tribune Publishing Company, Form 10-K, annual report for the fiscal year ending December 27, 2020 (March 8, 2021), from the US Securities and Exchange Commission website, https://sec.report/Document/0001593195-21-000020/.

79. "Lee Institutional Ownership—Lee Enterprises, Inc.," Fintel, https://fintel.io/so/ us/lee.

80. Lee Enterprises, Inc., Form 10-Q, quarterly report for the period ending June 27, 2021 (August 6, 2021), https://investors.lee.net/sec-filings/sec-filing/10-q/0001437749 -21-018907.

81. "McClatchy Files Asset Purchase Agreement with Chatham Asset Management That Retains Jobs and Benefits for All Employees: Paves Way to August 4 Hearing on Change in Control of 163-Year-Old News Company," *PR Newswire*, July 24, 2020.

82. Jonathan Randles and Lukas I. Alpert, "Fund Manager Wins McClatchy," *Wall Street Journal*, July 13, 2020, http://proxyau.wrlc.org/login?url=https://www.proquest.com/ newspapers/fund-manager-wins-mcclatchy/docview/2422935873/se-2?accountid=8285.

83. The McClatchy Company jointly filed with Chatham Asset Management, LLC, Schedule 13G (August 31, 2017), https://www.sec.gov/Archives/edgar/data/0001511989/ 000090571817000859/mcclatchy_13gaug312017.htm; McClatchy Company, Form 10-Q, quarterly report for the quarterly period ended July 1, 2018 (August 9, 2018), https:// content.edgar-online.com/ExternalLink/EDGAR/0001056087-18-000068.html?hash =4aa533c2106eb87e78489acc555abad007afcb48601bdf287492e458f9d6de40&dest=MNI -20180701EX1046F0090_HTM#MNI-20180701EX1046F0090_HTM.

84. Form 4, Statement of Changes in Beneficial Ownership (November 30, 2017), https:// www.sec.gov/Archives/edgar/data/0001056087/000090571817001010/xslF345X03/ chathamasset_fm4nov282017.xml.

85. McClatchy Company, Form 10-Q, quarterly report for the quarterly period ended July 1, 2018 (August 9, 2018).

86. McClatchy Company, July 1, 2018, quote appears on p. 6.

87. A list of McClatchy bankruptcy actions, claims, and petitions may be found here: https://www.kccllc.net/mcclatchy/register. Kevin G. Hall, "Hedge Fund Chatham Completes Purchase of McClatchy, Names Two Independent Board Members," McClatchy DC Bureau, September 4, 2020, https://www.mcclatchydc.com/article245490390.html #storylink=cpy.

88. S&P Capital IQ profile of September 6, 2021.

89. In conversation with the author, November 2021.

90. "McClatchy Acquired by Chatham Asset Management, LLC," McClatchy, accessed October 14, 2022, https://www.mcclatchy.com/about/news/mcclatchy-acquired-by -chatham-asset-management-llc/.

91. America Counts Staff, "Idaho Was the Second-Fastest Growing State Last Decade," US Census Bureau, US Department of Commerce, August 25, 2021, https://www.census .gov/library/stories/state-by-state/idaho-population-change-between-census-decade.html.

92. Teo Armus, "An Idaho Newspaper Editor Struggled to Get Excel Access for Staff. After Tweeting about It, She Was Fired," *Washington Post,* January 26, 2021, https://www .washingtonpost.com/nation/2021/01/26/idaho-statesman-editor-fired-excel/.

93. Keith Ridler, "Idaho Lawmakers Want Federal Public Land Appraised for Taxes," *AP News,* November 1, 2021, https://apnews.com/article/technology-business-idaho -property-taxes-congress-d9fc9fba592de45a929b5c3d6e9e07a5.

94. Kati Erwert, "Impact," *Seattle Times,* n.d., https://company.seattletimes.com/impact/.

95. Margaret Carmel, "Union Says Idaho Statesman's Top Editor Was Fired over Tweet, Demands Reinstatement," BoiseDev. Day365, LLC, January 25, 2021, https://boisedev .com/news/2021/01/25/idaho-statesman-union-blasts-mcclatchy-for-inappropriate-firing -of-editor-in-chief/.

96. Idaho News Guild, Twitter post, January 25, 2021, 6:22 p.m., https://twitter.com/ IdahoNewsGuild/status/1353845760853385218.

97. Christina Lords, "Welcome to the Idaho Capital Sun—the Gem State's Newest Nonprofit Journalism Outlet," *Idaho Capital Sun,* March 31, 2021, https://idahocapitalsun .com/2021/03/31/welcome-to-the-idaho-capital-sun-the-gem-states-newest-nonprofit -journalism-outlet/?fbclid=IwAR2qL6xnuB2mjKxpfm3Upe4oh7Qe7Y8sFMBKNEQSI _hy2zTp9ofV_EsDV6Q.

98. Chatham Asset Management, LLC, Form ADV, Uniform Application for Invest- ment Adviser Registration and Report by Exempt Reporting Advisers (May 17, 2021), from the US Securities and Exchange Commission website, https://reports.adviserinfo .sec.gov/reports/ADV/157517/PDF/157517.pdf.

99. "Press Release: Chatham Asset Management Sends Letter to Mohegan Tribal Gaming Authority," *Dow Jones Institutional News,* January 28, 2021, http://proxyau.wrlc.org/login ?url=https://www.proquest.com/wire-feeds/press-release-chatham-asset-management -sends/docview/2482457563/se-2?accountid=8285.

100. "One Call Names Thomas Warsop Chief Executive Officer," *PR Newswire,* February 4, 2020, https://www.proquest.com/wire-feeds/one-call-names-thomas-warsop-chief -executive/docview/2350300415/se-2?accountid=8285.

101. "About Our Values, Mission, People, and Commitments," R. R. Donnelley & Sons Company, n.d., https://www.rrd.com/about.

102. "R. R. Donnelley Responds to 13G Filing from Chatham, Open to Input from Holders," *The Fly,* August 2, 2021, https://thefly.com/landingPageNews.php?id=3347564 &headline=RRD-RR-Donnelley-responds-to-G-filing-from-Chatham-open-to-input -from-holders.

103. "Chatham Asset Management Calls for Continued Deleveraging at R. R. Donnel- ley," *The Fly,* September 1, 2021, https://thefly.com/landingPageNews.php?id=3366075

&headline=RRD-Chatham-Asset-Management-calls-for-continued-deleveraging-at -RR-Donnelley.

104. "Chatham Asset Management Completes Acquisition of RRD," accessed October 14, 2022, https://investor.rrd.com/news/news-details/2022/Chatham-Asset-Management -Completes-Acquisition-of-RRD/default.aspx.

105. Penelope Muse Abernathy, *The Rise of the New Media Baron and the Emerging Threats of News Deserts*, University of North Carolina at Chapel Hill Center for Innovation and Sustainability in Local Media, 2016, http://newspaperownership.com/newspaper -ownership-report/.

106. David Billings, "The Convergence of Hedge Funds and Private Equity Funds," *Hedge Fund Journal*, issue 7, accessed March 15, 2019, https://thehedgefundjournal.com/ the-convergence-of-hedge-funds-and-private-equity-funds/; John Morton, "The Hedge Fund Era: Financial Firms Are Investing Heavily in Newspapers. What Does That Mean for Journalism?," *American Journalism Review* 33, no. 1 (March 2011): 56, https://go.gale .com/ps/i.do?id=GALE%7CA252635088&sid=googleScholar&v=2.1&it=r&linkaccess= abs&issn=10678654&p=AONE&sw=w&userGroupName=anon%7Eecd07b69.

107. Mark Fitzgerald and Jennifer Saba, "The New Face of Newspapers?," *Editor & Publisher* 139, no. 1 (January 2006): quote appears in paragraph 6, ABI/INFORM.

108. Julie Reynolds, "Why Hedge Funds Shouldn't Own the News," *American Prospect*, October 1, 2020, https://prospect.org/economy/why-hedge-funds-shouldnt-own-the-news/.

109. Richard Siklos, "How Did Newspapers Land in This Mess?," *New York Times*, October 1, 2006, https://www.nytimes.com/2006/10/01/business/yourmoney/01frenzy.html.

110. John Hoff, "Avista Capital Partners Is the Devil," *Minnesota Daily*, October 1, 2007, https://mndaily.com/193008/opinion/avista-capital-partners-devil/.

111. Alex S. Jones, *Losing the News: The Future of the News That Feeds Democracy* (Oxford: Oxford University Press, 2009).

112. Katharine Q. Seelye, "McClatchy Sells the Star Tribune of Minneapolis to a Private Equity Firm," *New York Times*, December 27, 2006, https://www.nytimes.com/ 2006/12/27/technology/27iht-startrib.4027986.html.

113. In conversation with the author, January 2021.

114. "Avista Capital Partners: Minneapolis Paper to Cut 145 Positions as Sales Fall," *Wall Street Journal*, May 8, 2007, ABI/INFORM.

115. Chris Serres, "Bringing in Blackstone, Star Tribune Means Business," *McClatchy-Tribune Business News*, May 6, 2008, ABI/INFORM; David Phelps, "Paper's Largest Lender Is Local; Wayzata Investment Partners, Spun Off from a Former Cargill Subsidiary, Holds $58 Million of the Star Tribune's Debt. Court Papers Show the Economy's Effects on Advertising," *Star Tribune*, January 17, 2009, ABI/INFORM.

116. Form D Avista Capital Partners II, LP, US Securities and Exchange Commission, February 9, 2009, https://sec.report/Document/9999999997-09-004097/.

117. Robert Kuttner and Hildy Zenger, "Saving the Free Press from Private Equity," *American Prospect*, Winter 2018, 1–21.

118. Adam Belz, "Glen Taylor Finalizes Purchase of Star Tribune," *TCA Regional News*, July 1, 2014.

119. Glen Taylor, "Now More Than Ever, This Newspaper Is Essential to Minnesota," *Star Tribune*, May 16, 2020, https://www.startribune.com/now-more-than-ever-this-newspaper-is-essential-to-minnesota/570517952/.

120. Avista Capital Partners, Form ADV, Uniform Application for Investment Adviser Registration and Report by Exempt Reporting Advisers (March 24, 2021), from the US Securities and Exchange Commission website, https://sec.report/AdviserInfo/Firms/160750/Form-ADV-160750.pdf.

121. "Ariel Capital Management Raise Stakes in Tribune," Black Entrepreneurs & Executives Profiles, November 15, 2006, https://www.blackentrepreneurprofile.com/news/article/ariel-capital-management-raise-stakes-in-tribune.

122. "Interview: Charles Bobrinskoy," *Frontline*, October 30, 2006, https://www.pbs.org/wgbh/pages/frontline/newswar/interviews/bobrinskoy.html.

123. Norm Alster, "Paper Chase," *Institutional Investor*, 2006, 1, ABI/INFORM; Sarah Ellison and Julia Angwin, "Tribune Opens Door to Possible Sale; Board Forms Panel to Craft Strategy to Increase Value; Range of Options on the Table," *Wall Street Journal*, September 22, 2006, A3, ABI/INFORM.

124. Edward S. Herman, *Corporate Control, Corporate Power* (New York: Cambridge University Press, 1981), 12.

125. Vincent Mosco, *Political Economy of Communication* (London: Sage, 2009).

126. Aldo Svaldi and Steve Raabe, "MediaNews Makes Changes," *Denver Post*, January 19, 2011, https://www.denverpost.com/2011/01/18/medianews-makes-changes/.

127. Jonathan O'Connell, "As Gannett Merger Nears Completion, Union Claims 'Journalism Will Suffer' under Deal," *Washington Post*, November 9, 2019, https://www.washingtonpost.com/business/2019/11/08/gannett-merger-nears-completion-union-claims-deal-threatens-journalism/.

128. "About Apollo Global Management," Leadership & About Apollo Global Management | Apollo Global Management, accessed March 6, 2021, https://www.apollo.com/about-apollo.

129. Ted Bunker, "Private Equity Daily: Investors See Weaker in Terms to Bar Conflicts Beckelman on Secondaries | Apollo's SoftBank Loan | Bets Rise on Metal Miners," *WSJ Pro. Private Equity*, December 22, 2021, http://proxyau.wrlc.org/login?url=https://www.proquest.com/trade-journals/private-equity-daily-investors-see-weaker-terms/docview/2612372415/se-2?accountid=8285; "Apollo Doles Out $1.8b Loan for Newspaper Merger," *Financial Services Monitor Worldwide*, November 16, 2019.

130. Gannett Co., December 31, 2020, quote appears on p. 52.

131. Gannett Co., Inc., Schedule 14-A (April 28, 2021), https://d18rnop25nwr6d.cloudfront.net/CIK-0001579684/6ee6b199-e99e-4288-8998-b1bb54adfdd8.pdf.

132. "The Future of Media Project," *Index of US Mainstream Media Ownership*, Harvard University, May 11, 2021, https://projects.iq.harvard.edu/files/futureofmedia/files/us_media_ownership_may_2021.pdf.

133. "About BlackRock," BlackRock, Inc., n.d., https://www.blackrock.com/sg/en/about-us.

134. Dawn Lim, "BlackRock Closes In on the Once Unthinkable, $10 Trillion in Assets; Chief Executive Larry Fink Says Inflation Is Here to Stay," *Wall Street Journal*, July 14, 2021.

135. Jan Fichtner, Eelke M. Heemskerk, and Javier Garcia-Bernardo, "Hidden Power of the Big Three? Passive Index Funds, Re-concentration of Corporate Ownership, and New Financial Risk," *Business and Politics* 19, no. 2 (2017): 298–326, doi:10.1017/bap.2017.6.

136. BlackRock, Investment Stewardship annual report for the reporting period ending June 30, 2020 (September 2020), https://www.blackrock.com/corporate/literature/publication/blk-annual-stewardship-report-2020.pdf.

137. Jack Horgan-Jones, "Doing Business with the Hound of Hell," *Sunday Business Post*, September 29, 2016.

138. "Nurses Say Private Equity Firm Starving Massachusetts Hospitals," Communications Workers of America, December 21, 2011, https://cwa-union.org/news/entry/nurses_say_private_equity_firm_starving_massachusetts_hospitals-phe.

139. Bob Warner, "Newspapers' Owners Choose Philadelphia Media Network Inc. as Company's New Name," *McClatchy-Tribune Business News*, June 22, 2010.

140. "Why Can't Cerberus Foot the Bill?," editorial, *New York Times*, February 23, 2009, https://archive.nytimes.com/dealbook.nytimes.com/2009/02/23/why-cant-cerberus-foot-the-bill/.

141. "Potential Suitor Eyes High-Stakes Bet on Kannapolis, N.C.–Based Textile Firm," *Knight Ridder Tribune Business News*, May 10, 2003.

142. "Times-News Parent Company Sells Broadcast Properties," *McClatchy-Tribune Business News*, November 2, 2011.

143. Rimin Dutt, "Cerberus-Backed NewPage Launches Debt Swap Offers," *LBO Wire*, August 6, 2009.

144. "Cerberus in Talks to Buy Newspaper Owner Digital First Media–Bloomberg," *Dow Jones Institutional News*, January 23, 2015, ABI/INFORM; Ken Doctor, "What Are They Thinking? Apollo's Acquisition of Digital First Media," *Politico*, March 17, 2015, https://www.politico.com/media/story/2015/03/what-are-they-thinking-apollos-acquisition-of-digital-first-media-003573/.

145. Tribune Publishing Company, Schedule 13D (May 24, 2021), filed by Donnelley Financial Solutions, from US Securities and Exchange Commission website, https://sec.report/Document/0001193125-21-173983/.

146. James O'Shea, *The Deal from Hell: How Moguls and Wall Street Plundered Great American Newspapers* (New York: PublicAffairs, 2011), 346.

Chapter 4. Mergers and Acquisitions

1. Penelope Muse Abernathy, *The Rise of the New Media Baron and the Emerging Threats of News Deserts*, University of North Carolina at Chapel Hill Center for Innovation and Sustainability in Local Media, 2016, http://newspaperownership.com/newspaper-ownership-report/.

2. To Amend the Clayton Act to Modify the Standard for an Unlawful Acquisition, and for Other Purposes, S.B. 307, 116th Cong. (2019), https://www.congress.gov/116/bills/s307/BILLS-116s307is.pdf.

3. Jonathan A. Knee, Bruce C. Greenwald, and Ava Seave, *The Curse of the Mogul: What's Wrong with the World's Leading Media Companies* (New York: Penguin, 2009), 12.

4. Graeme K. Deans, Fritz Kroeger, and Stefan Zeisel, *Winning the Merger Endgame: A Playbook for Profiting from Industry Consolidation* (New York: McGraw-Hill, 2003), xiv.

5. Alex Jones, *Losing the News: The Future of the News That Feeds Democracy* (Oxford: Oxford University Press, 2009), 156–57.

6. Deans, Kroeger, and Zeisel, *Winning the Merger Endgame*, ix.

7. Paul Boselie and Bas Koene, "Private Equity and Human Resource Management: 'Barbarians at the Gate!' HR's Wake-Up Call?," *Human Relations* 63, no. 9 (2010): 1297–1319, https://doi.org/10.1177/0018726709349519, 1298.

8. Richard Tofel, "Bancroft Family Members Express Regrets at Selling Wall Street Journal to Murdoch," *ProPublica*, July 13, 2011, https://www.propublica.org/article/bancroft-family-members-express-regrets-at-selling-wall-street-journal-to-m; Anna Nicolaou and James Fontanella-Khan, "The Fight for the Future of America's Local Newspapers," FT.com, January 21, 2021, https://www.ft.com/content/5c22075c-f1af-431d-bf39-becf9c54758b.

9. "The History of the Scripps Concern," E. W. Scripps Papers, Mahn Center for Archives & Special Collections, Ohio University Libraries, https://media.library.ohio.edu/digital/collection/scripps/id/8364, quote on 9.

10. Edwin Emery, *The Press and America: An Interpretive History of the Mass Media* (New York: Prentice-Hall, 1972), 711.

11. "Scripps Networks Announces Strategic Reorganization," Scripps Howard, January 19, 2000, https://scripps.com/press-releases/232-scripps-networks-announces-strategic-reorganization/.

12. The E. W. Scripps Company, Form 10-K, annual report filed by the E. W. Scripps Company for the year ending December 31, 2015 (February 26, 2016), https://ir.scripps.com/static-files/b329c2d1-1dfb-4d88-bc31-3be15262704a.

13. "Cox Enterprises Announces Close of Cox Media Group Sale to Affiliates of Apollo Global Management," Cision PR Newswire, December 17, 2019, https://www.prnewswire.com/news-releases/cox-enterprises-announces-close-of-cox-media-group-sale-to-affiliates-of-apollo-global-management-300976507.html.

14. R. D. Gersh, "Bingham Family Newspapers Sold to Gannett," *Associated Press*, May 19, 1986, https://apnews.com/article/58b26571abb7b2d1e68003e1e0b1c94e; Susan E. Tifft and Alex S. Jones, *The Patriarch: The Rise and Fall of the Bingham Dynasty* (New York: Simon and Schuster, 1993).

15. Jolie Solomon and Laurie Hays, "Gannett Wins Bidding Contest to Acquire 2 Bingham Newspapers in Louisville, Ky.," *Wall Street Journal*, May 20, 1986, 8, ABI/INFORM.

16. Philip Meyer, *The Vanishing Newspaper: Saving Journalism in the Information Age* (Columbia: University of Missouri Press, 2009), 41.

17. Nick Penniman, "Goliath Getting Bigger," *American Prospect*, May 6, 2002, 8.

18. Stephen Taub, "Leon Cooperman to Convert Omega Advisors to Family Office at Year End," *Institutional Investor*, July 23, 2018, https://www.institutionalinvestor.com/article/b1964md24fs2fr/Leon-Cooperman-to-Convert-Omega-Advisors-to-Family-Office-at-Year-End.

19. Abernathy, *The Rise of a New Media Baron*.

20. Soontae An and Hyun Seung Jin, "Interlocking of Newspaper Companies with Financial Institutions and Leading Advertisers," *Journalism and Mass Communication Quarterly* 81, no. 3 (Autumn 2004): 578–600.

21. Suzanne M. Kirchhoff, "The U.S. Newspaper Industry in Transition," Congressional Research Service, September 9, 2010, https://sgp.fas.org/crs/misc/R40700.pdf.

22. Robert G. Picard, "Issues and Challenges," in *Corporate Governance of Media Companies*, ed. Robert G. Picard (Jönkoping, Sweden: Jönkoping International Business School, 2005), 1.

23. Picard, "Issues and Challenges," 1.

24. Robert Kuttner and Hildy Zenger, "Saving the Free Press from Private Equity," *American Prospect*, December 27, 2017, https://prospect.org/health/saving-free-press-private-equity/.

25. Lukas I. Alpert, "Gannett Looks to Spare Journalists' Jobs after Big Newspaper Merger; Deal to Combine USA Today Publisher Gannett with GateHouse Media Closes, Forming Company with 30% of Papers Sold Daily in U.S.," *Wall Street Journal*, November 19, 2019, https://www.wsj.com/articles/gannett-looks-to-spare-journalists-jobs-after-big-newspaper-merger-11574197800.

26. Greg Avery and Mark Harden, "Singleton to Step Down as CEO of Denver Post Owner MediaNews Group," *Denver Business Journal*, January 20, 2011, https://www.bizjournals.com/denver/news/2011/01/18/singleton.html.

27. Howard Kurtz, "Tribune to Buy Times Mirror Co.," *Washington Post*, March 14, 2000, https://www.washingtonpost.com/archive/politics/2000/03/14/tribune-to-buy-times-mirror-co/2573233d-41cc-4562-9c35-b7ff729170d0/; "Chandler Family," *Forbes*, 2015, https://www.forbes.com/profile/chandler/?sh=4dfd04336038.

28. David Shaw and Mitchell Landsberg, "L.A. Icon Otis Chandler Dies at 78," *Los Angeles Times*, February 27, 2006, https://www.latimes.com/la-me-chandler-obit-story.html.

29. David Halberstam, *The Powers That Be* (Urbana: University of Illinois Press, 1975), 94.

30. *In re Tribune Co., et al.*, Case No. 18–2909, 2020 WL 5035797 (3d Cir. Aug. 26, 2020).

31. David Shaw and Sallie Hofmeister, "Times Mirror Agrees to Merger with Tribune Co.," *Los Angeles Times*, March 13, 2000, https://www.latimes.com/archives/la-xpm-2000-mar-13-mn-9216-story.html.

32. Media Intelligence Center, Alliance for Audited Media, accessed October 12, 2021, https://auditedmedia.com.

33. Mark Fitzgerald and Jennifer Saba, "The New Face of Newspapers?," *Editor & Publisher* 139, no. 1 (January 2006): quote in paragraph 1, ABI/INFORM.

34. "Journal Register Co. Hopes Shares Attract Institutional Investors," *Wall Street Journal*, August 25, 1999, ABI/INFORM.

35. "Journal Register Company: Company Profile, Information, Business Description, History, Background Information on Journal Register Company," Reference for Business, Advameg, Inc., n.d., https://www.referenceforbusiness.com/history2/73/Journal-Register-Company.html.

36. Business Editors, "Warburg, Pincus Capital Company, L.P. to Distribute up to Five Million Shares of Journal Register Company Common Stock to Partners," *Business Wire*, August 23, 1999.

37. "Journal Register Company: Company Profile."

38. Hilary Rosenberg, *The Vulture Investors* (New York: John Wiley & Sons, 2000), 324.

39. Brian Steinberg, "Despite Woes, Newspapers Seen Hitting Targets: Ad-Revenue Growth Slows, Staff Shake-Ups Grow, but Bottom Lines Hold," *Wall Street Journal*, January 5, 1999, eastern edition, ABI/INFORM; Lucia Moses, "Soft Landing for Year-End Profits," *Editor & Publisher* 133, no. 50 (December 2000): 9–10, ABI/INFORM.

40. Business Editors, "Warburg Pincus Distributes 2.5 Million Shares of Journal Register Company Common Stock to Partners," *Business Wire*, June 18, 2002, ABI/INFORM.

41. Brian Steinberg, "Fund Scores with Untrendy Picks: Small-Capitalization Stocks Currently out of Favor Are Paying Off for Ariel," *Wall Street Journal*, July 10, 2002, ABI/INFORM; Norm Alster, "Paper Chase," *Institutional Investor* 12 (2006): 1, ABI/INFORM.

42. "Warburg Pincus Acquires SDI Media Group," *PR Newswire*, July 5, 2004; Peter Lauria, "Pulitzer on the Block," The Deal.com, November 25, 2004, 1, ABI/INFORM.

43. "Q2 2004 Journal Register Earnings Conference Call—Final," *Fair Disclosure Wire*, July 16, 2004, ABI/INFORM.

44. "Q2 2004 Mcg Capital Corporation Earnings Conference Call—Final," *Fair Disclosure Wire*, August 4, 2004, ABI/INFORM.

45. Dennis K. Berman, "Journal Register Cements Deal for 21st Century Newspapers," *Wall Street Journal*, July 6, 2004, ABI/INFORM.

46. Rob Garver, "The Journal Register Continues to Cluster," NJBIZ, August 9, 2005, https://njbiz.com/the-journal-register-continues-to-cluster-2/.

47. Jacques Steinberg, "Pulitzer to Be Acquired by Lee Enterprises," *New York Times*, February 1, 2005, https://www.nytimes.com/2005/02/01/business/media/pulitzer-to-be-acquired-by-lee-enterprises.html.

48. "Gannett to Acquire Hometown Communications Network," TEGNA Inc., November 19, 2004, https://www.tegna.com/gannett-to-acquire-hometown-communications-network/.

49. "Gannett to Acquire."

50. Dennis K. Berman, "Fortress Capital to Buy Publisher Liberty Group," *Wall Street Journal*, May 11, 2005, ABI/INFORM.

51. "Journal Register Company Acquires Suburban Lifestyles Community Newspaper Group," *Business Wire*, March 29, 2006.

52. Christopher Rowland, "Can Suburban Newspapers Deliver? Investors See Promise," *Knight Ridder Tribune Business News*, May 16, 2006, ABI/INFORM.

53. Judy McDermott, "GateHouse Media Seeks $762M in Loans," *Bank Loan Report,* May 15, 2006, 1, ABI/INFORM.

54. Mary Stone, "Majority Owner of GateHouse Presses a Market First with IPO," *Rochester Business Journal,* February 16, 2007, 1, ABI/INFORM.

55. Lynn Cowan, "GateHouse Media Rises 18% in IPO; Two Others Mixed," *Wall Street Journal,* October 26, 2006, eastern edition, https://www.wsj.com/articles/SB116181541143803910.

56. Ken Doctor, "Newsonomics: As McClatchy Teeters, a New Set of Money Men Enters the News Industry Spotlight," Nieman Lab, Nieman Foundation for Journalism at Harvard University, November 19, 2019, https://www.niemanlab.org/2019/11/newsonomics-as-mcclatchy-teeters-a-new-set-of-money-men-enters-the-news-industry-spotlight/.

57. Max Follmer, "The Reporting Team That Got Iraq Right," *HuffPost,* May 25, 2011, https://www.huffpost.com/entry/the-reporting-team-that-g_n_91981.

58. Knight Ridder, Inc., Form 10-K, annual report filed with the US Securities and Exchange Commission for the fiscal year ending December 26, 2004 (March 2, 2005), https://sec.report/Document/0001193125-05-041190/.

59. Charles Layton, "Sherman's March: How Naples, Florida, Money Manager Bruce S. Sherman Muscled Knight Ridder—the Nation's Second-Largest Newspaper Company—into Putting Itself up for Sale," *American Journalism Review* 28, no. 1 (2006): 18–25, https://ajrarchive.org/Article.asp?id=4037, quote appears in paragraph 1.

60. Layton, "Sherman's March," paragraph 7.

61. Lawrence C. Strauss, "Behind the Pressure on Knight Ridder," *Barron's,* November 21, 2005, 36.

62. Laura Smitherman, "Florida-Based Investment Firm's Quiet Leader Has Two-Decade Media Background," *Knight Ridder Tribune Business News,* November 4, 2005, ABI/INFORM.

63. Layton, "Sherman's March," paragraph 7.

64. Smitherman, "Florida-Based."

65. Private Capital Management, Form 13-G, report filed with the US Securities and Exchange Commission, February 14, 2006, https://www.sec.gov/Archives/edgar/data/93676/000089722606000073/0000897226-06-000073.txt, quote appears in exhibit 1.

66. Smitherman, "Florida-Based."

67. Fitzgerald and Saba, "The New Face?," 24–26, 28, 30–32.

68. David Folkenflik, "McClatchy Will Buy Knight Ridder for $4.5 Billion," *NPR,* March 13, 2006, https://www.npr.org/templates/story/story.php?storyId=5260417.

69. "Business: Press Gang; Newspapers in America," *The Economist,* November 19, 2005, 76.

70. John Soloski, "Taking Stock Redux: Corporate Ownership and Journalism of Publicly Traded Newspaper Companies," in *Corporate Governance of Media Companies,* ed. Robert G. Picard (Jönkoping, Sweden: Jönkoping International Business School, 2005), 59–76.

71. "McClatchy to Sell Four Knight Ridder Newspapers for $1 Billion," Hearst Communications, Inc., April 26, 2006, https://www.hearst.com/-/mcclatchy-to-sell-four-knight-ridder-newspapers-for-1-billion.

72. Rem Rieder, "The Conventional Wisdom Trap: When It Comes to Newspaper Ownership, Saviors Are Elusive," *American Journalism Review* 29, no. 1 (2007): 4–5, https://ajrarchive.org/Article.asp?id=4260, quote on 4.

73. "Journal Community Publishing Group Agrees to Sell Its Connecticut and Vermont Clusters to Hersam Acorn Community Publishing and Its Central Ohio Advertiser Network and Advantage Press to Gannett Co.," *Business Wire*, June 19, 2007, ABI/INFORM.

74. "Sealing Their Own Fates," *Editor & Publisher* 140, no. 1 (January 2007): 19, ABI/INFORM.

75. Journal Register Co., Form 10-K, annual report filed by Capital Systems with the US Securities and Exchange Commission for the fiscal year ending December 30, 2007 (March 14, 2008), from US Securities and Exchange Commission website, https://sec.report/Document/0000950136-08-001341/.

76. Steven Church and Dawn McCarty, "Journal Register Files for Bankruptcy," *Philadelphia Inquirer*, February 21, 2009, https://www.inquirer.com/philly/news/breaking/20090221_Journal_Register_files_for_bankruptcy.html.

77. GateHouse Media, Inc., Form 10-K, annual report for the fiscal year ending December 31, 2007 (March 17, 2008), https://www.sec.gov/Archives/edgar/data/1368900/000114420408015835/v096277_10k.htm, quote on 1.

78. "Morris Publishing Group to Sell Several Newspapers and Other Related Publications," *PR Newswire*, October 23, 2007, ABI/INFORM.

79. "GateHouse Buying 14 Dailies, Other Pubs, from Morris for $115 Million," *Editor & Publisher*, October 23, 2007, https://web.archive.org/web/20171201032124/http://www.editorandpublisher.com/news/gatehouse-buying-14-dailies-other-pubs-from-morris-for-115-million/.

80. "GateHouse Media Completes Acquisition of 9 Publications in Northeastern Ohio and Central Illinois," *Gannett*, April 4, 2007, https://investors.gannett.com/news/news-details/2007/GateHouse-Media-Completes-Acquisition-of-9-Publications-in-Northeastern-Ohio-and-Central-Illinois/default.aspx.

81. "GateHouse Media Completes Acquisition of Morris Publications," *Gannett*, December 3, 2007, https://investors.gannett.com/news/news-details/2007/GateHouse-Media-Completes-Acquisition-of-Morris-Publications/default.aspx.

82. Tom Lowry, "Hot News in Nowheresville: Fortress' GateHouse Media Is Snapping Up Small-Town Papers—and Turning a Nice Profit," *Bloomberg Businessweek*, February 19, 2007, 74, ABI/INFORM.

83. GateHouse Media, Inc., Form 10-K, December 31, 2007, 93.

84. Lowry, "Hot News in Nowheresville," 74.

85. "Knight Ridder Launches Internet Unit," *Editor & Publisher*, November 9, 1999, https://www.editorandpublisher.com/stories/knight-ridder-launches-internet-unit,99420, quote appears in paragraph 1.

86. "A New Story Lead for the Newspaper Industry: Newspaper Websites Are Contributing to Audience Growth; Online-Exclusive Newspaper Audience Accounts for 2% to 15% of Integrated Newspaper Audience; Industry Executives Comment on Online Au-

dience Growth in New White Paper from Scarborough," *PR Newswire*, August 23, 2006, ABI/INFORM.

87. Suzanne McGee and Matthew Rose, "Newspapers' Internet Stories Haven't Clicked with Investors," *Wall Street Journal*, July 11, 2000, eastern edition, ABI/INFORM.

88. "Business: Press Gang; Newspapers in America," *The Economist*, November 19, 2005, 76, ABI/INFORM.

89. Andrew Bary, "Printing Money," *Barron's*, April 9, 2007, 23, 25, quote appears in paragraph 1, ABI/INFORM.

90. Bill Pate to Sam Zell, memorandum, August 9, 2007, Equity Group Investments, LLC, EGI-LAW 00178270, https://admin.epiq11.com/onlinedocuments/trb/examiner reports/EX%200786.pdf.

91. David Carr and Tim Arango, "Tribune Chief Accepts Advice and Backs Out," *New York Times*, October 22, 2010, https://www.nytimes.com/2010/10/23/business/media/23tribune.htm.

92. William Pate, "Tribune First 100 Day Plan," email, 2007, https://admin.epiq11.com/onlinedocuments/trb/examinerreports/EX%200825.pdf.

93. Kurt Greenbaum, "Sifting the Dot-Com Wreckage for Lessons," *American Editor*, no. 817 (April 2001): 24–26.

94. In conversation with the author, September 2020.

95. "Lee Enterprises 2005 Annual Report," 2005, https://bloximages.chicago2.vip.town-news.com/lee.net/content/tncms/assets/v3/editorial/2/31/2310b45e-2bc6-11e4-98d2-001a4bcf887a/53fa3f2cb4366.pdf.

96. Gregory Cancelada, "Pulitzer Purchase Is Largest in History of Lee Enterprises," *Knight Ridder Tribune Business News*, January 31, 2005, ABI/INFORM.

97. Fitzgerald and Saba, "The New Face?"

98. Gannett Co. Inc., Form 10-K, annual report to investors for the fiscal year ending December 24, 2005 (February 24, 2006), https://investors.tegna.com/static-files/ba068c13-27b3-4941-b35e-7af2de1b1853.

99. In conversation with the author, October 2021.

100. In conversation with the author, October 2021.

101. New Media Investment Group, Inc., Form 10-K, annual report for the fiscal year ending December 29, 2013 (March 19, 2014), from the US Securities and Exchange Commission website, https://www.sec.gov/Archives/edgar/data/1579684/000119312514106565/d694452d10k.htm.

102. New Media Investment Group, Inc., Form 10-K, December 29, 2013.

103. "Gannett, GateHouse Media in Merger Talks—7th Update," *Dow Jones Institutional News*, May 30, 2019, ABI/INFORM.

104. Jennifer Wentz, "Central Penn Business Journal Parent Buys Newspapers in Philadelphia, Pittsburgh Suburbs," *Central Penn Business Journal*, June 19, 2017, ABI/INFORM.

105. "Press Club of Western PA Announces 2017 Golden Quill Winners," *PR Newswire*, May 25, 2017, ABI/INFORM.

106. In conversation with the author, October 2021.

107. Dean Starkman, *Columbia Journalism Review*, November/December 2011, https://archives.cjr.org/essay/confidence_game.php, quote appears in paragraph 17.

108. Jeffrey C. Hooke, *The Myth of Private Equity: An Inside Look at Wall Street's Transformative Investments* (New York: Columbia University Press, 2021), 174.

109. David Simon, "Testimony, U.S. Senate Commerce Committee, Hearing on the Future of Newspapers," *Audacity of Despair*, May 6, 2009, https://davidsimon.com/wire-creator-david-simon-testifies-on-the-future-of-journalism/.

110. James Fallows, "Our Towns: There's Hope for Local Journalism," *The Atlantic*, September 18, 2019, https://www.theatlantic.com/notes/2019/09/theres-hope-for-local-journalism/598225/.

111. Graeme K. Deans, Fritz Kroeger, and Stefan Zeisel, *Winning the Merger Endgame: A Playbook for Profiting from Industry Consolidation* (New York: McGraw-Hill Professional, 2003).

112. Fitzgerald and Saba, "The New Face?"

113. Andrew Ross Sorkin, "When a Bank Works Both Sides," *New York Times*, April 8, 2007, https://www.nytimes.com/2007/04/08/business/yourmoney/08deal.html.

114. Lauren Rich Fine, "Newspapers Should Come to Terms with Lower Margins Then Go Private," *CBS News*, October 22, 2018, https://www.cbsnews.com/news/amazon-return-to-office-3-days/, quote appears in paragraph 1.

115. Lauren Rich Fine, "Hard to Find the Silver Lining; Possibilities Include Bankruptcies, Funding Woes," *CBS News*, September 30, 2008, https://www.cbsnews.com/news/bankruptcy-filings-2022-company-personal-epiq/, quote appears in paragraph 3.

Chapter 5. The Debt

1. Matt Phillips, "Hungry for Investors, Some Companies Woo the Little Guy," *New York Times*, April 13, 2021, https://www.nytimes.com/2021/04/13/business/stock-market-investors.html.

2. A list of documents, including court opinions, motions, and exhibits such as Mr. Kauders's letter referenced in this chapter, may be found at https://dm.epiq11.com/case/tribune/info.

3. In conversation with the author, October 8, 2021.

4. In re Tribune Company Fraudulent Conveyance Litigation, Consolidated Multidistrict Action: Case No. 11 MD 2296 (RJS), No. 12 MC 2296 (RJS), No. 12 CV 6055 (RJS) (S.D.N.Y. August 2, 2013), https://www.akingump.com/a/web/24307/Kirschner-v.-Citigroup-File-Stamped-First-Amended-Complaint-R.pdf.

5. "For 'Vultures,' Slim Pickings," *Dow Jones Institutional News*, April 10, 2011.

6. Mark Fitzgerald and Jennifer Saba, "Owners Up to It?," *Editor & Publisher* 142, no. 12 (December 2009): 24–26, https://www.proquest.com/abicomplete/docview/194323623/A7AE10CE4FC04261PQ/1?accountid=8285.

7. Robert Kuttner and Hildy Zenger, "Saving the Free Press from Private Equity," *American Prospect*, Winter 2018, 1–21, 19. Hildy Zenger was at the time the pen name of a GateHouse reporter.

8. Eliza Ronalds-Hannon and Jeremy Hill, "McClatchy Bankruptcy Begins with Call to Probe Deals," *Bloomberg Wire Service*, June 26, 2020.

9. "Craig Newmark Endows the CUNY Graduate School of Journalism with a $20 Million Gift," Craig Newmark Graduate School of Journalism, City University of New York, June 11, 2018, https://www.journalism.cuny.edu/2018/06/now-craig-newmark -graduate-school-journalism-city-university-new-york/.

10. Kevin Phillips, *Bad Money: Reckless Finance, Failed Politics, and the Global Crisis of American Capitalism* (New York: Penguin, 2009), 43.

11. Irina Fox, "Protecting All Corporate Stakeholders: Fraudulent Transfer Law as a Check on Corporate Distributions," *Delaware Journal of Corporate Law* 44, no. 1 (2020): 81–120.

12. US Senate, Committee on Finance, *Hearing, Debt versus Equity: Corporate Integration Considerations*, §114–656 (114AD), https://www.govinfo.gov/content/pkg/CHRG -114shrg25851/pdf/CHRG-114shrg25851.pdf.

13. US Senate, Committee on Finance, *Hearing, Debt versus Equity*, 9.

14. "Chapter 11—Bankruptcy Basics," United States Courts, n.d., https://www.uscourts .gov/services-forms/bankruptcy/bankruptcy-basics/chapter-11-bankruptcy-basics.

15. US Senate, Committee on Finance, *Hearing, Debt versus Equity*.

16. Michelle M. Harner, "Activist Distressed Debtholders: The New Barbarians at the Gate," *Washington University Law Review* 89, no. 1 (2011): 155–206.

17. Stephen G. Moyer and John D. Martin, "Distressed Debt Investments," in *Private Equity: Opportunities and Risks*, ed. H. Kent Baker, Greg Filbeck, and Halil Kiymaz (New York: Oxford University Press, 2015), 100–120.

18. Edward I. Altman, "The Role of Distressed Debt Markets, Hedge Funds, and Recent Trends in Bankruptcy on the Outcomes of Chapter 11 Reorganizations," *American Bankruptcy Institute Law Review* 22, no. 1 (Winter 2014): 75–124, 84.

19. Moyer and Martin, "Distressed Debt Investments," 108.

20. Rashida K. La Lande, "Private Equity Strategies for Exiting a Leveraged Buyout," Practical Law Company, 2011, https://www.gibsondunn.com/wp-content/uploads/ documents/publications/LaLande-PrivateEquityStrategiesforExitingaLeveragedBuyout .pdf.

21. Fox, "Protecting All Corporate Stakeholders," 102.

22. Harner, "Activist Distressed Debtholders."

23. Dan Beighley, "Day of Reckoning for Private Equity?," *Orange County Business Journal* 31, no. 1 (January 2009): 15.

24. Kuttner and Zenger, "Saving the Free Press," paragraph 64.

25. Mark Fitzgerald and Jennifer Saba, "Time to Clip Dividends?," *Editor & Publisher* 141, no. 6 (June 2008): 24–29, ABI/INFORM, quote appears in paragraph 11.

26. David Cohn, "When Journalism's Digital Dimes Are Made of Silver," *MediaShift*, July 18, 2013, http://mediashift.org/2013/07/when-journalisms-digital-dimes-are-made -of-silver/.

27. Harner, "Activist Distressed Debtholders," 184.

28. Hiromi Cho, Hugh J. Martin, and Stephen Lacy, "An Industry in Transition: Entry and Exit in Daily Newspaper Markets, 1987–2003," *Journalism and Mass Communication Quarterly* 83, no. 2 (July 2006): 381–96.

29. Julie Leupold, "News of the Week," *Orange County Business Journal* 33, no. 19 (May 2010): 6.

30. Fitzgerald and Saba, "Owners Up to It?," quote appears in paragraph 1.

31. Aaron Elstein, "Ten Years On, Taking Stock of the Financial Crisis: The Great Recession's Lasting Impact on Careers, Markets and Politics," *Crain's New York Business*, March 11, 2019, 10.

32. Hilary Rosenberg, *The Vulture Investors* (New York: John Wiley & Sons, 2000), 21.

33. Andrew Ross Sorkin, "When a Bank Works Both Sides," *New York Times*, April 8, 2007, https://www.nytimes.com/2007/04/08/business/yourmoney/08deal.html.

34. In re Tribune Co., Case No. 08–13141 (Bankr. D. Del. November 1, 2010), 3, https://amlawdaily.typepad.com/tribunecreditorsuit.pdf.

35. In re Tribune Co., Case No. 08–13141 (KJC) (Bankr. D. Del. October 31, 2011).

36. James O'Shea, *The Deal from Hell: How Moguls and Wall Street Plundered Great American Newspapers* (New York: PublicAffairs, 2011).

37. Rufus T. Dorsey and Matthew M. Weiss, "Third Circuit's Warning Shot to Senior Creditors in re Tribune," *American Bankruptcy Institute Journal* 39, no. 12 (December 2020): 14–15, 51–52.

38. In re Tribune Company Fraudulent Conveyance Litigation.

39. "Faculty Profiles: Kenneth Klee," UCLA School of Law, Regents of the University of California, n.d., https://law.ucla.edu/faculty/faculty-profiles/kenneth-n-klee.

40. Daniel Bussel, "A Third Way: Examiners as Inquisitors," *CLS Blue Sky Blog*, Trustees of Columbia University in the City of New York, April 12, 2015, https://clsbluesky.law.columbia.edu/2015/04/12/a-third-way-examiners-as-inquisitors/.

41. Bussel, "A Third Way."

42. In re Tribune Co., Case No. 08–13141 (KJC) (Bankr. D. Del. October 31, 2011), vol. 1, "Report of Kenneth N. Klee, as Examiner."

43. Richard Kellerhals, *Tribune Bankruptcy Hits Another Holdup*, Bank Loan Report, vol. 25 (New York: SourceMedia, Inc., 2010), 1.

44. "Tribune Investors Sue Banks That Arranged Financing," *Reuters*, October 30, 2010, https://www.reuters.com/article/us-tribune-lawsuit/tribune-investors-sue-banks-that-arranged-financing-idUSTRE69T1C920101030.

45. The Tribune docket may be found at https://dm.epiq11.com/case/tribune/dockets.

46. In re Tribune Co., Case Nos. 14-3332 and 14-3333 (3d Cir. 2015), http://www2.ca3.uscourts.gov/opinarch/143332p.pdf.

47. Soma Biswas, "Neiman Marcus, in Debt Talks, Makes It Easier to Bet It Will Fail; Activist Hedge Fund Aurelius Capital Pushed for Language in Debt Proposal That Would Make It Easier to Profit if Luxury Retailer Defaults," *Wall Street Journal*, March 26, 2019, ABI/INFORM.

48. In re Tribune Media Co., 799 F.3d 272 (3d Cir. 2015), https://casetext.com/case/in-re-tribune-media-co-1.

49. Matthew DeBord, "Aurelius Capital Management: The Hedge Fund That's Keeping Tribune in Bankruptcy," 89.3 KPCC, American Public Media Group, January 4, 2012, https://archive.kpcc.org/blogs/economy/2012/01/04/4167/aurelius-capital-hedge -fund-s-keeping-tribune-bank/.

50. Michael Oneal, "Bankruptcy Inc.: Four Years Later, the Biggest Winners in Tribune Co.'s Chapter 11 Case Are the Investment Firms That Profit from the Boom-and-Bust Cycles of Wall Street," in *Chicago Tribune (1963)* (Chicago: Tribune Publishing Company, 2013).

51. In re Tribune Company Fraudulent Conveyance Litigation.

52. Jonathan Randles, "Supreme Court Declines to Hear Tribune Co. Creditors' Challenge to 2007 Buyout; Tribune Creditors' Latest Bid to Claw Back Billions of Dollars That Flowed to Shareholders through the Leveraged Buyout Was Turned Away Monday," *WSJ Pro.Bankruptcy*, April 19, 2021.

53. In re Tribune Company et al., Brief of Appellees Tribune Company Retirees (3d Cir. 2020), January 24, 2019, quote on 16.

54. Judith Miller, "News Deserts: No News Is Bad News," in *Urban Policy 2018*, ed. William Bratton et al., 59–76, quote on 70, Manhattan Institute for Policy Research, https:// media4.manhattan-institute.org/sites/default/files/MI_Urban_Policy_2018.pdf.

55. Keith J. Kelly, "LA Times Owner Patrick Soon-Shiong 'Despised' for Tribune Vote," *New York Post*, May 26, 2021, https://nypost.com/2021/05/25/la-times-owner-patrick -soon-shiong-despised-for-tribune-vote/; Robert Channick, "Hedge Fund Alden Closes $633 Million Tribune Publishing Acquisition; Newspaper Chain Is Delisted from Stock Market," *TCA Regional News*, May 24, 2021, ABI/INFORM.

56. Kelly, "LA Times Owner."

57. Tribune Publishing Co., Form 10-Q, quarterly report filed by Tronc, Inc., with the US Securities and Exchange Commission for the period ending March 28, 2021 (May 5, 2021), from US Securities and Exchange Commission website, https://sec.report/ Document/0001593195-21-000039/#ie9bc2321e28e4a41a77127aa34946502_16.

58. Matt Moore, "Alden Global Capital Buys Journal Register Co.," *San Diego Union-Tribune*, July 14, 2011, https://www.sandiegouniontribune.com/sdut-alden-global-capital -buys-journal-register-co-2011jul14-story.html, quote appears in paragraph 4.

59. David Lieberman, "Journal Register Files for Chapter 11 Bankruptcy Protection," *Deadline*, Penske Business Media, LLC, September 5, 2012, https://deadline.com/ 2012/09/journal-register-files-bankruptcy-329615/.

60. Alan D. Mutter, "What Went Wrong at JRC," *Reflections of a Newsosaur* (blog), April 13, 2008, http://newsosaur.blogspot.com/2008/04/what-went-wrong-at-jrc.html.

61. Steven Church and Dawn McCarty, "Journal Register Files for Bankruptcy," *Philadelphia Inquirer*, February 21, 2009, https://www.inquirer.com/philly/news/breaking/ 20090221_Journal_Register_files_for_bankruptcy.html.

62. Rachel Feintzeig, "Journal Register Heads to Auction Block with $122M Lead Offer," *LBO Wire*, December 20, 2012.

63. GateHouse Media, Inc., Form 10-K, annual report for the fiscal year ending December 30, 2012 (March 7, 2013), from the US Securities and Exchange Commission website,

https://www.sec.gov/Archives/edgar/data/1368900/000119312513096322/d475356d10k
.htm.

64. GateHouse Media, Inc. December 30, 2012, quote on 11.

65. GateHouse Media, Inc., Form 10-K, annual report for the fiscal year ending December 31, 2007 (March 17, 2008), from the US Securities and Exchange Commission website, https://www.sec.gov/Archives/edgar/data/1368900/000114420408015835/v096277_10k.htm.

66. US Senate, Committee on Finance, *Hearing, Debt versus Equity*.

67. GateHouse Media, Inc., Form 10-K, annual report for the fiscal year ending December 31, 2007.

68. GateHouse Media, Inc., Form 10-K, annual report for the fiscal year ending December 31, 2010 (March 1, 2011), from the US Securities and Exchange Commission, Mergent Archives Database.

69. Mike Spector and Emily Glazer, "Buyout Shops' Deals Play Both Sides," *Wall Street Journal*, January 2, 2014, eastern edition.

70. Mikolo Ilas, "GateHouse Emerges from Bankruptcy," *SNL Kagan Media & Communications Report*, November 28, 2013.

71. "Newcastle Completes Acquisition of Dow Jones Local Media Group & Plans to Restructure GateHouse Debt," *Business Wire*, September 4, 2013, https://www.businesswire.com/news/home/20130904006012/en/Newcastle-Completes-Acquisition-Dow-Jones-Local-Media.

72. Gatehouse Media, Inc., Chapter 11, filed in the United States Bankruptcy Court for the District of Delaware on November 4, 2013, from the US Securities and Exchange Commission website, https://www.sec.gov/Archives/edgar/data/1368900/000119312513437119/d625806dex21.htm.

73. "GateHouse Media Files Prepackaged Chapter 11 Bankruptcy to Complete Secured Debt Restructuring," *PR Newswire*, September 27, 2013, ABI/INFORM.

74. Gannett Co., Inc., Form 10-K, annual report for the fiscal year ended December 31, 2020 (February 26, 2021), from the Gannett Co., Inc., website, https://investors.gannett.com/financials/sec-filings/sec-filings-details/default.aspx?FilingId=14753779.

75. Gannett Co., Inc., Form 10-K, annual report for the fiscal year ended December 31, 2020.

76. Lukas I. Alpert, "Gannett Looks to Spare Journalists' Jobs after Big Newspaper Merger; Deal to Combine USA Today Publisher Gannett with GateHouse Media Closes, Forming Company with 30% of Papers Sold Daily in U.S.," *Wall Street Journal*, November 20, 2019.

77. Alpert, "Gannett Looks."

78. Gannett Co., Inc., Form 10-K, annual report for the fiscal year ended December 31, 2020.

79. Gannett Co., Inc., Form 10-K, annual report for the fiscal year ended December 31, 2020.

80. Elahe Izadi, "The Newsroom Was the Beating Heart of a Local Newspaper. What's Lost When the Owner Shuts It Down?," *Washington Post*, August 18, 2020, https://www.washingtonpost.com/lifestyle/media/the-newsroom-was-the-beating-heart-of-a-local

-newspaper-whats-lost-when-the-owner-shuts-it-down/2020/08/17/6e9840e4-dcd8
-11ea-8051-d5f887d73381_story.html.

81. Rosenberg, *The Vulture Investors*, xi.

Chapter 6. Layoffs

1. In conversation with the author, October 2021.

2. Kristen Doerschner, "Registered Sex Offenders Still May Work with Children," BishopAccountability.org, December 11, 2011, https://www.bishop-accountability.org/news2011/11_12/2011_12_11_Doerschner_RegisteredSex.htm.

3. "Frequently Asked Questions: Banks," Pennsylvania Interest on Lawyers' Trust Accounts Board, n.d., https://www.paiolta.org/faqs/banks/#faq-1.

4. "Past John Bull Award Winners," Pennsylvania NewsMedia Association, 2021, https://panewsmedia.org/wp-content/uploads/Awards/Keystone_Awards_Professional/Specialty_Categories/Past-John-Bull-Award-Winners2.pdf.

5. New Media Investment Group, Inc., Form 10-K, annual report for the fiscal year ending December 31, 2017 (February 28, 2018), from the US Securities and Exchange Commission website, https://www.sec.gov/Archives/edgar/data/1579684/000157968418000003/newm-20171231x10k.htm, 73.

6. In conversation with the author, October 2021.

7. New Media Investment Group, Inc., Form 10-K, annual report for the fiscal year ending December 30, 2018 (February 27, 2019), from the Gannett website, https://investors.gannett.com/financials/sec-filings/sec-filings-details/default.aspx?FilingId=13260522, 70.

8. "NewsGuild-CWA: GateHouse-Gannett Merger Threatens Journalism," NewsGuild–Communication Workers of America, n.d., 6, https://newsguild.org/wp-content/uploads/2019/11/Statement-on-GateHouse-Gannett-Merger.pdf.

9. In conversation with the author, October 2021.

10. "We Believe Truth Is Worth Fighting For. So Do You," petition, Save Our Courant, NewsGuild-CWA, February 11, 2019, https://www.saveourcourant.org/.

11. "Tell MediaNews Group to Stop Cutting Our Loveland Reporter-Herald," petition, Action Network, NewsGuild-CWA, n.d., https://actionnetwork.org/petitions/tell-medianews-group-to-stop-cutting-our-loveland-reporter-herald.

12. Howard Lee, "The Bulletin of Norwich Lays Off 7 Newsroom Employees," *McClatchy-Tribune Business News*, November 3, 2011, http://proxyau.wrlc.org/login?url=https://www.proquest.com/wire-feeds/bulletin-norwich-lays-off-7-newsroom-employees/docview/901604748/se-2?accountid=8285.

13. Benjamin Goggin, "Local Newspaper Giant GateHouse Media Laid Off at Least 60 Journalists across the US after a $30 Million Acquisition," *Business Insider*, February 10, 2019, US edition https://www.proquest.com/abicomplete/docview/2402546393/423E975635A34CE5PQ/1?accountid=8285; Goggin, "Local-Newspaper Giant Gatehouse Media Is Laying Off Journalists across the US in Cuts Their CEO Is Calling 'Immaterial,'" *Business Insider*, May 23, 2019, https://www.businessinsider.com/gatehouse-media-layoffs-after-poor-earnings-2019-5.

14. Benjamin Goggin, "7,800 People Lost Their Media Jobs in a 2019 Landslide," *Business Insider*, December 10, 2019, US edition.

15. Eve Hightower, "The Modesto Bee Offers Buyouts to Its Full-Time Employees," *McClatchy-Tribune Business News*, August 19, 2008.

16. David Carr and Tim Arango, "Tribune Chief Accepts Advice and Backs Out," *New York Times*, October 22, 2010, https://www.nytimes.com/2010/10/23/business/media/23tribune.html.

17. Rakel Cabanilla Iyel, "Newly Acquired San Diego Union-Tribune Slashes Jobs," *SNL Kagan Media & Communications Report*, May 28, 2015, ABI/INFORM.

18. Robert Channick, "Alden's Investment Brings New Uncertainty to Tribune Publishing," *TCA Regional News*, November 23, 2019.

19. "The 1986 Pulitzer Prize Winner in Public Service," Pulitzer Prizes, Columbia University, n.d., https://www.pulitzer.org/winners/denver-post.

20. Robert Channick, "Alden's Investment Brings New Uncertainty to Tribune Publishing," *TCA Regional News*, November 23, 2019, http://proxyau.wrlc.org/login?url=https://www.proquest.com/wire-feeds/alden-s-investment-brings-new-uncertainty-tribune/docview/2322643132/se-2?accountid=8285.

21. Michael Roberts, "Denver Post Lays Off Thirty Employees, Nearly One-Third of Newsroom Staff," *Westword*, March 14, 2018, https://www.westword.com/news/denver-lays-off-thirty-employees-nearly-one-third-of-newsroom-staff-10087469.

22. *Denver Post* Editorial Board, "Editorial: As Vultures Circle, the Denver Post Must Be Saved," *Denver Post*, April 15, 2019, https://www.denverpost.com/2018/04/06/as-vultures-circle-the-denver-post-must-be-saved/.

23. Laurel Wamsley, "'Denver Post' Calls Out Its 'Vulture' Hedge Fund Owners in Searing Editorial," NPR, 2018, https://www.npr.org/sections/thetwo-way/2018/04/09/600831352/denver-post-calls-out-its-vulture-hedge-fund-owners-in-searing-editorials.

24. Mark Fitzgerald and Jennifer Saba, "The New Face of Newspapers?," *Editor & Publisher* 139, no. 1 (January 2006): 24–26, 28, 30–32.

25. D. B. Hebbard, "Jann Wenner to Sell Majority Stake in Rolling Stone; Staff Cuts at Tronc and Gannett Newspapers," *Talking New Media*, September 15, 2017, https://www.talkingnewmedia.com/2017/09/18/jann-wenner-sell-majority-stake-rolling-stone-staff-cuts-tronc-gannett-newspapers/.

26. "Dow Jones Job Cuts, Reorganization," *Dow Jones Institutional News*, January 31, 2017.

27. "Gannett CEO Gets $7.9 Million in 2007," *Greeley Tribune*, May 13, 2020, https://www.greeleytribune.com/2011/05/11/gannett-ceo-gets-7-9-million-in-2007/.

28. Gannett Co., Inc., Schedule 14A, Definitive Proxy Statement, March 18, 2010, from US Securities and Exchange Commission website, https://www.sec.gov/Archives/edgar/data/39899/000119312510060017/ddef14a.htm#toc20271_24.

29. "Roll Call III: Say Goodbye to More of Your Friends," Gannett blog, Jim Hopkins, December 4, 2008, http://gannettblog.blogspot.com/2008/10/roll-call-iii-say-goodbye-to-more-of.html; Amanda Eisenberg and Kelsey Sutton, "'It Was a Total Bloodbath': USA Today Journalists Recount Layoffs," *American Journalism Review*, Philip Merrill College of Journalism, September 5, 2014, https://ajr.org/2014/09/05/total-bloodbath-usa

-today-journalists-recount-layoffs/; Keith Kelly, "Gannett Stages 'Mini Bloodbath' at New Jersey Newspapers," *New York Post*, September 15, 2017, https://nypost.com/2017/09/15/gannett-stages-mini-bloodbath-at-new-jersey-newspapers/; Kelly, "Gannett Bloodbath Claims as Many as 400 Jobs," *New York Post*, January 24, 2019, https://nypost.com/2019/01/24/gannett-bloodbath-claims-as-many-as-400-jobs/.

30. Gannett Co., Inc., Schedule 14A, "Definitive Proxy Statement," April 27, 2022, 38, https://d18rnop25nwr6d.cloudfront.net/CIK-0001579684/cc01730c-df41-483a-80a0-d9cf4ee8c44a.pdf

31. Goggin, "7,800 People."

32. Sara Fischer and Kerry Flynn, "Gannett Shed Nearly Half Its Workforce Since Gatehouse Merger," *Axios*, March 7, 2023, https://www.axios.com/2023/03/07/gannett-changes-leadership-workers.

33. Mason Walker, "U.S. Newsroom Employment Has Fallen 26% Since 2008," Pew Research Center, July 13, 2021, https://www.pewresearch.org/fact-tank/2021/07/13/u-s-newsroom-employment-has-fallen-26-since-2008/.

34. Elizabeth Grieco, "About a Quarter of Large US Newspapers Laid Off Staff in 2018," Pew Research Center, 2019, http://www.pewresearch.org/fact-tank/2019/08/01/large-us-newspapers-layoffs-2018.

35. Amy Mitchell and Jesse Holcomb, "State of the News Media," Pew Research Center, June 15, 2016, https://assets.pewresearch.org/wp-content/uploads/sites/13/2016/06/30143308/state-of-the-news-media-report-2016-final.pdf.

36. Scott Reinardy, "Newspaper Journalism in Crisis: Burnout on the Rise, Eroding Young Journalists' Career Commitment," *Journalism* 12, no. 1 (2011): 33–50.

37. Scott Reinardy, "Downsizing Effects on Personnel: The Case of Layoff Survivors in US Newspapers," *Journal of Media Business Studies* 7, no. 4 (2010): 1–19, 1, https://doi.org/10.1080/16522354.2010.11073512.

38. Carla Murphy, "The 'Leavers' Survey," *OpenNews*, 2020, https://opennews.org/projects/2020-leavers-survey/#why-leave.

39. In conversation with the author, December 2020.

40. Aaron Davis, George Kelly, Harry Harris, and Rick Hurd, "Oakland: Ghost Ship Fire Deadliest in the U.S. in 13 Years," *East Bay Times*, December 10, 2016, https://www.eastbaytimes.com/2016/12/07/oakland-ghost-ship-fire-search-nearly-finished-investigators-eye-refrigerator-as-cause/.

41. In conversation with the author, November 2021.

42. "The 2017 Pulitzer Prize Winner in Breaking News Reporting," Pulitzer Prizes, Columbia University, n.d., https://www.pulitzer.org/winners/staff-27.

43. Kristen Hare, "Layoffs Come to the East Bay Times after Pulitzer Win," *Poynter*, April 26, 2017, https://www.poynter.org/business-work/2017/layoffs-come-to-the-east-bay-times-after-pulitzer-win/.

44. Darwin Bond Graham, "Buy-Outs and Layoffs Hit East Bay Times and Other Bay Area News Group Papers: East Bay Express: Oakland, Berkeley & Alameda," *East Bay Express*, January 30, 2018, https://eastbayexpress.com/buy-outs-and-layoffs-hit-east-bay-times-and-other-bay-area-news-group-papers-2-1/.

45. James T. Hamilton, *Democracy's Detectives* (Cambridge, MA: Harvard University Press, 2017), 207.

46. In conversation with the author, October 2020.

47. Nikki Usher, *News for the Rich, White, and Blue: How Place and Power Distort American Journalism* (New York: Columbia University Press, 2021).

48. David Simon, "Testimony, U.S. Senate Commerce Committee, Hearing on the Future of Newspapers," Audacity of Despair, May 6, 2009, https://davidsimon.com/wire-creator-david-simon-testifies-on-the-future-of-journalism/.

49. Pengjie Gao, Chang Lee, and Dermot Murphy, "Financing Dies in Darkness? The Impact of Newspaper Closures on Public Finance," *Journal of Financial Economics* 135, no. 2 (2020): 445–67, 445, https://doi.org/10.1016/j.jfineco.2019.06.003.

50. Joshua P. Darr, Matthew P. Hitt, and Johanna L. Dunaway, *Home Style Opinion: How Local Newspapers Can Slow Polarization* (New York: Cambridge University Press, 2021).

51. Lindsey Meeks, "Undercovered, Underinformed: Local News, Local Elections, and US Sheriffs," *Journalism Studies* 21, no. 12 (2020): 1609–26, https://doi.org/10.1080/1461670X.2020.1781546.

52. Mike Schneider, "Report: PR Pros Outnumber Journalists by a 6-to-1 Ratio," *PR Daily*, September 19, 2018, https://www.prdaily.com/report-pr-pros-outnumber-journalists-by-a-6-to-1-ratio/.

53. In conversation with the author, October 2021.

54. "Report of Investigation," December 5, 2019, US Department of Labor Employee Benefits Security Administration, File No. 60–107584 (48), 1–10.

55. Sabrina Moreno (@sabrinamorenoo), Twitter post, "After acquiring Tribune . . . ," November 22, 2021, 10:37 a.m., https://twitter.com/sabrinaamorenoo/status/1462807566292037639.

56. "News-Guild-CWA Membership Totals 2015–2021," n.d.

57. Robert Bruno, "Evidence of Bias in the Chicago Tribune Coverage of Organized Labor: A Quantitative Study from 1991 to 2001," *Labor Studies Journal* 34, no. 3 (2009): 385–407.

58. Walter M. Brasch, *With Just Cause: Unionization of the American Journalist* (Lanham, MD: University Press of America, 1991), xxii.

59. Philip M. Glende, "'We Used Every Effort to Be Impartial': The Complicated Response of Newspaper Publishers to Unions," *American Journalism* 29, no. 2 (2012): 37–65, https://doi.org/10.1080/08821127.2012.10677825.

60. William J. Puette, *Through Jaundiced Eyes: How the Media View Organized Labor* (Ithaca, NY: ILR Press, 1992).

61. Wendy M. Weinhold, "Newspaper Negotiations: The Crossroads of Community Newspaper Journalists' Values and Labor," *Journalism Practice* 2, no. 3 (2008): 476–86, https://doi.org/10.1080/17512780802281222.

62. Jennifer M. Proffitt, "Solidarity in the Newsroom? Media Concentration and Union Organizing: A Case Study from the Sunshine State," *Journalism* 22, no. 9 (2021): 2165–81, 2175, https://doi.org/10.1177/1464884919860030.

63. Kitty Weiss Krupat, "Save the News: Campaigning to Preserve Jobs and Democratize Journalism; A Conversation with Jon Schleuss," *New Labor Forum* 30, no. 1 (2021): 52–58.

64. Peter Rossman and Gerard Greenfield, "Financialization: New Routes to Profit, New Challenges for Trade Unions," *Labour Education: The Quarterly Review of the ILO Bureau for Workers' Activities* 1, no. 142 (2006): 55–62.

65. Andrea Hunter, "'It's Like Having a Second Full-Time Job': Crowdfunding, Journalism and Labour," *Journalism Practice* 10, no. 2 (2016): 217–32, https://doi.org/10.1080/17512786.2015.1123107.

66. Gannett Co., Inc., Form 10-K, annual report for the fiscal year ended December 31, 2020 (February 26, 2021), https://d18rnop25nwr6d.cloudfront.net/CIK-0001579684/738c2ddb-7f33-48c7-80f9-0c2a79094433.pdf.

67. Los Angeles Daily News Publishing Company et al., and Media Guild of the West, TNG-CWA Local 39213, Case 21-RC-273230, National Labor Relations Board, https://www.nlrb.gov/case/21-RC-273230.

68. In re: Journal Register Co., 488 B.R. 835, 2013 Bankr. LEXIS 1068, 57 Bankr. Ct. Dec. 192 (United States Bankruptcy Court for the Southern District of New York March 21, 2013, Decided).

69. Hamilton, *Democracy's Detectives*, 222.

70. In conversation with the author, August 2020.

71. Marvin Kalb, *Enemy of the People: Trump's War on the Press, the New McCarthyism, and the Threat to American Democracy* (Washington, DC: Brookings Institution Press, 2018).

Chapter 7. Neglected Audiences

1. In conversation with the author, July 2020.

2. Carol Kammen, "Ithaca History: First Newspaper Published 200 Years Ago," *Ithaca Journal*, April 27, 2015, https://www.ithacajournal.com/story/news/local/2015/04/27/ithaca-history-first-newspaper/26457093/.

3. Gannett Co., Inc., Form 10-K, annual report for the fiscal year ended December 25, 2005 (February 24, 2006), from the US Securities and Exchange Commission website, https://www.sec.gov/Archives/edgar/data/39899/000119312506038810/d10k.htm.

4. Gannett Co., Inc., Form 10-K, annual report for the fiscal year ended December 25, 2005, 21.

5. "Livonia-Based Observer & Eccentric Newspapers Have Made Their First Layoffs Since They Were Acquired by Gannett Corp. in March 2005," *Crain's Detroit Business*, April 3, 2006, Dow Jones Factiva.

6. Jim Hopkins, "Digital Divide: Along a Journey to Transformation, an Aging Publisher Stumbles at a Critical Crossroads," *Gannett Blog*, December 8, 2013, https://gannettblog.blogspot.com/search?q=dubow&max-results=20&by-date=true.

7. Amy Mitchell and Jesse Holcomb, "State of the News Media," Pew Research Center, June 15, 2016, https://assets.pewresearch.org/wp-content/uploads/sites/13/2016/06/30143308/state-of-the-news-media-report-2016-final.pdf.

8. Penelope Muse Abernathy, "News Deserts and Ghost Newspapers: Will Local News Survive?," Center for Innovation and Sustainability in Local Media, Hussman School of Journalism and Media, University of North Carolina at Chapel Hill, 2020, https://www.usnewsdeserts.com/wp-content/uploads/2020/06/2020_News_Deserts_and_Ghost _Newspapers.pdf.

9. Charles St. Cyr, Stephen Lacy, and Susana Guzman-Ortega, "Circulation Increases Follow Investments in Newsrooms," *Newspaper Research Journal* 26, no. 4 (2005): 50–60.

10. Danny Hayes and Jennifer L. Lawless, "The Decline of Local News and Its Effects: New Evidence from Longitudinal Data," *Journal of Politics* 80, no. 1 (2018): 332–36.

11. Stephen Lacy and Alan Blanchard, "The Impact of Public Ownership, Profits, and Competition on Number of Newsroom Employees and Starting Salaries in Mid-Sized Daily Newspapers," *Journalism & Mass Communication Quarterly* 80, no. 4 (2003): 949–68.

12. Hsiang Iris Chyi and Ori Tenenboim, "Charging More and Wondering Why Readership Declined? A Longitudinal Study of US Newspapers' Price Hikes, 2008–2016," *Journalism Studies* 20, no. 14 (2019): 2113–29; Danny Hayes and Jennifer L. Lawless, *News Hole: The Demise of Local Journalism and Political Engagement* (Cambridge: Cambridge University Press, 2021).

13. Warren Buffett, letter to the shareholders of Berkshire Hathaway, Inc., March 1, 2013, https://www.berkshirehathaway.com/letters/2012ltr.pdf.

14. Andrea Wenzel and Jacob L. Nelson, "Introduction to 'Engaged' Journalism: Studying the News Industry's Changing Relationship with the Public," *Journalism Practice* 14, no. 5 (2020): 515–17, https://doi.org/10.1080/17512786.2020.1759126.

15. James Hamilton, *All the News That's Fit to Sell: How the Market Transforms Information into News* (Princeton, NJ: Princeton University Press, 2004); Adithya Pattabhiramaiah, Eric Overby, and Lizhen Xu, "Spillovers from Online Engagement: How a Newspaper Subscriber's Activation of Digital Paywall Access Affects Her Retention and Subscription Revenue," *Management Science* 68, no. 5 (2021): 3528–48, https://doi.org/10.1287/mnsc.2021.4092; Adithya Pattabhiramaiah, S. Sriram, and Puneet Manchanda, "Paywalls: Monetizing Online Content," *Journal of Marketing* 83, no. 2 (2019): 19–36, https://doi.org/10.1177/0022242918815163.

16. Philip M. Napoli, *Audience Evolution: New Technologies and the Transformation of Media Audiences* (New York: Columbia University Press, 2011).

17. Chris W. Anderson, "Deliberative, Agonistic, and Algorithmic Audiences: Journalism's Vision of Its Public in an Age of Audience Transparency," *International Journal of Communication* 5 (2011): 19, https://ijoc.org/index.php/ijoc/article/view/884.

18. Tim P. Vos, Martin Eichholz, and Tatsiana Karaliova, "Audiences and Journalistic Capital: Roles of Journalism," *Journalism Studies* 20, no. 7 (2019): 1009–27, https://doi.org/10.1080/1461670X.2018.1477551.

19. Irene Costera Meijer, "Valuable Journalism: A Search for Quality from the Vantage Point of the User," *Journalism* 14, no. 6 (2013): 754–70, https://doi.org/10.1177/1464884912455899.

20. Chris Peters and Tamara Witschge, "From Grand Narratives of Democracy to Small Expectations of Participation: Audiences, Citizenship, and Interactive Tools in Digital

Journalism," *Journalism Practice* 9, no. 1 (2015): 19–34, https://doi.org/10.1080/17512786.2014.928455.

21. Magda Konieczna and Elia Powers, "What Can Nonprofit Journalists Actually Do for Democracy?," *Journalism Studies* 18, no. 12 (2017): 1542–58, https://doi.org/10.1080/1461670X.2015.1134273.

22. Wiebke Loosen and Jan-Hinrik Schmidt, "Between Proximity and Distance: Including the Audience in Journalism," in *The Routledge Companion to Digital Journalism Studies*, ed. Bob Franklin and Scott Eldridge II (New York: Routledge, 2016), 354–63.

23. Matt Carlson and Nikki Usher, "News Startups as Agents of Innovation: For-Profit Digital News Startup Manifestos as Metajournalistic Discourse," *Digital Journalism* 4, no. 5 (2016): 563–81, https://doi.org/10.1080/21670811.2015.1076344; Andrea D. Wenzel, Sam Ford, and Efrat Nechushtai, "Report for America, Report about Communities: Local News Capacity and Community Trust," *Journalism Studies* 21, no. 3 (2020): 287–305, https://doi.org/10.1080/1461670X.2019.1641428; Lindita Camaj, "The Monitorial Role of Crowdsourced Journalism: Audience Engagement in Corruption Reporting in Nonprofit Newsrooms," *Journalism Practice*, August 3, 2021, 1–19, 1, https://doi.org/10.1080/17512786.2021.1960587.

24. Rodrigo Zamith, "Quantified Audiences in News Production: A Synthesis and Research Agenda," *Digital Journalism* 6, no. 4 (2018): 418–35, https://doi.org/10.1080/21670811.2018.1444999.

25. Jacob L. Nelson, *Imagined Audiences: How Journalists Perceive and Pursue the Public* (New York: Oxford University Press, 2021).

26. Raul Ferrer-Conill and Edson C. Tandoc Jr., "The Audience-Oriented Editor: Making Sense of the Audience in the Newsroom," *Digital Journalism* 6, no. 4 (2018): 436–53, https://doi.org/10.1080/21670811.2018.1440972.

27. Caitlin Petre, *All the News That's Fit to Click: How Metrics Are Transforming the Work of Journalists* (Princeton, NJ: Princeton University Press, 2021), 48.

28. Valerie Belair-Gagnon, Jacob L. Nelson, and Seth C. Lewis, "Audience Engagement, Reciprocity, and the Pursuit of Community Connectedness in Public Media Journalism," *Journalism Practice* 13, no. 5 (2019): 558–75, https://doi.org/10.1080/17512786.2018.1542975.

29. Robert G. Picard, "Funding Digital Journalism: The Challenges of Consumers and the Economic Value of News," in Franklin and Eldridge, *The Routledge Companion*, 146–54.

30. Hsiang Iris Chyi and Yee Man Margaret Ng, "Still Unwilling to Pay: An Empirical Analysis of 50 US Newspapers' Digital Subscription Results," *Digital Journalism* 8, no. 4 (2020): 526–47, https://doi.org/10.1080/21670811.2020.1732831; Angela Ross, Libby Lester, and Claire Konkes, "Audience Perspectives on Paying for Local News: A Regional Qualitative Case Study," *Journalism Studies* 22, no. 8 (2021): 1066–82, https://doi.org/10.1080/1461670X.2021.1916985.

31. Manuel Goyanes, "An Empirical Study of Factors That Influence the Willingness to Pay for Online News," *Journalism Practice* 8, no. 6 (2014): 742–57, https://doi.org/10.1080/17512786.2014.882056.

32. Manuel Goyanes, "The Value of Proximity: Examining the Willingness to Pay for Online Local News," *International Journal of Communication* 9 (2015): 18, https://ijoc .org/index.php/ijoc/article/view/3388.

33. Nic Newman, Richard Fletcher, Anne Schulz, Simge Andi, and Rasmus Kleis Nielsen, "Digital News Report 2020," Reuters Institute, Oxford University, 2020, https:// reutersinstitute.politics.ox.ac.uk/sites/default/files/2020-06/DNR_2020_FINAL.pdf.

34. Stuart Hall, *Encoding/Decoding* (New York: Routledge, 2003).

35. Ingunn Hagen and Janet Wasko, "Introduction: Consuming Audiences? Production and Reception in Media Research," in *Consuming Audiences? Production and Reception in Media Research*, ed. Ingunn Hagen and Janet Wasko (New York: Hampton Press, 2000), 3–29.

36. Dallas W. Smythe, "On the Audience Commodity and Its Work," *Media and Cultural Studies: Keyworks* 230 (1981): 256.

37. Graham Murdock, "Commodities and Commons," in *The Audience Commodity in a Digital Age: Revisiting a Critical Theory of Commercial Media*, ed. Lee McGuigan and Vincent Manzerolle (New York: Peter Lang, 2014), 229–44.

38. James S. Ettema and D. Charles Whitney, *Audiencemaking: How the Media Create the Audience* (New York: SAGE Publications, 1994), 5.

39. Douglas Kellner, *Media Culture: Cultural Studies, Identity and Politics between the Modern and the Post-modern* (New York: Routledge, 2003).

40. Douglas Kellner, "Toward a Critical Media/Cultural Studies," in *Media/Cultural Studies: Critical Approaches*, ed. Rhonda Hammer and Douglas Kellner (New York: Peter Lang, 2009), 5–24.

41. Douglas Kellner and Jeff Share, "Critical Media Education and Radical Democracy," in *The Routledge International Handbook of Critical Education*, ed. Michael W. Apple, Wayne Au, and Luis Armando Gandin (New York: Routledge, 2009), 281–95.

42. Sut Jhally and Bill Livant, "Watching as Working: The Valorization of Audience Consciousness," *Journal of Communication* 36, no. 3 (1986): 124–43, https://doi.org/ 10.1111/j.1460-2466.1986.tb01442.x.

43. Meenakshi Gigi Durham and Douglas M. Kellner, eds., *Media and Cultural Studies: Keyworks* (New York: John Wiley & Sons, 2012).

44. Matthew Crain, *Profit over Privacy: How Surveillance Advertising Conquered the Internet* (Minneapolis: University of Minnesota Press, 2021).

45. Kenza Lamot and Peter Van Aelst, "Beaten by Chartbeat? An Experimental Study on the Effect of Real-Time Audience Analytics on Journalists' News Judgment," *Journalism Studies* 21, no. 4 (2020): 477–93, https://doi.org/10.1080/1461670X.2019.1686411.

46. Ignacio Siles and Pablo J. Boczkowski, "Making Sense of the Newspaper Crisis: A Critical Assessment of Existing Research and an Agenda for Future Work," *New Media & Society* 14, no. 8 (2012): 1375–94, https://doi.org/10.1177/1461444812455148.

47. Irene Costera Meijer and Tim Groot Kormelink, "Audiences for Journalism," in *The International Encyclopedia of Journalism Studies*, ed. Tim P. Vos and Folker Hanuschu (Hoboken, NJ: Wiley Blackwell, 2019), 1–7, https://doi.org/10.1002/9781118841570 .iejs0002.

48. Michael Barthel and Kirsten Worden, "Newspaper Fact Sheet," Pew Research Center, June 29, 2021, https://www.pewresearch.org/journalism/fact-sheet/newspapers/.

49. Abernathy, "News Deserts."

50. In conversation with the author, July 2020.

51. In conversation with the author, July 2020.

52. This was the only audience interview conducted by Zoom because the participant did not have access to a reliable phone.

53. In conversation with the author, August 2020.

54. In conversation with the author, July 2020.

55. In conversation with the author, July 12, 2020.

56. Katie Robertson, "Major Newspaper Company Will Stop Endorsing National and Statewide Candidates," *New York Times*, October 6, 2022, https://www.nytimes.com/2022/10/06/business/media/alden-newspaper-candidate-endorsements.html.

57. In conversation with the author, August 10, 2020.

58. In conversation with the author, August 2020.

59. In conversation with the author, July 2020.

60. In conversation with the author, July 2020.

61. In conversation with the author, June 25, 2020.

62. In conversation with the author, October 2, 2020.

63. In conversation with the author, October 2020.

64. Alliance for Audited Media, Audit Report Daily News Media, Hartford Courant, March 31, 2019.

65. Lauren Smiley, "As You Like It," *Columbia Journalism Review*, 2019, https://www.cjr.org/special_report/as-you-like-it.php.

66. Priyanjana Bengani, "Hundreds of 'Pink Slime' Local News Outlets Are Distributing Algorithmic Stories and Conservative Talking Points," Tow Center for Digital Journalism, Columbia's Graduate School of Journalism, December 18, 2019, https://www.cjr.org/tow_center_reports/hundreds-of-pink-slime-local-news-outlets-are-distributing-algorithmic-stories-conservative-talking-points.php.

67. Jeff Kaye and Stephen Quinn, *Funding Journalism in the Digital Age: Business Models, Strategies, Issues and Trends* (New York: Peter Lang, 2010).

68. In conversation with the author, July 2020.

69. Rick Edmonds, "At Gannett's Ithaca Journal, Local News Staffing Is Down to One Reporter," *Poynter*, June 10, 2020, https://www.poynter.org/locally/2020/at-gannetts-ithaca-journal-local-news-staffing-is-down-to-one-reporter/.

Conclusion: Ending the Era

1. Michael Gold and Tony Closson, "What We Know about Daniel Prude's Case and Death," *New York Times*, April 16, 2021, https://www.nytimes.com/article/what-happened-daniel-prude.html.

2. Steve Orr, "How Daniel Prude Suffocated as Rochester Police Restrained Him," *Rochester Democrat and Chronicle*, September 9, 2020, https://www.democratandchronicle

.com/story/news/2020/09/02/daniel-prude-rochester-ny-police-died-march-2020-after-officers-restrained-him/5682948002/.

3. Carolyn Thompson, "Prude's Family Says Videos Show Crime; Officers Say No," *Associated Press*, February 25, 2021, https://apnews.com/article/new-york-rochester-crime-police-daniel-prude-34563dd3491615fecec1026f68dbe21e.

4. Gold and Closson, "What We Know."

5. James Brown, "Neighbor on Daniel Prude's Death: 'It's Not Fair. It Says That You're Less Than,'" *WXXI News*, September 3, 2020, https://www.wxxinews.org/local-news/2020-09-03/neighbor-on-daniel-prudes-death-its-not-fair-it-says-that-youre-less-than.

6. Special Investigations and Prosecutions Unit, New York State Office of the Attorney General, *Report on the Investigation into the Death of Daniel Prude*, n.d., https://ag.ny.gov/sipu/footage/daniel-prude.

7. Atyia Collins, "Newspaper Merger Could Shake Up Industry with Strong Rochester Roots," *RochesterFirst*, August 6, 2019, https://www.rochesterfirst.com/news/business/gannett-gatehouse-merger-could-shake-up-newspaper-industry/; staff reports, "Gannett Lays Off Workers, Including 8 in Rochester," *Democrat and Chronicle*, October 25, 2016, https://www.democratandchronicle.com/story/money/business/2016/10/25/gannett-layoffs-rochester-democrat-chronicle/92722882/.

8. Doug Cunningham, "Rochester, N.Y., to Pay $12M in Daniel Prude Wrongful Death Suit," *United Press International*, October 6, 2022.

9. Stephen Lacy and Alan Blanchard, "The Impact of Public Ownership, Profits, and Competition on Number of Newsroom Employees and Starting Salaries in Mid-Sized Daily Newspapers," *Journalism & Mass Communication Quarterly* 80, no. 4 (2003): 949–68, https://doi.org/10.1177/107769900308000413.

10. Vincent Mosco, *The Political Economy of Communication*, 2nd ed. (London: SAGE, 2009).

11. Hamish Boland-Rudder, "'Investigating the Bastards': ICIJ's Founder on How He Learned to Love Nonprofit Journalism," International Consortium of Investigative Journalists, May 1, 2018, https://www.icij.org/inside-icij/2018/05/investigating-bastards-icijs-founder-learned-love-nonprofit-journalism/.

12. Robert G. Picard and Victor Pickard, *Essential Principles for Contemporary Media and Communications Policymaking*, Reuters Institute, Oxford University, April 2017, https://reutersinstitute.politics.ox.ac.uk/sites/default/files/research/files/Essential%2520Principles%2520for%2520Contemporary%2520Media%2520and%2520Communications%2520Policymaking.pdf; Victor Pickard, *Democracy without Journalism? Confronting the Misinformation Society* (New York: Oxford University Press, 2020), 89.

13. Federal Communications Commission v. Prometheus Radio Project, 592 U.S. (2021), https://www.supremecourt.gov/opinions/20pdf/19-1231_i425.pdf.

14. Michael Roberts, "Dean Singleton on Resigning from the Post: 'They've Killed a Great Newspaper,'" *Westword*, May 7, 2018, https://www.westword.com/news/dean-singleton-on-resigning-from-the-denver-post-theyve-killed-a-great-newspaper-10287146.

15. "Your Partner to Improve Performance and Drive Value," Cerberus Capital Management, LP, n.d., https://www.cerberus.com.

16. Dan Margolies, "With Deal for McClatchy, Kansas City Star Will See Its Fifth Owner in Four Decades," Kansas City Public Radio, July 13, 2020, https://www.kcur.org/news/2020-07-13/with-deal-for-mcclatchy-kansas-city-star-will-see-its-fifth-owner-in-four-decades.

17. "Apollo Global Management, Inc. Reports Third Quarter 2021 Results," Apollo Global Management, Inc., November 2, 2021, https://www.apollo.com/~/media/Files/A/Apollo-V3/press-release/2021/earnings-release-3q-2021.pdf; Jonathan Berr, "Finally, Gannett Has Some Good News to Tell," *Forbes*, January 29, 2021, https://www.forbes.com/sites/jonathanberr/2021/01/29/finally-gannett-has-some-good-news-to-tell/?sh=60d9cdab2518.

18. Charles E. Schumer to Heath Freeman, US Senate, February 21, 2019, https://www.democrats.senate.gov/imo/media/doc/Letter%20to%20Mr%20Freeman%20Alden%20Global%20MNG%202-21-19.pdf.

19. "Private Equity Firm's Bid for Gannett Is Bad News for IndyStar, Indianapolis," *Indianapolis Business Journal*, January 18, 2019, 10, https://www.ibj.com/articles/72086-private-equity-firms-bid-for-gannett-is-bad-news-for-indystar-indianapolis.

20. US House of Representatives, Committee on Financial Services, "America for Sale: An Examination of the Practices of Private Funds," §. Serial No. 116–66 (116AD), https://www.congress.gov/event/116th-congress/house-event/110248.

21. Richard J. Durbin and Tammy Duckworth to Heath Freeman, Alden Global Capital president, March 12, 2020, https://dfmworkers.org/wp-content/uploads/2020/04/Letter-to-Alden-Global-Capital-FINAL.pdf.

22. Heath Freeman of Alden Global Capital, to Richard J. Durbin and Tammy Duckworth, US Senate, March 27, 2020, https://www.documentcloud.org/documents/6826199-Alden-Response-to-Durbin-and-Duckworth-Letter.html

23. "Agencies Lobbied by BlackRock Inc., 2018," OpenSecrets, https://www.opensecrets.org/federal-lobbying/clients/agencies?cycle=2018&id=D000021872.

24. Kevin Phillips, *Bad Money: Reckless Finance, Failed Politics, and the Global Crisis of American Capitalism* (New York: Penguin, 2009), vii.

25. "Securities & Investment: Background," OpenSecrets, December 2021, https://www.opensecrets.org/industries/background.php?ind=F07, quote appears in paragraph 1.

26. "Industry Profile: Securities & Investment," OpenSecrets, https://www.opensecrets.org/federal-lobbying/industries/summary?cycle=2011&id=F07.

27. "Client Profile: Fortress Investment Group," OpenSecrets, https://www.opensecrets.org/federal-lobbying/clients/summary?cycle=2009&id=D000021989.

28. "Issues Lobbied by Fortress Investment Group, 2009," OpenSecrets, https://www.opensecrets.org/federal-lobbying/clients/issues?cycle=2009&id=D000021989&spec=BNK&specific_issue=Bankruptcy#specific_issue.

29. Alexandra Wolfe, "Wesley Edens Is an Investor with an Affinity for the Underdog; The Fortress Investment Group Co-founder and Milwaukee Bucks Co-owner Likes a

Counterintuitive Bet," *Wall Street Journal*, July 20, 2018, https://www.wsj.com/articles/wesley-edens-is-an-investor-with-an-affinity-for-the-underdog-1532111122; Shelly Sigo, "Brightline, with Trains Parked Since March, Launches Bond Remarketing," *Bond Buyer*, December 3, 2020, https://www.bondbuyer.com/news/brightline-with-trains-parked-since-march-launches-bond-remarketing.

30. Barbara Allen, "Gannett Layoffs Underway at Combined New Company," Poynter Institute for Media Studies, February 27, 2020, https://www.poynter.org/business-work/2020/gannett-layoffs-underway-at-combined-new-company/; Sigo, "Brightline."

31. "John W. Snow," Cerberus Capital Management, n.d., https://www.cerberus.com/our-firm/leadership/john-w-snow/.

32. Demitri Diakantonis, "The Stars Come Out for Private Equity," *Mergers and Acquisitions* 57, no. 3 (May/June 2022): 10–13, ABI/INFORM.

33. "Wally Adeyemo," US Department of the Treasury, April 5, 2021, https://home.treasury.gov/about/general-information/officials/Wally-Adeyemo.

34. "OpenSecrets: Following the Money in Politics," https://www.opensecrets.org/.

35. "Top Contributors to Romney Victory PAC," Open Secrets, based on Federal Election Commission data released on March 25, 2013, https://www.opensecrets.org/pres12/jfc_detail.php?name=Romney+Victory+PAC&id=C00518282.

36. "Sen. Orrin G. Hatch—Campaign Finance Summary," OpenSecrets, https://www.opensecrets.org/members-of-congress/orrin-g-hatch/summary?cid=N00009869.

37. Craig I. Forman, "Solutions to America's Local Journalism Crisis: Consolidated Literature Review," Shorenstein Center on Media, Politics and Public Policy, Harvard Kennedy School, October 12, 2021, https://shorensteincenter.org/solutions-americas-local-journalism-crisis-consolidated-literature-review/.

38. US Congress, House, *A Bill to Provide Tax Incentives That Support Local Newspapers and Other Local Media, and for Other Purposes*, H.R. 7640, 116th Cong., 2nd sess., introduced in the House July 16, 2020, https://www.congress.gov/116/bills/hr7640/BILLS-116hr7640ih.pdf.

39. Rick Edmonds, "A Window of Opportunity Has at Last Opened for Federal Aid to Support Local Journalism," Poynter Institute for Media Studies, Inc., October 14, 2021, https://www.poynter.org/business-work/2021/a-window-of-opportunity-has-at-last-opened-for-federal-aid-to-support-local-journalism/.

40. Marc Tracy, "Local News Outlets Could Reap $1.7 Billion in Build Back Better Aid," *New York Times*, November 28, 2021, https://www.nytimes.com/2021/11/28/business/media/build-back-better-local-news.html.

41. US Congress, House, *Local Journalism Sustainability Act*, H.S. 3940, 117th Cong., introduced in House June 16, 2021, https://www.congress.gov/bill/117th-congress/house-bill/3940/text.

42. Michael McCann and Robert Raiola, "Cubs 'Disguised Sale' Leads to Tax Court Loss for Tribune Media," *Sportico*, November 16, 2021, https://www.sportico.com/law/analysis/2021/chicago-cubs-ricketts-1234646564/.

43. Gilbert Cranberg and Randall Bezanson, "What's to Stop a New Kind of 'Family-Owned' Newspaper?," *Nieman Watchdog*, Nieman Foundation for Journalism at Harvard University, May 13, 2008, http://www.niemanwatchdog.org/index.cfm ?fuseaction=Background.view&backgroundid=249.

44. "Guide to Antitrust Laws," Federal Trade Commission, n.d., https://www.ftc.gov/ tips-advice/competition-guidance/guide-antitrust-laws/antitrust-laws.

45. "Summary of Section 7 of the Clayton Act," American Antitrust Institute, Washington, DC, October 11, 2011, https://www.antitrustinstitute.org/wp-content/uploads/ 2018/09/Section-7.pdf.

46. Judith A. Witterschein, "Antitrust-Interlocking Directorates: Section Eight of Clayton Act Bars Interlocking Directorates between Banks That Compete with Non-banks," *Seton Hall Law Review* 12, no. 3 (1981): 568–80, quote on 568.

47. "Horizontal Merger Guidelines," US Department of Justice, August 19, 2010, https:// www.justice.gov/atr/horizontal-merger-guidelines-08192010, quote appears in paragraph 6 of the overview.

48. Robert Jay Preminger, "Deputization and Parent-Subsidiary Interlocks under Section 8 of the Clayton Act," *Washington University Law Quarterly* 59 (1981): quote on 943.

49. Michelle M. Harner, "Disciplining Corporate Boards and Debtholders through Targeted Proxy Access," *Indiana Law Journal* 92, no. 1 (2016): 227–76, quote on 227.

50. Steven Waldman, "A Replanting Strategy: Saving Local Newspapers Squeezed by Hedge Funds," Center for Journalism and Liberty, November 12, 2020, https://www.journalismliberty .org/publications/replanting-strategy-saving-local-newspapers-squeezed-by-hedge-fund.

51. Tribune Publishing Company, Schedule 13D, filed by Alden Global Capital (May 24, 2021), from the US Securities and Exchange Commission website, https://sec.report/ Document/0001193125-21-173983/.

52. Paul M. Goldschmid, "More Phoenix Than Vulture: The Case for Distressed Investor Presence in the Bankruptcy Reorganization Process," *Columbia Business Law Review* 2005, no. 1 (2005): 191–274, 191, https://doi.org/10.7916/cblr.v2005i1.2997.

53. United States Securities and Exchange Commission, Form 13F Information Table, from the US Securities and Exchange website, https://www.sec.gov/Archives/edgar/ data/1616882/000156761920010364/xslForm13F_X01/form13fInfoTable.xml.

54. Anna Nicolaou and James Fontanella-Khan, "The Fight for the Future of America's Local Newspapers," FT.com, January 21, 2021.

55. Adam J. Saffer, Deborah L. Dwyer, Jennifer L. Harker, Christopher E. Etheridge, Mariam Turner, and Daniel Riffe, "Interlocking among American Newspaper Organizations Revisited: 'Pressure from the Top' and Its Influence on Newsroom and Content," *Mass Communication and Society* 24, no. 3 (2021): 441–469, https://doi.org/10.1080/15205436 .2020.1868523.

56. Soontae An and Hyun Seung Jin, "Interlocking of Newspaper Companies with Financial Institutions and Leading Advertisers," *Journalism & Mass Communication Quarterly* 81, no. 3 (2004): 578–600.

57. Jennifer L. Harker, "The United States of America's Interlocked Information Industry: An Examination into Seven US Media Sectors' Boards of Directors," *Journal of Media Business Studies* 17, no. 2 (2020): 219–42, 236, https://doi.org/10.1080/16522354.2020.1726671.

58. Jeffrey Manns, "The Case for Preemptive Oligopoly Regulation," *Indiana Law Journal* 96, no. 3 (Spring 2021): 751–802, 755, https://www.repository.law.indiana.edu/ilj/vol96/iss3/3?utm_source=www.repository.law.indiana.edu%2Filj%2Fvol96%2Fiss3%2F3&utm_medium=PDF&utm_campaign=PDFCoverPages.

59. "Mergers," Federal Trade Commission, n.d., https://www.ftc.gov/tips-advice/competition-guidance/guide-antitrust-laws/mergers.

60. US Congress, Senate, *A Bill to Amend the Clayton Act to Modify the Standard for an Unlawful Acquisition, and for Other Purposes*, S. 307, 116th Cong., introduced in the Senate January 31, 2019, https://www.congress.gov/bill/116th-congress/senate-bill/307?q=%7B%22search%22%3A%5B%22klobuchar+mergers%22%5D%7D&r=3&s=1.

61. Cecilia Kang and David McCabe, "Efforts to Rein in Big Tech May Be Running Out of Time," *New York Times*, January 20, 2022, https://www.nytimes.com/2022/01/20/technology/big-tech-senate-bill.html.

62. James Fallows, "Our Towns: There's Hope for Local Journalism," *The Atlantic*, September 18, 2019, https://www.theatlantic.com/notes/2019/09/theres-hope-for-local-journalism/598225/.

63. Waldman, "A Replanting Strategy."

64. Victor Pickard and Timothy Neff, "Op-Ed: Strengthen Our Democracy by Funding Public Media," *Columbia Journalism Review*, June 2, 2021, https://www.cjr.org/opinion/public-funding-media-democracy.php.

65. Robert W. McChesney and John Nichols, "The Local Journalism Initiative: A Proposal to Protect and Extend Democracy," *Columbia Journalism Review*, November 30, 2021, https://www.cjr.org/business_of_news/the-local-journalism-initiative.php.

66. Siva Vaidhyanathan, *Antisocial Media: How Facebook Disconnects Us and Undermines Democracy* (New York: Oxford University Press, 2018).

67. "Uncovered: Shining a Light on South Carolina Corruption and Misconduct," *Post and Courier*, 2021, https://www.postandcourier.com/uncovered/.

68. In conversation with the author, October 2021.

69. Tony Bartelme, Glenn Smith, Joseph Cranney, and Avery G. Wilks, "Uncovered: News Deserts and Weak Ethics Laws Allow Corruption to Run Rampant in SC," *Post and Courier*, February 12, 2021, https://www.postandcourier.com/uncovered/news-deserts-and-weak-ethics-laws-allow-corruption-to-run-rampant-in-sc/article_df3f64fe-5a63-11eb-aa62-4fb6abe764b6.html, quote appears in paragraph 31.

70. "The 2015 Pulitzer Prize Winner in Public Service," Pulitzer Prizes, Columbia University, n.d., https://www.pulitzer.org/winners/post-and-courier.

71. "Streets of Despair," *Hartford Courant*, February 2, 1992, https://www.courant.com/news/connecticut/hc-xpm-1992-02-02-0000206238-story.html.

72. Katie Robertson, "The Hartford Courant's Newsroom Is Closing Down," *New York Times*, December 31, 2020, https://www.nytimes.com/2020/12/04/business/media/the-hartford-courants-newsroom-is-closing-down.html; Bradley Clift and Bob Sudyk, "13 Years in Hell," *Hartford Courant*, May 2, 1999, https://www.courant.com/news/connecticut/hc-xpm-1999-05-02-9910270071-story.html.

73. Tribune Publishing Company, Form 10-K, annual report filed by Tribune Publishing Company for the fiscal year ending December 27, 2020 (March 8, 2021), from the US Securities and Exchange Commission website, https://sec.report/Document/0001593195-21-000020/tpco-20201227.htm.

74. Mike Gorrell, "A Brief History of Salt Lake Tribune Owners Since Its Birth—with Photos of the Paper through the Years," *Salt Lake Tribune*, April 22, 2016, https://www.sltrib.com/news/2016/04/22/a-brief-history-of-salt-lake-tribune-owners-since-its-birth-with-photos-of-the-paper-through-the-years/.

75. "Our Nonprofit Model," *Salt Lake Tribune*, March 25, 2021, https://www.sltrib.com/footer/2020/01/09/our-nonprofit-model/.

76. Lauren Gustus, "From Hedge Fund Ownership to Nonprofit Status: How We're Investing in 2022," *Salt Lake Tribune*, November 10, 2021, https://www.sltrib.com/news/business/2021/11/10/hedge-fund-ownership/.

77. Magda Konieczna, *Journalism without Profit: Making News When the Market Fails* (New York: Oxford University Press, 2018), 5.

78. In conversation with the author, July 2020.

79. In conversation with the author, July 2020.

80. "Eden Tesfay Owned a Store on the Corner of Summit and Sixth Street in Weinland Park for Years. That Store Is Now Rubble," *Matter News*, n.d., https://www.matternews.org/cornering-stores.

81. "The Tributary: A Northeast Florida Journalism Collective," https://jaxtrib.org.

82. Epicenter NYC, n.d., https://epicenter-nyc.com/.

83. S. Mitra Kalita, "A Letter to the New Yorker Who Made It This Far," Epicenter NYC, n.d., https://epicenter-nyc.com/a-letter-to-the-new-yorker-who-made-it-this-far/.

84. Kim Kelly, "This Is a Horror Story: How Private Equity Vampires Are Killing Everything," *The Nation*, November 5, 2019, https://www.thenation.com/article/archive/private-equity-deadspin/.

85. "Defector Annual Report, September 2020–August 2021," *Defector*, October 4, 2021, https://defector.com/defector-annual-report-year-one/.

86. Tim Evans and Mark Alesia, "Former USA Gymnastics Doctor Accused of Abuse," *Indianapolis Star*, January 24, 2018, https://www.indystar.com/story/news/2016/09/12/former-usa-gymnastics-doctor-accused-abuse/89995734/.

87. Julie Brown, "Perversion of Justice: Jeffrey Epstein," *Miami Herald*, December 19, 2019, https://www.miamiherald.com/topics/jeffrey-epstein.

88. Reuters, "Leon Black, Billionaire Co-founder and CEO of Apollo Hedge Fund, Steps Down after Review of Ties to Epstein," NBCNews.com, January 26, 2021, https://

www.nbcnews.com/business/business-news/leon-black-billionaire-co-founder-ceo
-apollo-hedge-fund-steps-n1255654.

89. Adam Lewis, "Apollo Doles Out $1.8B Loan for Newspaper Merger," Pitchbook,
November 15, 2019, https://pitchbook.com/news/articles/apollo-doles-out-18b-loan-for
-newspaper-merger

90. Jonas Heese, Gerardo Pérez-Cavazos, and Caspar David Peter, "When the Local Newspaper Leaves Town: The Effects of Local Newspaper Closures on Corporate Misconduct,"
n.d., https://s3.documentcloud.org/documents/22187014/local-corp-crime.pdf.

91. Bill McKibben, "Money Is the Oxygen on Which the Fire of Global Warming Burns,"
New Yorker, September 17, 2019, https://www.newyorker.com/news/daily-comment/
money-is-the-oxygen-on-which-the-fire-of-global-warming-burns.

92. In conversation with the author, October 2020.

93. Perry Parks, "Researching with Our Hair on Fire: Three Frameworks for Rethinking
News in a Postnormative World," *Journalism & Mass Communication Quarterly* 97, no. 2
(June 2020): 393–415, https://doi.org/10.1177/1077699020916425.

94. J. P. Darr, M. P. Hitt, and J. L. Dunaway, "Newspaper Closures Polarize Voting
Behavior," *Journal of Communication* 68, no. 6 (2018): 1007–28, https://doi.org/10.1093/
joc/jqy051; Asa Royal and Philip Napoli, "Local Journalism without Journalists? Metric
Media and the Future of Local News," *Journal of Creative Industries and Cultural Studies*,
no. 8 (2020): 118–147, https://doi.org/10.56140/JOCIS-v8-2.

95. "Chevron PR Firm Launches 'News' Sites in Journalism-Starved Regions," EcoWatch,
August 19, 2022, https://www.ecowatch.com/chevron-greenwashing-permian-proud.html.

96. Priyanjana Bengani, "Hundreds of 'Pink Slime' Local News Outlets Are Distributing
Algorithmic Stories and Conservative Talking Points," Tow Center for Digital Journalism, Columbia's Graduate School of Journalism, December 18, 2019, https://www.cjr
.org/tow_center_reports/hundreds-of-pink-slime-local-news-outlets-are-distributing
-algorithmic-stories-conservative-talking-points.php.

97. Karen Yourish, Danielle Ivory, Aaron Byrd, Weiyi Cai, Nick Corasaniti, Meg Felling,
Rumsey Taylor, and Jonathan Weisman, "How Election Lies Took Over the Republican Ticket
Nationwide," *New York Times*, October 13, 2022, https://www.nytimes.com/interactive/
2022/10/13/us/politics/republican-candidates-2020-election-misinformation.html.

98. John Creamer, Emily A. Shrider, Kalee Burns, and Frances Chen, "Poverty in the
United States: 2021," US Census Bureau, September 13, 2022, https://www.census.gov/
library/publications/2022/demo/p60-277.html#:~:text=Highlights-,Official%20Poverty
%20Measure,and%20Table%20A%2D1.

Index

MARGOT SUSCA is an assistant professor in the School of Communication at American University.

The History of Communication

Selling Free Enterprise: The Business Assault on Labor and Liberalism, 1945–60
  Elizabeth A. Fones-Wolf
Last Rights: Revisiting *Four Theories of the Press*   *Edited by John C. Nerone*
"We Called Each Other Comrade": Charles H. Kerr & Company, Radical Publishers
  Allen Ruff
WCFL, Chicago's Voice of Labor, 1926–78   *Nathan Godfried*
Taking the Risk Out of Democracy: Corporate Propaganda versus Freedom and Liberty
  Alex Carey; edited by Andrew Lohrey
Media, Market, and Democracy in China: Between the Party Line and the Bottom Line
  Yuezhi Zhao
Print Culture in a Diverse America   *Edited by James P. Danky and Wayne A. Wiegand*
The Newspaper Indian: Native American Identity in the Press, 1820–90   *John M. Coward*
E. W. Scripps and the Business of Newspapers   *Gerald J. Baldasty*
Picturing the Past: Media, History, and Photography   *Edited by Bonnie Brennen*
  and Hanno Hardt
Rich Media, Poor Democracy: Communication Politics in Dubious Times
  Robert W. McChesney
Silencing the Opposition: Antinuclear Movements and the Media in the Cold War
  Andrew Rojecki
Citizen Critics: Literary Public Spheres   *Rosa A. Eberly*
Communities of Journalism: A History of American Newspapers and Their Readers
  David Paul Nord
From Yahweh to Yahoo!: The Religious Roots of the Secular Press   *Doug Underwood*
The Struggle for Control of Global Communication: The Formative Century   *Jill Hills*
Fanatics and Fire-eaters: Newspapers and the Coming of the Civil War   *Lorman A. Ratner*
  and Dwight L. Teeter Jr.
Media Power in Central America   *Rick Rockwell and Noreene Janus*
The Consumer Trap: Big Business Marketing in American Life   *Michael Dawson*
How Free Can the Press Be?   *Randall P. Bezanson*
Cultural Politics and the Mass Media: Alaska Native Voices   *Patrick J. Daley*
  and Beverly A. James
Journalism in the Movies   *Matthew C. Ehrlich*
Democracy, Inc.: The Press and Law in the Corporate Rationalization of the Public Sphere
  David S. Allen
Investigated Reporting: Muckrakers, Regulators, and the Struggle over Television
  Documentary   *Chad Raphael*
Women Making News: Gender and the Women's Periodical Press in Britain   *Michelle Tusan*
Advertising on Trial: Consumer Activism and Corporate Public Relations in the 1930s
  Inger L. Stole
Speech Rights in America: The First Amendment, Democracy, and the Media   *Laura Stein*
Freedom from Advertising: E. W. Scripps's Chicago Experiment   *Duane C. S. Stoltzfus*

The University of Illinois Press
is a founding member of the
Association of University Presses.

————————————————

Composed in 10.75/13 Arno Pro
with Avenir LT Std display
by Lisa Connery
at the University of Illinois Press
Manufactured by Sheridan Books, Inc.

University of Illinois Press
1325 South Oak Street
Champaign, IL 61820-6903
www.press.uillinois.edu